Technology Tools for Teachers

• Third Edition •

Lynne C. Levy • Frank J. Orlando

College of Education
Rowan University

KENDALL/HUNT PUBLISHING COMPANY
4050 Westmark Drive   Dubuque, Iowa 52002

Pages 50-56   Reprinted with permission form *National Educational Technology Standards for Teachers,* copyright © 2000, ISTE (International Society for Technology in Education), 800.336.5191 (U.S. & Canada) or 541.302.3777 (Int'l), iste@iste.org, www.iste.org. All rights reserved. Permission does not constitute an endorsement by ISTE. For more information about the NETS Project, contact Lajeane Thomas, Director, NETS Project, 318.257.39223. lthomas@latech.edu.

Page 220   Photo courtesy of Ellison.

Cover image courtesy of Rowan University

ISBN 10: 0-7575-3458-9
ISBN 13: 978-0-7575-3458-4

Printed in the United States of America
10 9 8 7 6 5 4 3 2 1

CONTENTS

Part II - Standards

Part III - Internet Technology

Introduction

Technology tools continue to transform the face of teaching, learning, and teacher education across the nation and in the world. Schools are constantly being challenged to infuse the existing and emerging technology into their classrooms and curricula so students are technologically literate. To achieve this goal, schools must make the technology available to teachers, and teachers must be able to effectively use the technology.

Teacher education programs play a critical role in achieving this goal. In order to prepare teachers for the future, programs must be based on a model that incorporates technology as a central element. Graduates of teacher education programs must have an understanding of technology and know how to effectively use technology as a tool for teaching and learning.

The College of Education of Rowan University has made significant program changes to enhance the preparation of its graduates. One such change has been the implementation of a required course titled Educational Technology. In this course, students are introduced to a variety of technology-related resources that are available to them at Rowan University. They also purchase a subscription to *TaskStream*, a Web-based tool that is used by students to electronically submit their lesson plans, units, and other assignments. This account also serves as the repository for the student to develop and maintain a portfolio of evidence for courses, the program exit assessment, and job seeking.

This third edition of ***Technology Tools for Teachers*** is intended to serve two purposes. It is the text for the course Educational Technology, and it is an instructional resource for assignments and activities that are part of the College of Education's programs of study. To effectively address these various needs, topics have been grouped under five headings: Rowan University, Standards, Internet Technology, Contemporary Instructional Technology Tools, and Traditional Instructional Technology Tools. Knowledge and skills in each of these areas is essential to the successful completion of all teacher education programs in the College of Education of Rowan University.

We wish you well in your quest to become a teacher.

Lynne C. Levy, Ed.D.
Frank J. Orlando, Ed.D.

Part I

Rowan University

CHAPTER 1

Technology at Rowan University

1.1 - Introduction

Information Resources at Rowan University hosts a wealth of information about technology resources available to students at Rowan. These are housed at www.rowan.edu/toolbox. At that address, the screen below appears. At the time of this writing, the **Technology Toolbox** was still under construction. You will, however, find a screen similar to the one below. The menu on the left takes you to topics that are important to know. Some of these are described in this chapter. Searching *the Rowan Knowledgebase* on the right takes you to a search engine of questions about these topics.

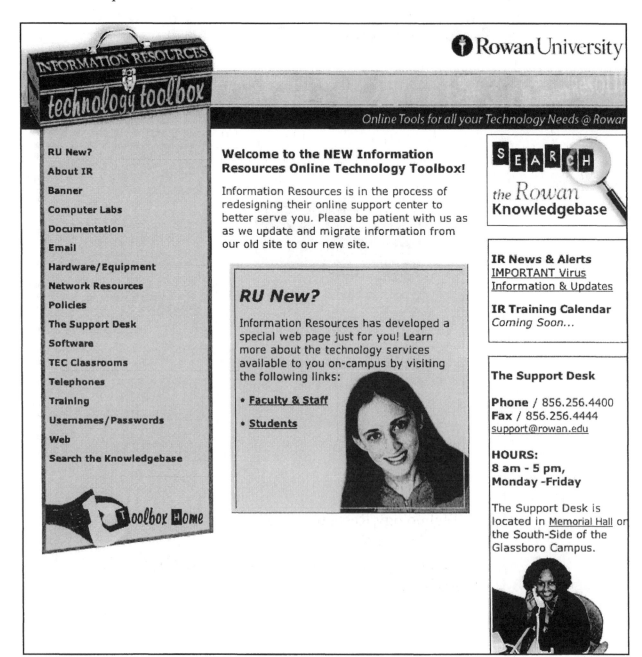

1.2 - Technology Resources at Rowan University

From the *Technology Toolbox*, "Students" links to the menu below: The TOP TEN things you need to know. Most of these are described here, with more detail on the Rowan network provided in Section 1.3 of this chapter.

Username and Password: Your Rowan network account is used to access most resources on the Rowan network, including WebCT, e-mail, your home directory, your personal Web site, and the Openarea. If you do not have a Rowan ID, or if you want to change your password, go to www.rowan.edu/password/reset. The system will ask you to verify personal information about yourself, including your Social Security Number and home address.

Using the Rowan Network: This has four components that will be detailed in the next section. Your Home Directory (H Drive) is a personal folder on Rowan's servers where you can safely store files. These files can be accessed on or off campus. Using any Web editor, you can create a Web page and save it in your Home Directory. The Openarea is a folder on the network where faculty members can share files with students.

Student E-Mail: You can access your e-mail by visiting the Student Portal page at cp.rowan.edu. For details and assistance, follow the links in #3.

#1 : Username and Password Info

#2 : Using the Rowan Network

- Home directory
- Openarea
- Personal Web Space
- Accessing Files from Off-Campus

#3 : Accessing Your E-Mail

#4 : Using Your Telephone

#5 : Student Self-Service (Web for Students)

#6 : WebCT

#7 : Network Cables/Mini-Hubs/Wireless

#8 : Downloading Software

#9 : Need your Computer Repaired?

AND #10 :

Support Desk Contact Information

WebCT: This is online management software that aids students in their classes by creating, managing, organizing, and housing a Web-based learning environment. On this site, faculty can post lecture notes and information, grades, and past quizzes. WebCT also contains a chat area and bulletin board. Its biggest advantage is that it allows students access to information at any time of the night or day. This can be accessed through the Student Portal at cp.rowan.edu, or directly from the Rowan WebCT address: webct.rowan.edu.

Banner for Students: You can register for classes, obtain your class schedule, add/drop classes, access your grades, view your transcript, apply for financial aid, review loan status, and more by visiting banner.rowan.edu. You will first be asked for your Rowan network username and password. Begin *Banner* by selecting "Start Banner Self Service," then choose "Enter Secure Area." You will then be asked for your User Identification Number and PIN. This is different than your network ID. If you do not know this, go to www.rowan.edu/mybanner. Once logged in, select the "Student and Financial Aid" menu. Online training videos are available to help you take advantage of the *Banner* services. To access these, go to www.rowan.edu/ir/training; click "Banner," then "Students."

Network Cables and Computer Repair: Students can pick up a network cable from the NSS Workshop located in Memorial Hall South. These cables are 14 feet in length and are free for all registered students living in the residence halls. If you are having a problem with your computer, NSS has technicians available to assist you. The fastest way to get your computer repaired is to take it to the NSS Workshop. If you have a desktop computer, just take the computer itself. The  other parts, such as monitor, keyboard, mouse, etc., are not needed by the workshop. If you do not want to take your computer to the workshop, you can put in a work order by calling the Support Desk at 856-256-4400. Please note that machines are usually repaired in the workshop within 48 hours, while it may take up to two weeks for a technician to come to you.

Downloading Software: You can download licensed and free software on Rowan University's Download Page. On this page you will find the following licensed software available for your use:
- *McAfee® Anti-Virus* Software
- Latest *McAfee Anti-Virus* Update (keep your virus software up-to-date)
- *Cisco VPN client* (used for accessing your files from home)
- *Secure FX®* (FTP Program)
- *Secure CRT®* (Terminal Emulator)

You will also find free software including:
- *Stinger* for *Windows®* (a free virus tool that identifies and eliminates the top high-risk viruses from your computer)
- *Ad-Aware™* (an application built to find and remove adware and spyware)
- *Adobe® Acrobat® Reader™*
- *Fetch* (an FTP program for Macs®)
- Various Web browsers
- Multimedia utilities such as Macromedia's® *Flash™* and *Shockwave™*

Support Desk Contact Information: The Support Desk is located in Memorial Hall. The entrance is the main set of doors closest to the Greenhouse. You can call the Support Desk at 856-256-4400 or send e-mail to support@rowan.edu. The Support Desk's hours are 8:00 a.m. to 5:00 p.m., Monday through Friday. The Support Desk has extended hours, 8:00 a.m. to 6:30 p.m., during the first two weeks of school.

Useful Rowan Links (all links will open in a new window)

- www.rowan.edu/myhome - Find your Home Directory location
- www.rowan.edu/password/reset - Find or reset Rowan ID
- www.rowan.edu/ph - Online telephone and e-mail address directory
- users.rowan.edu - Personal Web site directory
- www.rowan.edu/map - Campus maps
- cp.rowan.edu - Student Portal
- sinfo.rowan.edu - Student self-service (Web for Students)
- webct.rowan.edu - WebCT

1.3 - The Rowan Network

"H" Drive at Rowan (for saving files)

Your home directory (also known as your H Drive) is a personal folder created for you on one of Rowan's servers. Saving your files and documents there allows them to be accessed from any computer, on campus or off. Your home directory is also backed up every night to ensure that you will never lose your files if your computer breaks or even if you accidentally delete your files. To find the location of your H Drive, go to www.rowan.edu/myhome. To access your H Drive, follow the steps below.

In the Computer Labs/Residence Halls:

Most of the labs on campus are configured so that when you log in, the default for saving your files is to your H Drive. Unless you change where files will be saved, they will go to your H Drive.

In Labs and Residence Halls (if not saved as above):

Windows PC users can access their home directory (H Drive) by double clicking the "My Computer" icon on the desktop (or from the Start menu, depending on how *Windows XP* looks on the computer) and double clicking the H Drive, which will be named "nwuser2.rowan.edu," for example. The number will change depending on the location of your specific home server (see above). Once you click "OK" you will be prompted for your Rowan username and password.

Mac OSX users can access their home directory by clicking "Go" on the Finder menu, then selecting "Connect to Server" and entering their home server (e.g., nwuser2.rowan.edu). Once you click "Connect" you will be prompted for your Rowan username and password.

Using either of the above, your H Drive should appear. If it does not, open the home server icon, click on "Students," then click on your Rowan username.

Off Campus

You can access files on the Rowan network from your home computer using the *VPN Client*. The *VPN (Virtual Private Network) Client* allows you to access Rowan University network resources from home as if you were on campus. A *VPN* is a secured private network connection built on top of publicly accessible infrastructure.

Rowan provides two VPNs, available as free downloads. The "RowanVPN" connection is for normal use; the "RowanLibrary" connection is specifically used for connecting to the library's databases and should only be used for that purpose. Both of these VPNs can be downloaded from www.rowan.edu/toolbox/network/off_campus. Directions are also available there to "Install the VPN Client," "Connect to Rowan Using the VPN Client," "Connect to Your Home Directory," "Connect to the Openarea," and "Connect to the Library's Databases."

Creating a Personal Web Page

All student home directories automatically contain a folder called "public.www". Using any Web editor, you can create Web pages and save them to your "public.www" folder. The first page must be titled "index.htm." That "index.html" page will be your personal home page. You can reach this page by visiting *http://users.rowan.edu/~yourusername*.

1.4 - Technology-Enhanced Classrooms (TEC)

The Department of Instructional Technology maintains a number of technology-enhanced classrooms in every academic building. TEC rooms at Rowan are generally equipped with:

- TEC Room Networked Computer (Mac and/or PC)
- VCR
- DVD Player
- Cassette and CD Player
- Document Imaging Camera
- Projector w/ Controllable Screen
- Touch Screen Control

The information and directions that follow are for the equipment in Education Hall. All classrooms are TEC rooms; however, most do not have Document Imaging Cameras and do not need the Touch Screen Control. All images are projected on the large screen at the front on the room; speakers are mounted next to the screen. DVDs are played through the computer in the room.

Log-in is required to access the Rowan network. Your Rowan ID and password are your log-in.

Turning on the Projector: Controls for turning on the projector are on the computer. Therefore, the desktop computer must be on for all projections. Push the power button on the front of the computer and monitor to turn them on. After logging in, a *Projector Controls* panel will appear. Click on the first icon to turn the projector on. Choose whether you want to use the desktop computer, a laptop, or a VCR. Turn off the projector when finished.

Power, network, audio, and VGA connections are on the laptop plate on the top of the desk.

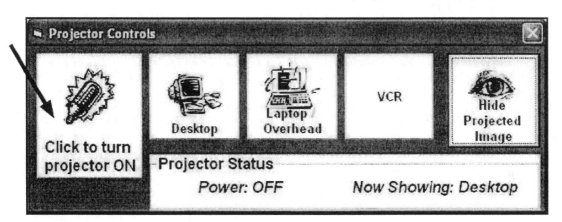

To Use a Mac Laptop:
1. Follow *Log-in* and *Turning on the Projector* directions (above).
2. Using the VGA - DVI connector cable (about 6" long) that came with your computer (not provided in room), connect the DVI end to the DVI port on the side of your laptop, and connect the VGA end to the VGA port on the plate on the desk.
3. For network access, plug an Ethernet cable (in drawer of desk) into the laptop and the plate on the desk.
4. Turn on the laptop.
5. For mirror image (see on laptop and screen), press F7 on the keyboard.
6. For audio, connect the audio cable (in drawer of desk) to the laptop and the plate on the desk.

To Use a PC Laptop:
1. Follow *Log-in* and *Turning on the Projector* directions (above).
2. Connect the VGA cable (in drawer of desk) to the back of the laptop and the plate on the desk.
3. For network access, plug an Ethernet cable (in drawer of desk) into the laptop and the plate on the desk.
4. Turn on the laptop.
5. For mirror image (see on laptop and screen), use one of these function keys (depending of brand of computer): 4, 5, 6, or 8.
6. For audio, connect the audio cable (in drawer of desk) to the laptop and the plate on the desk.

To Play and Display a VHS Tape:
1. Follow *Log-in* and *Turning on the Projector* directions (page 9).
2. Click *VCR* on the Projector Controls screen.
3. Wait until "Projector Status ON; Now Showing: VCR" appears.
4. Insert the VHS tape; the unit is powered and the tape will begin.
5. Use the controls on the VCR unit to Rewind, Fast Forward, and/or Stop.
6. Control sound using the volume keys on the top right of the keyboard.
7. To display a camera using S-video from the VCR, plug the camera into the front of the VCR using an S-video cable, and use "Channel Up" and "Channel Down" to select the F1 input.

To Play and Display a DVD:
1. Follow *Log-in* and *Turning on the Projector* directions (page 9).
2. Click on the *Desktop* button (the DVD is in the desktop computer).
3. Insert the DVD into the CD/DVD tray in the computer.
4. A dialog box will appear; select "Play DVD Video using Windows Media Player;" select "OK."
5. Play and navigate the movie with the controls at the bottom left of the screen.
6. To view the movie full screen, go to *View* (in menu bar) – *Full screen*.
7. Use volume keys on the keyboard to control sound.

1.5 - Activities

• Activity One •

Go to Rowan's *Technology Toolbox*. Choose three items of interest to you. Read the material. Write a paragraph on each item, explaining how it can benefit you while you are at Rowan.

• Activity Two •

Locate your H Drive in a lab on Rowan's campus. Save a *Word* file there. Access your H Drive from your Rowan residence or your home computer (by downloading and installing the appropriate software). Retrieve the *Word* file; modify and re-save.

• Activity Three •

Create a personal Web page using *Word* or *Netscape* [see Chapter 11]. Save the first page as "index.html." Save in your *Public WWW* file in your H Drive. Display the page in a Web browser using your Web address as described in this chapter.

CHAPTER 2

The Professional Teaching Portfolio

Portfolio

Edward A. Sample
Fall 2006

2.1 - Introduction

Maintaining a portfolio has been a common practice for many years for photographers and other artists. It is a vehicle to document their growth and development over a period of time. In recent years, the educational community has recognized the value of professional portfolios and has encouraged their development and use on a number of fronts. This is largely attributable to the resurgence of, and support for, teacher assessment and accountability and the emergence of standards as a key factor in education.

Most teacher education programs now require their students to begin keeping a portfolio during their first year of classes and to maintain it throughout the program. The student's portfolio is frequently a critical program exit and completion requirement. Portfolios are the most frequently used and required means to document your qualifications when seeking employment in the teaching profession. They are also a common tool when seeking additional certifications and/or job advancement.

2.2 - Types of Professional Teaching Portfolios

Although a variety of terms are used in the literature to describe portfolios developed by members of the educational community, three major types of professional teaching portfolios—based on their use—can be identified. They are the *product portfolio*, the *working portfolio*, and the *showcase portfolio*.

The Product Portfolio

The product portfolio consists of a series of artifacts and reflections developed over a short period of time for a specific purpose. Usually tied to a course, product portfolios are similar in content for everyone in the course. This type of portfolio is usually the starting point for the creation of a working portfolio.

The Working Portfolio

A working portfolio is also called a documentation portfolio, a developmental portfolio, and a process portfolio. It is a formative portfolio that is basically a work-in-progress. This portfolio documents the pre-service teacher's progress on the road to becoming a teacher. The intention is to facilitate the pre-service teacher's development by serving as a holding place for artifacts and reflections that are tied to program objectives. It will eventually become the source for evidence that will be placed in the showcase portfolio.

Portfolio

Teaching:
An Introduction
to the Profession

Fall 2006

Edward A. Sample

Portfolio

Edward A. Sample
• Secondary Science •

The Showcase Portfolio

The showcase portfolio is sometimes referred to as a presentation portfolio, an exit portfolio, or a display portfolio. It is a summative portfolio that documents the pre-service teacher's mastery of the requirements to be certified as a teacher.

The evidence, which should be comprehensive and compelling, should include artifacts, reflections, and validation entries such as observations. The contents of a showcase portfolio are selected to "showcase" the abilities and skills of the developer.

The showcase portfolio can also serve as a marketing or interview portfolio when seeking employment in the field of education.

2.3 - Portfolio Formats

When developing a professional teaching portfolio, there are two primary formats that can be adopted: the traditional "paper-based" portfolio and the electronic portfolio. In many cases, pre-service and inservice teachers develop and maintain portfolios in both formats. When a portfolio must be presented, the specific situation determines which format is appropriate.

Traditional (Paper-Based) Portfolio

The traditional (paper-based) portfolio often begins in a 3-ring binder with a set of dividers. As the documentation grows, the size of the binder and the number of dividers used will increase. This working portfolio is frequently transferred to a larger holding device such as an expandable folder, a plastic storage crate with hanging folders, or just a cardboard box with file folders. When a product or showcase portfolio is required, materials are selected from the larger set of evidence and it is usually organized and placed in a 3-ring binder.

Electronic Portfolios

Like traditional portfolios, electronic portfolios consist of a collection of evidence intended to document the preparer's knowledge, skills, and dispositions regarding teaching and learning. They differ in that the documentation is stored and presented electronically or in a digital format. This allows for the inclusion of audio, video, the Internet, and other technologies that are not easily included in the traditional portfolio.

Electronic portfolios can be created using a structure developed by the preparer or a commercial program especially designed for this purpose. The College of Education at Rowan University has adopted *TaskStream*, a Web-based system, as the tool for pre-service teachers to use to create, submit, and manage their electronic portfolios (see Chapter 3, *TaskStream*: Overview and Instructional Design and Chapter 4, *TaskStream*: Web Folios and Web Pages).

With *TaskStream*, the user can create a custom portfolio from scratch, or a template developed by the professor or the department can be selected.

Create a portfolio from scratch

○ **Custom portfolio** [More info/Preview]
Build your own portfolio without the use of a pre-set template.

OR... Select a template designed for your learning community

○ **Ed. Tech. Spring 2006** [More info/Preview]
Created by Lynne Levy on 2/14/2006

Example: Link to a template for the Educational Technology course

In addition, the user has the option of selecting one of several preset portfolio templates.

OR... Select a general purpose template

○ **Class Portfolio** [More info/Preview]
Use this template to collect and highlight the best examples of your students' work.

○ **Employment Portfolio** [More info/Preview]
Use this template to create a portfolio of your best work for potential employers.

○ **Professional Development Portfolio** [More info/Preview]
Use this template to demonstrate professional growth over the course of the year.

○ **Reflective Portfolio (Pre-Service)** [More info/Preview]
Create a reflective portfolio that demonstrates your professional growth and your readiness to enter the teaching profession. Useful for certification and program requirements.

○ **Showcase Portfolio** [More info/Preview]
Use this template to collect and highlight the best examples of your work.

○ **Standards-Based Folio** [More info/Preview]
Use this template to demonstrate how you have met professional certification standards.

Subtopics in *TaskStream* templates:

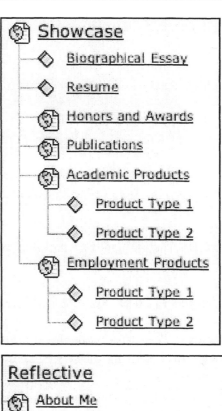

Portfolio Advantages and Disadvantages

	Advantages	Disadvantages
Traditional (paper-based) Portfolio	• Can be reviewed anywhere • No technical skills required • No special equipment required	• Difficult to deliver at a distance • Space intensive • Single copy
Electronic Portfolio	• Easily shared with others • Large storage capacity • Demonstrates technical skills	• Requires appropriate technology • Preparation is time consuming • Cannot receive written comments

2.4 - Portfolio Evidence

There is a wide range of artifacts that can become part of the evidence you provide in your professional teaching portfolio. This evidence is intended to document your knowledge, skills, and dispositions regarding teaching and learning. The following list identifies some of these items.

• Assessment instruments	• Philosophy of teaching and learning
• Bulletin board layouts	• Photographs
• Case studies	• Professional development plans
• Certificates and awards	• Professional memberships
• Classroom arrangement diagrams	• Projects
• Classroom management plans	• Reflections
• Cooperative learning plans	• Resume or vitae
• Descriptions of volunteer work	• Rubrics
• Evaluations	• Student contracts
• Examples of the use of technology	• Student feedback
• Individualized Education Plans (IEPs)	• Student work samples
• Instructional strategies	• Teacher-home communications
• Interdisciplinary lesson plans	• Teacher-made instructional materials
• Journal entries	• Teaching experiences
• Learning centers	• Teaching honors/awards
• Lesson plans	• Transcripts
• Letters of reference	• Unit plans
• Observation reports	• Videotapes of your teaching
• Personal goals	• Work experiences
• Personal Web site	

2.5 - Activities

• Activity One •

Reflect on your past, current, and anticipated future experiences relating to becoming a teacher. Using this information, prepare a detailed table of contents for a traditional portfolio. Be as specific as possible. Items that have not yet been prepared and experiences yet to be done should be underlined.

• Activity Two •

Examine two examples of an electronic teaching portfolio. Compare and contrast the organizational structure and the evidence provided. Develop a list of ideas you can incorporate into your electronic portfolio.

CHAPTER 3

TaskStream: Overview and Instructional Design

Task Stream
Tools of Engagement

3.1 - Introduction

TaskStream is a Web-based system specifically designed for pre-service teachers and K-12 learning communities. It is composed of a set of tools, resources, and methodologies to assist in the production of electronic portfolios, Web pages, standards-based unit and lesson plans, rubrics, and related items. State and national standards are available for incorporation as needed. Being Web-based, you can access and use it on any computer with an Internet connection.

With *TaskStream*, you can create, submit, and manage electronic portfolios. These can then be submitted to your professor(s) for review and evaluation. You will work with Collaborative Programs and/or Folio Assessment Programs. A Collaborative Program is specific to a class, or can be generated by the student (e.g., as a portfolio for employment or other purposes). A Folio Assessment Program includes a Directed Response Folio (DRF). A DRF is a folio specific to Rowan that outlines the requirements and work submissions necessary for graduation. You will be enrolled in different programs for different classes.

TaskStream is infused in many upper-level education classes at Rowan University. Education majors are required to subscribe to *TaskStream* in a designated class. The subscription is purchased directly through *TaskStream*. It is recommended that each student purchase a four-year subscription, providing access during your education classes, student teaching/clinical practice, job-searching, and the first year of teaching.

TaskStream is a Web-based tool.

Teacher candidates can use the design tools:
- Lesson Builder
- Unit Builder
- Rubric Wizard
- Standards Manager

...to develop standards-based learning activities (which integrate subject areas and technology, address standards, and use assessment rubrics);
...which can be sent to their professors for feedback and evaluation.

Once teacher candidates have completed their templates, attached lessons, images, etc., they can:
- publish their portfolio on their own Web site
- publish their portfolio to a CD
- send their work to their professor for review/evaluation

Faculty and students can:
- communicate via e-mail and instant messaging systems
- participate in discussion groups
- send lesson plans, unit plans, and portfolios back and forth for review/evaluation

3.2 - Logging On and Getting Help

When you are ready to purchase your account, go to www.taskstream.com. Click on the *Subscribe Today* button and proceed from there. Be sure to register as a Rowan student. Use a username and password you can remember, possibly your Rowan ID. Write it down so you can remember it for the next few years! When asked if you want the Teacher Productivity Pack, indicate that you do want this.

Once you have registered and have a *TaskStream* account, go to www.taskstream.com to log in and get started.

Downloadable Guides
Access an index of guides that you can download and print.

As you are working, there are **various ways to get assistance**. First, try the navigation bar on the left of the screen. Go to *General: Help*. Read through the sections you find there. On the right, you will find an option to obtain downloadable guides (in PDF format).

In addition to *Downloadable Guides* in the *Help* section, you can find out *What's New*; read *Frequently Asked Questions*, which can help with your problems; download free *Software*, such as Web browsers and utilities; and get *Supplemental Resources*.

For assistance with your Rowan work, and general questions, you can e-mail your professor(s) at his/her Rowan address.

For **direct assistance** from *TaskStream*, call 1-800-311-5656; ask for Mentoring Services. Refer to *General: Help* on the navigation bar to get their hours.

For help via e-mail, contact help@taskstream.com, or click *Request Support* under *General: Help*. *TaskStream* recommends that you add help@taskstream.com to your e-mail address book to ensure return messages from *TaskStream* are not blocked by spam software/settings you may have on your computer.

Teacher Productivity Pack: If you do not have the *Lesson Builder, Unit Builder, and Rubrics Wizard* in an area labeled *Instructional Design* on the navigation bar on the left, you did not enable the *Teacher Productivity Pack* when you registered. If you are unable to access any of these, go to *My Account Info*, click on the *Enable* link located under the *Subscriber Preferences (Teacher Productivity Pack)*. You should then have access to all of these features.

Internet Browsers: *TaskStream* supports most browsers. It is best to use *Internet Explorer* 5.17 and above, *Netscape*® 7.0 and above, *AOL*® 9.0 and above (10.3 for Mac OSX), *FireFox*® 1.0, or *Safari*™ 1.2 for Macintosh®. To be able to use HTML formatting (change text fonts, sizes, etc.) on a Mac, *Safari* must be used.

3.3 - Getting Around

Home **Help Index**

Programs & Resources

→ **My Programs**

→ Standards Manager

→ Resource Manager
(Mybrary/Cybrary)

Web Publication

□ Web Folio Builder

□ Web Page Builder

Instructional Design

→ Unit Builder

→ Lesson Builder

→ Rubric Wizard

Communications

→ Message Center
(E-mail)

→ TS Instant Messenger

→ Discussion Board

→ Calendar

→ Announcements

General

□ Help

□ Log Out

□ New Log In

□ My Account Info

□ Manage Online
Storage

There is a navigation bar on the left of your screen (as shown here).

My Programs admits you to programs set up by your Rowan professor so your work can be sent to him/her for review and evaluation. Once reviewed, feedback from professors can be accessed here. Ongoing discussions between you and your professor can be accessed here, as you get comments in the various areas of your folio.

Standards Manager is a database of state, national, and international standards. Most of the standards have been published by national or professional organizations, or state departments of education. All can easily be added to lesson plans and folios.

Resource Manager includes *Cybrary*, *Mybrary*, *Manage Online Storage* and *Pack-It-Up* (save work offline).

> **Mybrary** is a compilation of all of the documents you have created in *TaskStream*, including lesson plans, unit plans, rubrics, DRFs, Web folios, and Web pages.

> **Cybrary** is a compilation of **lesson plans** (over 5,000) from other *TaskStream* users. You will also find **Educational Web Sites Search** containing over 450 Web sites for teachers.

The **Web Folio Builder** is where you go to begin creating a Resource Folio, a Presentation Portfolio, or a DRF (Directed Response Folio). Files, *TaskStream* work, and standards can be added to these folios.

The **Web Page Builder** makes it easy to publish your own Web page. *TaskStream* will assist you in receiving a Web address. Your page can be password protected so only those with the password can view your work. Web pages can be created to demonstrate proficiency, showcase work, and share work with others for employment consideration.

Instructional Design includes three **Teaching Productivity Tools**. The **Unit Builder** helps to put together a unit plan, while the **Lesson Builder** allows you to create standards-based classroom activities. The Lesson Builder can include standards, uploaded documents, Web links, and rubrics. The **Rubric Wizard** is an easy way to create rubrics for grading the students' work. You can create your own rubric, or modify one from the database of rubrics in *TaskStream*.

The **Message Center** allows you to communicate with other *TaskStream* users (students and faculty). It is an internal e-mail system; therefore, you can only receive and send messages to other *TaskStream* users. At the top right of the *Home* screen, you are notified of new messages.

Using **TS Instant Messenger**, you can communicate with any users when they are online.

The **Discussion Board** allows you to participate in site-wide discussions or local discussions set up by your professor.

Calendar and Announcements are ways for your professor to post dates and information you need to know about your class(es). At the top right of the screen, you are notified of new announcements.

Items in the **General** area are self-explanatory and can be accessed when needed.

For more detailed information on any of these items, go to the **Home Page** and click on *More...* under each heading. Each is explained in detail there.

3.4 - Creating a Lesson Plan (*Lesson Builder*)

Click on *Lesson Builder*; assign a title. Under *Choose a Format*, choose *Rowan University Lesson Plan*. Click on *Create It*. After lesson plans have been created, they are shown in the menu *Edit or view an existing lesson plan* (below *Create a new lesson*). You can choose any lesson from the list to use, or modify it.

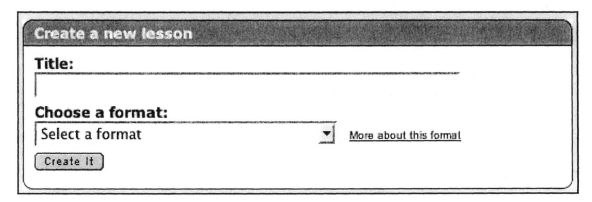

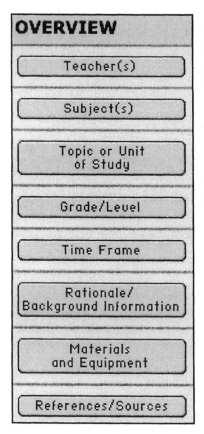

In the Lesson Builder, click on each topic; fill in the material you will be including in your lesson plan. Be sure to save your work as you progress by clicking *Save and Close Window*.

Subjects and *Grade/Level* are topical lists. You fill in information for the other categories.

Attachments and *Web Links* can also be added in some of the areas.

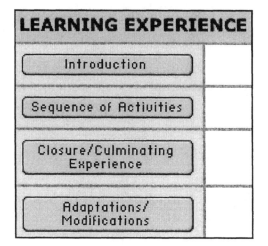

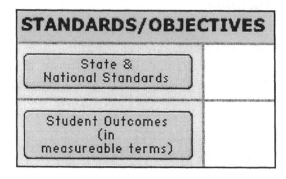

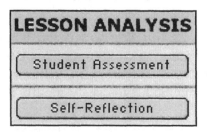

Standards Management within the Lesson Plan

To add standards, click on *Standards* within your lesson plan format (see the menus on the next page). In most cases you will use the New Jersey Core Curriculum Content Standards (NJCCCS). You can also access national standards for your subject area here (including NETS for technology areas), as well as the New Jersey Standards for Teachers and School Leaders.

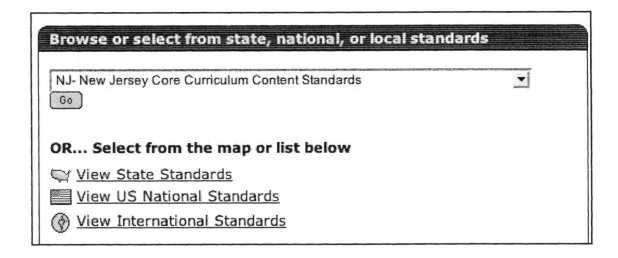

New Jersey Standards
NJ- Excel Standards Framework (Draft 11-04-02)
NJ- New Jersey Core Curriculum Content Standards
NJ- New Jersey Core Curriculum for Students with Severe Disabilities
NJ- New Jersey English Language Proficiency Standards
NJ- New Jersey Preschool Teaching & Learning Expectations:Standards ...
NJ- New Jersey Standards for Professional Development
NJ- Professional Standards for Teachers and School Leaders

Choose the standard(s) you want to include for your lesson plan, working down through the standards and grade levels. When you find the one you need, click the *Accept and Return* button. This places the standard(s) into your lesson plan.

Attachments

Clicking on the button for *Student Assessment* takes you to the menu below. Here you can attach Rubrics, Attachments (such as quizzes), or Web Links.

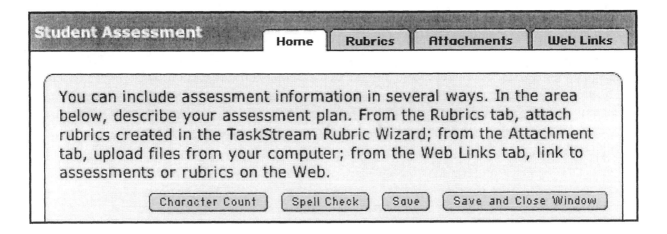

Completing Your Lesson Plan

Your work is saved each time you close a pop-up window. Once your lesson plan is completed, you can *Print* it, *E-mail* it, or *Request Feedback* from your professor. (*Publish* places it in the *Cybrary*.)

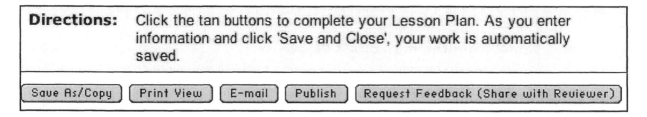

To add your lesson plan to your folio, click on *Lesson Plan* in the navigation bar (such as the one for Educational Technology), then click on *Attachments*. Your lesson plan can be found in *My TaskStream Work*, under *Lessons*.

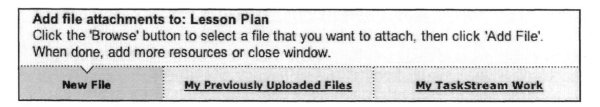

You can view all of the lesson plans you have created in *Lesson Builder* or *Mybrary*.

To **request feedback** *(Share with a Reviewer),* click the *Request Feedback* button at the top of the screen. Select your Reviewer, then click the *Submit for Review* button. You can add comments in either the *General Comment* area or the *Add Comment* area in each category.

If you are working on this lesson plan with someone else in your class, you can e-mail it to them and choose *Allow TaskStream recipients to copy this lesson for editing.*

3.5 - Creating Assessment Rubrics (*Rubric Wizard*)

A rubric is one way to assess the responses to the tasks you assign your students. In a rubric, the performance criteria that you identify defines the expectations for the activity. At the bottom of your lesson plan, you can attach the assessment(s). You can access the *Rubric Wizard* within *TaskStream* and construct a new rubric, or adapt an existing rubric for your assessment.

To create or adapt a rubric, go to *Rubric Wizard* under *Instructional Design* on the left of the screen. Before creating your own rubric, look at the sample rubrics to see if you can use one as a starting point.

```
                                                    Rubric Wizard

Directions:    To create a new rubric, place a title in the box below and click
               "Create it". You may also adapt a sample rubric by selecting it and
               clicking "Open". To view or edit, click the title on the list below.

  Create a new rubric

  Title:                                    Columns:
  [                                    ]     [Select ▼]  [ Create It ]

  OR... Adapt a sample rubric

  [ Select a sample rubric from this menu ▼ ]  [ Open ]
```

When adapting a sample rubric, first select the rubric to adapt. For each row of criteria you want to include in your rubric, click in the box on the right. Then click *Save and Return to Rubric*.

Levels / Criteria	1	2	3	4	☐ Select all
Links and Layout	Positioning of symbols is not used to convey overall relationships or meaning and links are missing and unlabeled.	Positioning of symbols is uneven and most links are unlabeled or mislabeled.	The diagram in general shows the logical relationships among most components but has some omissions.	The diagram captures all the logical relationships among all the conceptual components.	☐

Enter a title for your rubric. The criteria you chose will go into a new rubric. To edit this, click in the text area and make your changes. By clicking *Add Row*, you can add additional rows. While working on the rubric, you can add or delete rows, reorder rows and columns, spell check, etc.

Once your rubric is completed you can link it to your lesson plan. Open your lesson plan under *Lesson Builder*. Click on the *Student Assessment* button. Click the *Rubrics* tab. Here you will find a list of any rubrics you have created. Click the one you want to attach, then *Save and Close Window*.

3.6 - Creating a Unit Plan (*Unit Builder*)

Unit plans are similar to lesson plans, with a few differences.

When creating a unit plan, enter the basic information, then click on *Learning Activities*. This takes you to the *Assemble Activities/Lessons* window. Once your lesson plans are assembled, here you can easily sequence the lessons, bringing the lesson information into your unit.

When clicking on *Learning Activities*, you get the screen below. This is where you attach lessons previously constructed.

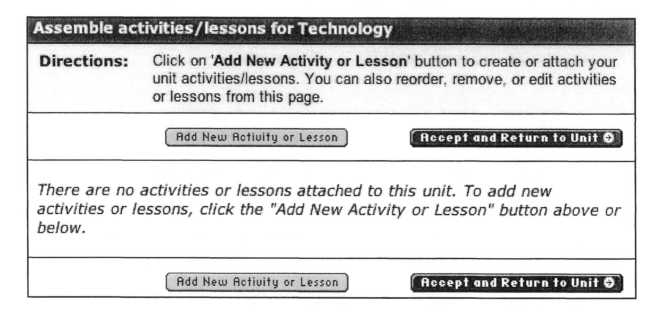

In addition to putting your lessons together here, you can also aggregate standards. As you attach lesson plans, standards in these lessons become aggregated. Since you have already created lessons by the time you build a unit, you will be able to navigate the screens, as they are similar to the *Lesson Builder*.

3.7 - Activities

• Activity One •

Using a lesson plan you are creating this semester, or one you created last semester, re-create it using the Rowan University Lesson Plan format in *TaskStream*. Identify the related New Jersey Core Curriculum Content Standards, along with a rubric for assessment.

CHAPTER 4

TaskStream: Web Folios and Web Pages

4.1 - Introduction

Electronic portfolios are constructed for various purposes: evaluation within a course or program, certification, or employment (to name a few). You can create different portfolios for each purpose. There are three types of Web folios in *TaskStream*. Each type can be shared with an instructor for assessment, burned to a CD, or published as a Web page.

> **The Resource Folio:** A Working Portfolio. This is an archive where you can store all of your documents. You can keep all of your papers, photos, and other work here in online files to access them when needed. Folios can be organized in various ways, as shown below.

Create a resource folio from scratch

⊙ **Custom resource folio** [More info/Preview]
Build your own resource folio without the use of a pre-set template.

OR... Select a general purpose template

⊙ **Curricular Resources** [More info/Preview]
Use this template to organize your resources for a topic or unit you plan to teach.

⊙ **Digital Archive/Working Folio** [More info/Preview]
Use this template to collect, organize, and/or archive your work products.

⊙ **Favorite Web Sites** [More info/Preview]
You can use this template to collect and organize your favorite web resources. Feel free to add/remove or rename any of the folders, to further personalize the resource folio.

⊙ **Syllabus** [More info/Preview]
Publish a class or course syllabus on a single web page. Outline the scope and sequence of the course, and post assignments, readings, and more.

⊙ **Teacher's File Cabinet** [More info/Preview]
Use this template to organize your curriculum, class, and web resources, and to keep a record of communication between you and students, parents, and administrators.

⊙ **Weekly Plans** [More info/Preview]
Organize your curriculum by sorting lessons and units into weekly folders. The outcome is a scope and sequence plan.

> **The Presentation Portfolio:** A Showcase Portfolio. This is an area to create your own portfolio for various purposes—Employment, Professional Development, Showcase, etc., or complete one set up for one of your classes. You have control of how it is constructed and what is included in the portfolio (see Chapter 2: The Professional Teaching Portfolio). As with the Resource Folio, various types can be constructed, or your professor will create a template for you to complete.

> **The Directed Response Folio (DRF):** An Assessment Portfolio. This is a performance-based assessment portfolio set up for you by your Rowan professors. The DRF must be completed to meet graduation/certification requirements. More structured than the Presentation Portfolio, here you will find requirements for each of your classes. During each class, you will add to the required signature assignments. Work in your folio will be assessed according to the standards you are required to address in your education program.

4.2 - Constructing a Presentation Portfolio

Learning the process for creating a Presentation Portfolio will assist in working with Directed Response Folios and Web Pages. The format is the same, with only minor variations.

For practice, begin by choosing *Web Folio Builder* from the navigator bar. Choose *Presentation Portfolios*. Enter the name of your portfolio: Call it "Practice." Click on *Create It*.

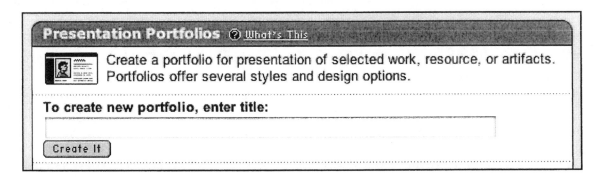

Instead of creating a portfolio yourself, you can use a template designed for your learning community or by *TaskStream*. **To use a template for one of your classes, select the name of the template, as shown below (you will not see this screen until you name your portfolio).**

OR... Select a template designed for your learning community
○ **Ed. Tech. Spring 2006** [More info/Preview]
Created by Lynne Levy on 2/14/2006

Click *Next Step* at the top or bottom of the screen. *Choose a Style*; *Next Step*.

You are now ready to add information.

In the template, click on each of the sub-headings to add information. For instance, in the **Employment Portfolio template**, Click on *Contact Information*; then *Edit*. Add your personal information. Do the same for your *Employment Objective*, explaining what you hope to do after graduation. This text can go in the *Introductory Text* area. For additional information, use the *Main Text* area. Along with entering new text, files can be copied from a word processor file and pasted here (use the clipboard icon for *Paste*).

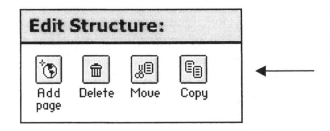

The categories in the *Edit Structure* can be changed with the tools on the top. Any of the categories can be deleted if not relevant or moved to a different area. Additional areas can be added. They can also be renamed when editing.

The box below will also appear; use this to add another section in any area.

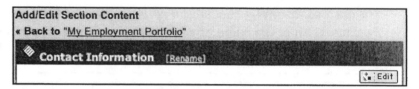

Clicking *Edit* takes you to a screen to input your information in the *Content Editor*.

When doing any writing, you can edit it (font, style, size) using a small HTML formatting palette in *TaskStream*. (For Macintosh, this is only available when using the browser *Safari*.) The character count for the text is 9,000 characters (about three pages). Anything larger than this must be included using an attachment. Be sure to use the *Spell Check* button to check spelling. When adding an attachment, always include *Introductory Text* so the reader knows what you are including and why.

If you want to include an image, click on *Image*. You will see stock images, or you can upload one. Be sure the image has the extension *.gif* or *.jpeg*.

To add a file as an attachment, click on *Attachments*. Text in an attachment will not show on the screen in *TaskStream*, but will download to the desktop so the reader can open it. Anything larger than 9,000 characters must be added as an attachment. Be sure to use only programs you know the reader will have. For instance, many do not have *Inspiration®*; therefore, you must save your document as a *.jpeg* document. Saving text files as *.rtf* (Rich Text Format) might allow any user to open your word processing file.

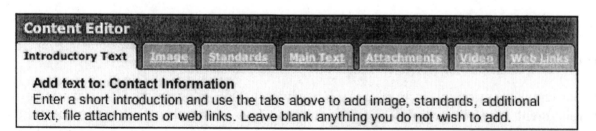

When adding attachments, ensure the file extension is included (*PowerPoint®-.ppt*; *Word-.doc*; *Rich Text Format-.rtf*; *Inspiration-.isf, Excel®-.xls*, etc.).

To add an attachment, refer to the screen illustrated on the next page. *Browse* will take you to the location of your original file (your computer, USB drive, etc.). Once you choose the file, it is uploaded to your *TaskStream* storage area (you have 100 MB of space allocated). All of your uploaded files are stored under *My Previously Uploaded Files*. Those created in *TaskStream* (lessons, units, rubrics) are stored under *My TaskStream Work*. These will remain for use in any of your *TaskStream* folios. To locate your file, choose the category it is in, then the file name.

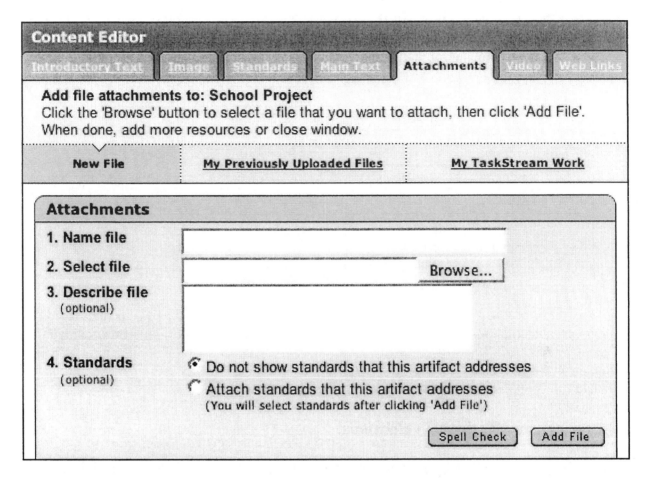

Scanned images can also be included as attachments. When scanning an image, do not store it as a *.tiff* extension; this takes up too much room. Make another choice such as *.gif*, or *.jpeg* for photographs.

Video can also be added here. It must be taken with a digital camcorder, or converted into a digital file using a digitizer. If Web links or standards are a part of your presentation, they can also be inserted in the Content Editor.

Converting a Folio to a Web Page

At the top right of the Folio Builder you will see *Publish/Share*. Then in the center, click on *Publish Options*. Seeing the screen below, click on *Publish* and follow instructions—your folio will be converted to a Web page. You have the option here to have your Web page password protected.

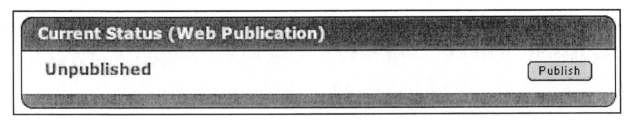

Sharing Work with a Reviewer

Most of your *TaskStream* work will be sent to your class professor for grading. To do this, click on *Publish/Share* in your Folio Builder area.

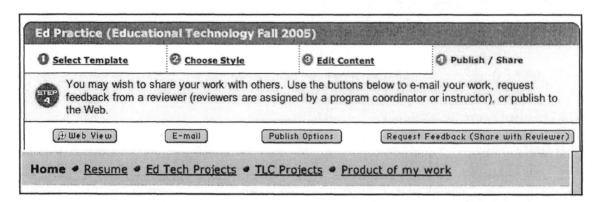

Next, click on *Request Feedback (Share with Reviewer)*. Choose *Entire Folio*, unless you are given other instructions. Choose your professor(s) from the available list. Add a comment, if desired (in *General Comments*, or in any area). To see what your work looks like as a Web page, click on *Web View*.

Receiving your Reviews/Evaluations

To see if you have any feedback from your professors, click *My Programs* on the navigation bar. Click *My Work* to view what you have shared. A *New* icon will appear next to items with comments to read. Click the title of your folio to read the comments. You can also go into *Web Folio Builder*. In **red** you will see *New Comments*. Click on *Publish/Share* to read your comments.

E-mailing a Portfolio

Choosing the e-mail option, you can e-mail your folio to someone else. When doing this, you can make your work available for copying (i.e., you are doing a project with someone else). To do this check *Allow TaskStream recipients to copy this folio* box.

Copying and Deleting a Portfolio

To make a copy of your portfolio, click *Save As/Copy*. This is similar to *Save As* in a word processor. It will be saved under a different name in order to make another version. To delete a portfolio, click *Delete* next to the portfolio title. Be sure you want to delete it—you cannot get it back!

4.3 - Directed Response Folio (DRF)

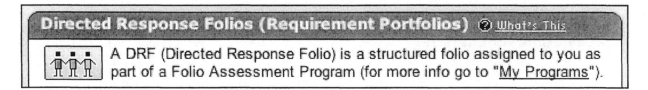

Signature assignments for each of your education classes are located in a DRF under *Folio Builder* and *My Programs (Work on DRF)*. This folio structures requirements you must complete in your program. It is a way for you to demonstrate competency of a predetermined set of skills, standards, or objectives. Each of your class professors will tell you when to use this method to submit a folio. This DRF can be published separately, as above, or it can be combined as part of another folio. Editing is the same as any other folio.

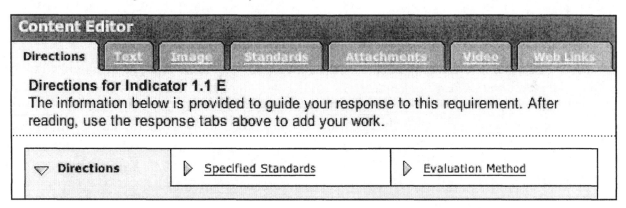

When you click on *Add/Edit Work*, the screen above appears. You will receive directions on the assignments to complete, the standards to assess, and a rubric for evaluation of your DRF.

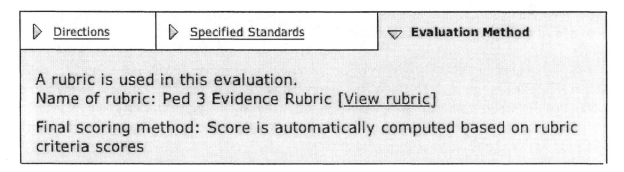

Submitting your DRF is somewhat different than your other folios. You can send this via *Publish/Share* in the beginning. There is, however, another component here. You will see another tab labeled *Evaluation*. This means your portfolio will be evaluated by your class professor using a rubric. You cannot edit the structure here, as in other folios. To send your DRF for grading, click on *Submit for Evaluation*. It will say "submitting will lock your work so no further editing will be possible." This means as you send it, you are ready for it to be graded. Once graded and returned, you can make changes if your professor marks it *Needs Revision*.

In this step, you will submit completed work for evaluation by clicking the **'Submit'** or **'Re-submit'** button (the submit button will only appear if work has been started). All evaluation results will be posted on this page, under "Evaluation Outcome" column.

Evaluation Summary [Print View]

Once your DRF has been evaluated, your status changes to *Evaluated*. A rubric with your scores will be sent to you. To see this, click the *Evaluation* link in the *Web Folio Builder*.

Status	Submit Work	Evaluation outcome
Evaluated		Pass; 50 points

Your DRF can be converted into a Presentation Portfolio. Go to **Web Folio Builder**. Click on *View/edit my Directed Response Folios*. Your DRF may include directions, which you may not want to be part of your folio. To eliminate these, choose *Save as Copy* in the Folio Builder. Name your DRF portfolio. After clicking *Submit*, a new portfolio without directions will appear. To **add your DRF to another folio**, add the title to the *Edit Structure* of your folio. Go to *Attachments*: Your DRF will be under *My TaskStream Work*. Select *Web Folios*, then the name of your DRF.

4.4 - Creating a Web Page

Your work can be submitted as a folio to your professor, "Packed Up" to burn to a CD, or made into a Web page (see page 31, Converting a Folio to a Web Page).

Instead of converting a folio to a Web page, you can also make a Web page from scratch. To begin this process, go to *Web Page Builder* in the navigation bar. The process is the same as creating a Presentation Portfolio (see Section 4.2). The **Web Page Builder** contains templates, making it easy to design a Web page. You can even create a classroom Web page when student teaching, or for classes at your field placements.

OR... Select a general purpose template

○ **Course Home Page** [More info/Preview]
Use this template to create a home page for your college or university course.

○ **Educator's Web Site** [More info/Preview]
Use this template to create a web site which highlights your professional information and interests.

○ **Electronic Exhibit Room** [More info/Preview]
This template makes it is easy to prepare for accreditation visits or display work samples, reports, faculty web pages, and other evidence.

Files attached for other portfolios can be attached to your Web page. These are found in the *Attachments* tab, under *Previously Uploaded Files*. Anything you developed in *TaskStream* will be in *My TaskStream Work*.

As in the Presentation Portfolio, **new pages** can be added in the *Edit Structure* area. Pages can also be rearranged here.

Your Web page can be **previewed** at anytime by clicking on *Web View*.

When you are ready to **publish**, click on *Publish/Share* at the top of the Web Page Builder screen. Then choose *Publish Options*. You will see the screen below.

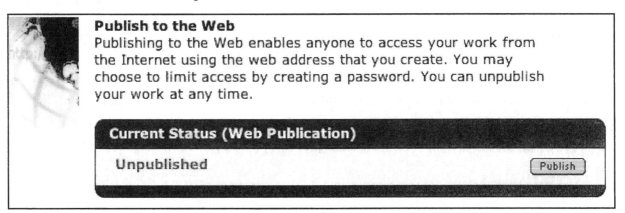

After clicking *Publish*, the screen below appears. You can modify the title in the box and decide if you want your page password protected. *Publish* now sends this address to *TaskStream* for confirmation. Your new Web address will appear in a few seconds.

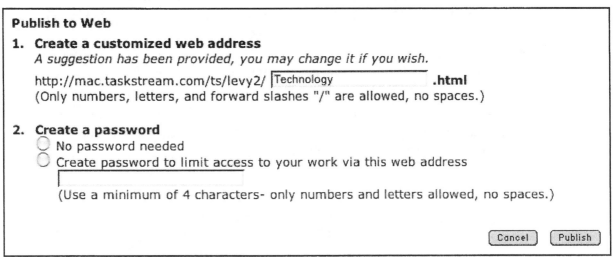

Once your address is confirmed, it will always appear in the Web Page Builder with the Web page.

4.5 - Creating a CD

To create a CD, go to "Pack-It-Up" in the **Resource Manager**. In this process, *TaskStream* takes your files and compresses them to store on a CD. You may request up to five packages per year. The package, which takes about two hours to process, is available for 30 days. Once "packed up" by *TaskStream*, you can place the files on a CD for burning.

4.6 - Printing

When printing *TaskStream* screens, be sure to first click in the frame you want to print. To select the frame, click somewhere in the information you want to print. Then go to *File: Print*, or use the print icon in the menu bar.

4.7 - Activities

• Activity One •

Create a Web page that can be used in your future classroom, the classroom you are in for your field experience, or in your student teaching assignment. Include: the class calendar (planned activities for one month), student assignments, and Web sites to assist students with their homework.

• Activity Two •

Go into the *My Programs* area of *TaskStream*. Access a *Presentation Portfolio* or *DRF* for a class in which you are now enrolled. Complete the portfolio and send it to your professor for review or evaluation.

> **See *TaskStream Summary*
> in the *Appendix*.**

Part II

Standards

Content Area Standards

5.1 - Introduction

The current emphasis on standards-based instruction stems from a 1983 report from the National Commission on Excellence in Education titled *A Nation at Risk: The Imperative for Education Reform*. In the years following this report, content area standards were developed by national subject-matter organizations. This movement was replicated on the state level with the issuance of content area standards developed by state departments of education. Today, educators need to be aware of the standards mandated by their state department of education, as well as the standards set forth by the professional organization(s) in the content area. These standards set forth the knowledge, skills, and dispositions that are essential at each grade level. Teachers in New Jersey must also be cognizant of the New Jersey Core Curriculum Content Standards and the supporting documentation and resources (e.g., Content Area Frameworks) provided by the New Jersey State Department of Education.

5.2 - Professional Associations

Professional associations exist for all of the content areas. In many cases these associations have developed a set of content area standards that have been adopted by the educational community. In other instances, the association has developed guidelines to address the content area. The following list identifies the leading professional associations in the educational community that have developed standards or guidelines to address content coverage.

- **American Alliance for Health, Physical Education, Recreation and Dance (AAHPERD)**
  www.aahperd.org
  > The largest organization of professionals supporting and assisting those involved in physical education, leisure, fitness, dance, health promotion, and education and all specialties related to achieving a healthy lifestyle.

- **American Association of Family and Consumer Sciences (AAFCS)**
  www.aafcs.org
  > The only national forum where K-12 teachers, university educators, and corporate executives collaborate to improve the quality of individual and family life.

- **American Council on the Teaching of Foreign Languages (ACTFL)**
  www.actfl.org
  > The only national organization dedicated to the improvement and expansion of the teaching and learning of all languages at all levels of instruction throughout the United States.

- **Association for Career and Technical Education (ACTE)**
  www.acteonline.org
  > The largest national education association dedicated to the advancement of education that prepares youth and adults for careers.

- **Association for the Advancement of Computing in Education (AACE)**
  www.aace.org
  > An international, educational, and professional organization dedicated to the advancement of the knowledge, theory, and quality of learning and teaching at all levels with information technology.

- **Council for Exceptional Children (CEC)**
  www.cec.sped.org
  > The largest international professional organization dedicated to improving educational outcomes for individuals with exceptionalities, students with disabilities, and/or the gifted.

- **Family and Consumer Sciences Education Organization (FCSEA)**
  www.cwu.edu/~fandcs/fcsea
  > An organization of family and consumer sciences educators and others associated with or interested in family and consumer sciences instruction in schools and colleges.

- **International Reading Association (IRA)**
  www.reading.org
  > The world's leading organization of literacy professionals involved in teaching reading to learners of all ages.

- **International Society for Technology in Education (ISTE)**
  www.iste.org
  > A professional organization with a worldwide membership of leaders and potential leaders in educational technology.

- **International Technology Education Association (ITEA)**
  www.iteaconnect.org/A6.html
  > The largest professional educational association, principal voice, and information clearinghouse devoted to enhancing technology education through technology, innovation, design, and engineering experiences at the K-12 school levels.

- **Music Teachers National Association (MTNA)**
  www.mtna.org
  > The mission of MTNA is to advance the value of music study and music making to society and to support the professionalism of music teachers.

- **National Art Education Association (NAEA)**
  www.naea-reston.org
  > NAEA promotes art education through professional development, service, advancement of knowledge, and leadership.

- **National Association for Bilingual Education (NABE)**

  www.nabe.org

  > The National Association for Bilingual Education is the only professional organization at the national level wholly devoted to representing both English language learners and bilingual education professionals.

- **National Association for the Education of Young Children (NAEYC)**

  www.naeyc.org

  > NAEYC is dedicated to improving the well-being of all young children, with particular focus on the quality of educational and developmental services for all children from birth through age 8.

- **National Association for Gifted Children (NAGC)**

  www.nagc.org

  > An organization of parents, teachers, educators, other professionals, and community leaders who unite to address the unique needs of children and youth with demonstrated gifts and talents, as well as those children who may be able to develop their talent potential with appropriate educational experiences.

- **National Association for Music Education (MENC)**

  www.menc.org

  > The mission of MENC, The National Association for Music Education, is to advance music education by encouraging the study and making of music by all.

- **National Business Education Association (NBEA)**

  www.nbea.org

  > The nation's largest professional organization devoted exclusively to serving individuals and groups engaged in instruction, administration, research, and dissemination of information for and about business.

- **National Council of Teachers of English (NCTE)**

  www.ncte.org

  > NCTE is devoted to improving the teaching and learning of English and the language arts at all levels of education.

- **National Council of Teachers of Mathematics (NCTM)**

  www.nctm.org

  > As the world's largest mathematics education organization, NCTM is a public voice of mathematics education, providing vision, leadership, and professional development to support teachers in ensuring mathematics learning of the highest quality for all students.

- **National Council for the Social Studies (NCSS)**

  www.socialstudies.org

  > The largest association in the country devoted solely to social studies education.

• **National Science Teachers Association (NSTA)**
  www.nsta.org
>   The largest organization in the world committed to promoting excellence and innovation in science teaching and learning for all.

• **Teachers of English to Speakers of Other Languages (TESOL)**
  www.tesol.org
>   TESOL is a global education association whose mission is to ensure excellence in English language teaching to speakers of other languages.

5.3 - New Jersey Core Curriculum Content Standards
(Selected material from the NJCCCS Web site.)

In 1996, the New Jersey State Board of Education adopted the New Jersey Core Curriculum Content Standards, an ambitious framework for educational reform in the state's public schools. New Jersey's standards were created to improve student achievement by clearly defining what all students should know and be able to do at the end of thirteen years of public education. Since the adoption of those standards, the New Jersey Department of Education has continuously engaged in discussion with educators, business representatives, and national experts about the impact of the standards on classroom practices. To assist teachers and curriculum specialists in aligning curriculum with the standards, the department provided local school districts with a curriculum framework for each content area. The frameworks provided classroom teachers and curriculum specialists with sample teaching strategies, adaptations, and background information relevant to each of the content areas. In addition, the statewide assessments were aligned to the Core Curriculum Content Standards. This alignment of standards, instruction, and assessment was unprecedented.

The 2004 New Jersey Core Curriculum Content Standards provide a level of specificity and depth of content that will better prepare students for post secondary education and employment. The standards are based on the latest research in each of the content areas and identify the essential core of learning for all students. They are clear, concise, and appropriate for the benchmarked grade levels and enhance a student's capacity to access new information, problem solve, employ research methods, and ask questions across disciplines.

The New Jersey Core Curriculum Content Standards are not meant to serve as a statewide curriculum guide. Local school districts must use the standards to develop and/or align curriculum to ensure that students achieve the expectations.

Since the adoption of the original 1996 New Jersey Core Curriculum Content Standards, the State Board approved administrative code that implements all aspects of standards-based reform. N.J.A.C. 6A:8 requires districts to: align all curriculum to the standards; ensure that teachers provide instruction according to the standards; ensure student performance is assessed in each content area; and provide teachers with opportunities for professional development that focuses on the standards. The regulations also include the state's accountability system for schools and districts, including new high school graduation requirements.

New Jersey's standards-based reform agenda has also been impacted by the adoption of the federal No Child Left Behind Act of 2001 (NCLB). NCLB requires states to develop challenging content standards and academic assessments and it holds states and local districts accountable for results. Each state must create annual assessments, based on the state's standards, which measure what children know and are able to do in reading and mathematics in grades 3 through 8, and at grade 11. Science will also be assessed at grades 4, 8, and 11. NCLB further requires that students be taught by highly qualified teachers and that research-based methodologies be used in the classroom.

Implementation

The New Jersey Core Curriculum Content Standards are intended for all students. This includes students who are college-bound or career-bound, gifted and talented, those whose native language is not English, students with disabilities, and students from diverse socioeconomic backgrounds. Insistence on the core curriculum means that every student will be involved in experiences addressing all of the expectations set forth in all nine content areas. A core curriculum does not mean that all students will be enrolled in the same courses. Different groups of students should address the standards at different levels of depth and should complete the core curriculum according to different timetables. Depending on their interests, abilities, and career plans, many students will and should development knowledge and skills that go beyond the specific indicators on the Core Curriculum Content Standards. Nevertheless, all students should complete all elements of the core curriculum.

While New Jersey's Core Curriculum Content Standards and cumulative progress indicators have been developed in terms of separate academic disciplines, this familiar approach was chosen primarily for the sake of organizational convenience and simplicity of communication. The results expected of New Jersey's students could have been described in more integrative terms, which would have reflected more accurately how students would someday apply what they have learned in school. Because students obtain knowledge and skills in a multiplicity of ways, it is most productive to concentrate on how we can best use resources to achieve higher order results across an array of content areas. Each content area focuses on the development of higher order thinking skills and requires students to read, write, think, and create. Although the standards have been organized into separate academic disciplines, this is not meant to imply that each standard can only be met through content-specific courses. The very nature of learning lends itself to an integrated approach with reinforcement through experiences beyond the school's walls, such as community service, mentorships, and structured learning experiences.

All schools must have, as their common goal, student achievement of these standards. However, the standards themselves will not result in major improvements unless there is continued commitment to their implementation in each and every school. Changing a school's instructional program to implement the vision of these standards will be a continuous, ongoing process. Of key importance to the successful implementation of these standards is teacher preparation and on-going, high quality professional development. Teacher preparation programs must focus on both content and pedagogy. Programs must focus on the increasing complexity of content set forth in these standards.

Format and Organization

Since our schools need to produce both excellent thinkers and excellent doers, the New Jersey Core Curriculum Content Standards describe what students should know and be able to do in nine academic areas: visual and performing arts, comprehensive health and physical education, language arts literacy, mathematics, science, social studies, world languages, technological literacy, and career education and consumer, family, and life skills. The last two standards areas replace the cross-content workplace readiness standards, adopted in 1996. Each of the nine content sections in this document begins with an introduction that articulates the vision for the content area and provides information on the revision process. Each content area has numbered standards (e.g., 3.1, 5.2), followed by a descriptive statement. The descriptive statement provides a brief overview of the content and skills enumerated in the standard.

The content standards themselves are concerned with the knowledge students should acquire and the skills they should develop in the course of their PK-12 experience. They are broad outcome statements that provide the framework for strands and cumulative progress indicators (CPIs). Strands are organizational tools that help teachers locate specific content and skills. Under each strand is a number of CPIs at specific benchmark grades. The CPIs provide the specific content or skills to be taught and are cumulative; that is, the progress indicators begin at a foundational or basic level and increase in complexity as the student matures, requiring more complex interaction with the content.

The Standards

1. Visual and Performing Arts
   1.1 <u>Aesthetics</u>: All students will use aesthetic knowledge in the creation of and in response to dance, music, theater, and visual art.
   1.2 <u>Creation and Performance</u>: All students will utilize those skills, media, methods, and technologies appropriate to each art form in the creation, performance, and presentation of dance, music, theater, and visual art.
   1.3 <u>Elements and Principles</u>: All students will demonstrate an understanding of the elements and principles of dance, music, theater, and visual art.
   1.4 <u>Critique</u>: All students will develop, apply, and reflect upon knowledge of the process of critique.
   1.5 <u>History/Culture</u>: All students will understand and analyze the role, development, and continuing influence of the arts in relation to world cultures, history, and society.

2. Comprehensive Health and Physical Education
   2.1 <u>Wellness</u>: All students will learn and apply health promotion concepts and skills to support a healthy, active lifestyle.
   2.2 <u>Integrated Skills</u>: All students will use health-enhancing personal, interpersonal, and life skills to support a healthy, active lifestyle.
   2.3 <u>Drugs and Medicine</u>: All students will learn and apply information about alcohol, tobacco and other drugs, and medicines to make decisions that support a healthy, active lifestyle.

2.4 <u>Human Relationships and Sexuality</u>: All students will learn the physical, emotional, and social aspects of human relationships and sexuality and apply these concepts to support a healthy, active lifestyle.

2.5 <u>Motor Skill Development</u>: All students will utilize safe, efficient, and effective movement to develop and maintain a healthy, active lifestyle.

2.6 <u>Fitness</u>: All students will apply health-related and skill-related fitness concepts and skills to develop and maintain a healthy, active lifestyle.

3. Language Arts Literacy

3.1 <u>Reading</u>: All students will understand and apply the knowledge of sounds, letters, and words in written English to become independent and fluent readers, and will read a variety of materials and texts with fluency and comprehension.

3.2 <u>Writing</u>: All students will write in clear, concise, organized language that varies in content and form for different audiences and purposes.

3.3 <u>Speaking</u>: All students will speak in clear, concise, organized language that varies in content and form for different audiences and purposes.

3.4 <u>Listening</u>: All students will listen actively to information from a variety of sources in a variety of situations.

3.5 <u>Viewing and Media Literacy</u>: All students will access, view, evaluate, and respond to print, nonprint, and electronic texts and resources.

4. Mathematics

4.1 <u>Number and Numerical Operations</u>: All students will develop number sense and will perform standard numerical operations and estimations on all types of numbers in a variety of ways.

4.2 <u>Geometry and Measurement</u>: All students will develop spatial sense and the ability to use geometric properties, relationships, and measurement to model, describe, and analyze phenomena.

4.3 <u>Patterns and Algebra</u>: All students will represent and analyze relationships among variable quantities and solve problems involving patterns, functions, and algebraic concepts and processes.

4.4 <u>Data Analysis, Probability, and Discrete Mathematics</u>: All students will develop an understanding of the concepts and techniques of data analysis, probability, and discrete mathematics, and will use them to model situations, solve problems, and analyze and draw appropriate inferences from data.

4.5 <u>Mathematical Processes</u>: All students will use mathematical processes of problem solving, communication, connections, reasoning, representations, and technology to solve problems and communicate mathematical ideas.

5. Science

5.1 <u>Scientific Processes</u>: All students will develop problem-solving, decision-making, and inquiry skills, reflected by formulating usable questions and hypotheses, planning experiments, conducting systematic observations, interpreting and analyzing data, drawing conclusions, and communicating results.

5.2 <u>Science and Society</u>: All students will develop an understanding of how people of various cultures have contributed to the advancement of science and technology, and how major discoveries and events have advanced science and technology.

5.3 <u>Mathematical Applications</u>: All students will integrate mathematics as a tool for problem-solving in science, and as a means of expressing and/or modeling scientific theories.

5.4 <u>Nature and Process of Technology</u>: All students will understand the interrelationships between science and technology and develop a conceptual understanding of the nature and process of technology.

5.5 <u>Characteristics of Life</u>: All students will gain an understanding of the structure, characteristics, and basic needs of organisms and will investigate the diversity of life.

5.6 <u>Chemistry</u>: All students will gain an understanding of the structure and behavior of matter.

5.7 <u>Physics</u>: All students will gain an understanding of natural laws as they apply to motion, forces, and energy transformations.

5.8 <u>Earth Science</u>: All students will gain an understanding of the structure, dynamics, and geophysical systems of the earth.

5.9 <u>Astronomy and Space Science</u>: All students will gain an understanding of the origin, evolution, and structure of the universe.

5.10 <u>Environmental Studies</u>: All students will develop an understanding of the environment as a system of interdependent components affected by human activity and natural phenomena.

6. Social Studies

6.1 <u>Social Studies Skills</u>: All students will utilize historical thinking, problem solving, and research skills to maximize their understanding of civics, history, geography, and economics.

6.2 <u>Civics</u>: All students will know, understand, and appreciate the values and principles of American democracy and the rights, responsibilities, and roles of a citizen in the nation and the world.

6.3 <u>World History</u>: All students will demonstrate knowledge of world history in order to understand life and events in the past and how they relate to the present and the future.

6.4 <u>United States and New Jersey History</u>: All students will demonstrate knowledge of United States and New Jersey history in order to understand life and events in the past and how they relate to the present and future.

6.5 <u>Economics</u>: All students will acquire an understanding of key economic principles.

6.6 <u>Geography</u>: All students will apply knowledge of spatial relationships and other geographic skills to understand human behavior in relation to the physical and cultural environment.

7. World Languages

7.1 <u>Communication</u>: All students will be able to communicate in at least one world language in addition to English. They will use language to engage in conversation, understand and interpret spoken and written language, present information, concepts, and ideas while making connections with other disciplines, and compare the language/culture studied with their own.

7.2 <u>Culture</u>: All students will demonstrate an understanding of the perspectives of a culture(s) through experiences with its products and practices.

8. Technological Literacy

8.1 <u>Computer and Information Literacy</u>: All students will use computer applications to gather and organize information and to solve problems.

8.2 <u>Technology Education</u>: All students will develop an understanding of the nature and impact of technology, engineering, technological design, and the designed world as they relate to the individual, society, and the environment.

9. Career Education and Consumer, Family, and Life Skills

9.1 <u>Career and Technical Education</u>: All students will develop career awareness and planning, employability skills, and foundational knowledge necessary for success in the workplace.

9.2 <u>Consumer, Family, and Life Skills</u>: All students will demonstrate critical life skills in order to be functional members of society.

The Standards Online

The most recent versions of the New Jersey Core Curriculum Content Standards, as well as the supporting Frameworks for each set of standards can be found online at the following Web site: www.nj.gov/njded/cccs.

5.4 - Activities

• Activity One •

Select a professional organization from those identified in section 5.2 and go to their Web site. Examine the online materials available and identify three resources that will be of value to you as a teacher. Using this information, write a two-page (word processed, double-spaced) report that describes the resources and identifies when and how you could use them.

• Activity Two •

Go to the New Jersey Core Curriculum Content Standards (NJCCCS) online at: www.nj.gov/njded/cccs. Select a content area and go to that page. Review the Rationale, Vision, and Standards that are identified. Click on the Framework link and scan the extent and detail of the materials provided. Based on your review of these materials, write a two-page (word processed, double-spaced) paper that discusses how and when you could use these materials as a teacher.

CHAPTER 6

National Educational Technology Standards (NETS)

6.1 - Introduction

The International Society for Technology in Education (ISTE) is the largest international, non-profit organization in the area of educational technology. Since its inception, ISTE has been in the forefront of providing leadership and resources for educational technology professionals. ISTE has been the driving force in the development of Technology Standards for Students and Teachers. These standards address what teachers should learn about technology, and what they should teach.

The primary goal of the ISTE NETS Project is to enable stakeholders in PreK-12 education to develop national standards for educational uses of technology that facilitate school improvement in the United States. The NETS Project will work to define standards for students, integrating curriculum technology, technology support, and standards for student assessment and evaluation of technology use. (NETS home page: cnets.iste.org)

The *National Educational Technology Standards for Students* (NETS•S), the *Profiles for Technology Literate Students,* and the *National Educational Standards for Teachers* (NETS•T) are provided in this chapter. *Profiles for Technology Literate Teachers* can be found at ISTE's Web site: cnets.iste.org/teachers/t_profiles.html.

[The following sections are reproductions of material found at the ISTE Web site (www.iste.org).]

6.2 - National Educational Technology Standards for Students

The National Educational Technology Standards for Students is designed to provide teachers, technology planners, teacher preparation institutions, and educational decision-makers with frameworks and standards to guide them in establishing enriched learning environments supported by technology.

The technology foundation standards for students are divided into six broad categories. Standards within each category are to be introduced, reinforced, and mastered by students. These categories provide a framework for linking performance indicators within the *Profiles for Technology Literate Students* to the standards. Teachers can use these standards and profiles as guidelines for planning technology-based activities in which students achieve success in learning, communication, and life skills.

Technology Foundation Standards for Students

1. Basic operations and concepts
   - Students demonstrate a sound understanding of the nature and operation of technology systems.
   - Students are proficient in the use of technology.

2. Social, ethical, and human issues
   - Students understand the ethical, cultural, and societal issues related to technology.
   - Students practice responsible use of technology systems, information, and software.
   - Students develop positive attitudes toward technology uses that support lifelong learning, collaboration, personal pursuits, and productivity.

3. Technology productivity tools
   - Students use technology tools to enhance learning, increase productivity, and promote creativity.
   - Students use productivity tools to collaborate in constructing technology-enhanced models, prepare publications, and produce other creative works.

4. Technology communications tools
   - Students use telecommunications to collaborate, publish, and interact with peers, experts, and other audiences.
   - Students use a variety of media and formats to communicate information and ideas effectively to multiple audiences.

5. Technology research tools
   - Students use technology to locate, evaluate, and collect information from a variety of sources.
   - Students use technology tools to process data and report results.
   - Students evaluate and select new information resources and technological innovations based on the appropriateness for specific tasks.

6. Technology problem-solving and decision-making tools
   - Students use technology resources for solving problems and making informed decisions.
   - Students employ technology in the development of strategies for solving problems in the real world.

6.3 - Profiles for Technology Literate Students

The Profiles for Technology Literate Students provide performance indicators describing the technology competence students should exhibit upon completion of the following grade ranges:

- Grades PreK - 2
- Grades 6 - 8
- Grades 3 - 5
- Grades 9 - 12

These profiles are indicators of achievement at certain stages in PreK-12 education. They assume that technology skills are developed by coordinated activities that support learning throughout a student's education. These skills are to be introduced, reinforced, and finally mastered, and thus, integrated into an individual's personal learning and social framework. They represent essential, realistic, and attainable goals for lifelong learning and a productive citizenry. The standards and performance indicators are based on input and feedback from educational technology experts as well as parents, teachers, and curriculum experts. In addition, they reflect information collected from professional literature and local, state, and national documents.

[Numbers in parentheses following each performance indicator refer to the standards category to which the performance is linked.]

GRADES PreK - 2

Prior to completion of Grade 2, students will:

1. Use input devices (e.g., mouse, keyboard, remote control) and output devices (e.g., monitor, printer) to successfully operate computers, VCRs, audiotapes, and other technologies. (1)

2. Use a variety of media and technology resources for directed and independent learning activities. (1, 3)

3. Communicate about technology using developmentally appropriate and accurate terminology. (1)

4. Use developmentally appropriate multimedia resources (e.g., interactive books, educational software, elementary multimedia encyclopedias) to support learning. (1)

5. Work cooperatively and collaboratively with peers, family members, and others when using technology in the classroom. (2)

6. Demonstrate positive social and ethical behaviors when using technology. (2)

7. Practice responsible use of technology systems and software. (2)

8. Create developmentally appropriate multimedia products with support from teachers, family members, or student partners. (3)

9. Use technology resources (e.g., puzzles, logical thinking programs, writing tools, digital cameras, drawing tools) for problem solving, communication, and illustration of thoughts, ideas, and stories. (3, 4, 5, 6)

10. Gather information and communicate with others using telecommunications, with support from teachers, family members, or student partners. (4)

GRADES 3 - 5

Prior to completion of Grade 5, students will:

1. Use keyboards and other common input and output devices (including adaptive devices when necessary) efficiently and effectively. (1)

2. Discuss common uses of technology in daily life and the advantages and disadvantages those uses provide. (1, 2)

3. Discuss basic issues related to responsible use of technology and information and describe personal consequences of inappropriate use. (2)

4. Use general purpose productivity tools and peripherals to support personal productivity, remediate skill deficits, and facilitate learning throughout the curriculum. (3)

5. Use technology tools (e.g., multimedia, authoring, presentation, Web tools, digital cameras, scanners) for individual and collaborative writing, communication, and publishing activities to create knowledge products for audiences inside and outside the classroom. (3, 4)

6. Use telecommunications efficiently to access remote information, communicate with others in support of direct and independent learning, and pursue personal interests. (4)

7. Use telecommunications and online resources (e.g., e-mail, online discussions, Web environments) to participate in collaborative problem-solving activities for the purpose of developing solutions or products for audiences inside and outside the classroom. (4, 5)

8. Use technology resources (e.g., calculators, data collection probes, videos, educational software) for problem solving, self-directed learning, and extended learning activities. (5, 6)

9. Determine which technology is useful and select the appropriate tool(s) and technology resources to address a variety of tasks and problems. (5, 6)

10. Evaluate the accuracy, relevance, appropriateness, comprehensiveness, and bias of electronic information sources. (6)

GRADES 6 - 8

Prior to completion of Grade 8, students will:

1. Apply strategies for identifying and solving routine hardware and software problems that occur during everyday use. (1)

2. Demonstrate knowledge of current changes in information technologies and the effect those changes have on the workplace and society. (2)

3. Exhibit legal and ethical behaviors when using information and technology, and discuss consequences of misuse. (2)

4. Use content-specific tools, software, and simulations (e.g., environmental probes, graphing calculators, exploratory environments, Web tools) to support learning and research. (3, 5)

5. Apply productivity/multimedia tools and peripherals to support personal productivity, group collaboration, and learning throughout the curriculum. (3, 6)

6. Design, develop, publish, and present products (e.g., Web pages, videotapes) using technology resources that demonstrate and communicate curriculum concepts to audiences inside and outside the classroom. (4, 5, 6)

7. Collaborate with peers, experts, and others using telecommunications and collaborative tools to investigate curriculum-related problems, issues, and information, and to develop solutions or products for audiences inside and outside the classroom. (4, 5)

8. Select and use appropriate tools and technology resources to accomplish a variety of tasks and solve problems. (5, 6)

9. Demonstrate an understanding of concepts underlying applications to learning and problem solving. (1, 6)

10. Research and evaluate the accuracy, relevance, appropriateness, comprehensiveness, and bias of electronic information sources concerning real-world problems. (2, 5, 6)

GRADES 9 - 12

Prior to completion of Grade 12, students will:

1. Identify capabilities and limitations of contemporary and emerging technology resources and assess the potential of these systems and services to address personal, lifelong learning, and workplace needs. (2)

2. Make informed choices among technology systems, resources, and services. (1, 2)

3. Analyze advantages and disadvantages of widespread use and reliance on technology in the workplace and in society as a whole. (2)

4. Demonstrate and advocate for legal and ethical behaviors among peers, family, and community regarding the use of technology and information. (2)

5. Use technology tools and resources for managing and communicating personal/professional information (e.g., finances, schedules, addresses, purchases, correspondence). (3, 4)

6. Evaluate technology-based options, including distance and distributed education, for lifelong learning. (5)

7. Routinely and efficiently use online information resources to meet needs for collaboration, research, publications, communications, and productivity. (4, 5, 6)

8. Select and apply technology tools for research, information analysis, problem-solving, and decision-making in content learning. (4, 5)

9. Investigate and apply expert systems, intelligent agents, and simulations in real-world situations. (3, 5, 6)

10. Collaborate with peers, experts, and others to contribute to a content-related knowledge base by using technology to compile, synthesize, produce, and disseminate information, models, and other creative works. (4, 5, 6)

6.4 - National Educational Technology Standards for Teachers

Building on the NETS for Students, the ISTE NETS for Teachers (NETS•T), which focus on pre-service teacher education, define the fundamental concepts, knowledge, skills, and attitudes for applying technology in educational settings. All candidates seeking certification or endorsements in teacher preparation should meet these educational technology standards. It is the responsibility of faculty across the university and at cooperating schools to provide opportunities for teacher candidates to meet these standards.

The six standards areas with performance indicators listed below are designed to be general enough to be customized to fit state, university, or district guidelines and yet specific enough to define the scope of the topic. Performance indicators for each standard provide specific outcomes to be measured when developing a set of assessment tools. The standards and the performance indicators also provide guidelines for teachers currently in the classroom.

I. TECHNOLOGY OPERATIONS AND CONCEPTS

Teachers demonstrate a sound understanding of technology operations and concepts.
Teachers:

- A. Demonstrate introductory knowledge, skills, and understanding of concepts related to technology (as described in the ISTE National Education Technology Standards for Students).
- B. Demonstrate continual growth in technology knowledge and skills to stay abreast of current and emerging technologies.

II. PLANNING AND DESIGNING LEARNING ENVIRONMENTS AND EXPERIENCES

Teachers plan and design effective learning environments and experiences supported by technology. Teachers:

- A. Design developmentally appropriate learning opportunities that apply technology-enhanced instructional strategies to support the diverse needs of learners.
- B. Apply current research on teaching and learning with technology when planning learning environments and experiences.
- C. Identify and locate technology resources and evaluate them for accuracy and suitability.
- D. Plan for the management of technology resources within the context of learning activities.
- E. Plan strategies to manage student learning in a technology enhanced environment.

III. TEACHING, LEARNING, AND THE CURRICULUM

Teachers implement curriculum plans that include methods and strategies for applying technology to maximize student learning. Teachers:

- A. Facilitate technology-enhanced experiences that address content standards and student technology standards.
- B. Use technology to support learner-centered strategies that address the diverse needs of students.
- C. Apply technology to develop students' higher order skills and creativity.
- D. Manage student learning activities in a technology-enhanced environment.

IV. ASSESSMENT AND EVALUATION

Teachers apply technology to facilitate a variety of effective assessment and evaluation strategies. Teachers:

- A. Apply technology in assessing student learning of subject matter using a variety of assessment techniques.
- B. Use technology resources to collect and analyze data, interpret results, and communicate findings to improve instructional practice and maximize student learning.
- C. Apply multiple methods of evaluation to determine students' appropriate use of technology resources for learning, communication, and productivity.

V. PRODUCTIVITY AND PROFESSIONAL PRACTICE

Teachers use technology to enhance their productivity and professional practice.
Teachers:

- A. Use technology resources to engage in ongoing professional development and lifelong learning.

B. Continually evaluate and reflect on professional practice to make informed decisions regarding the use of technology in support of student learning.
C. Apply technology to increase productivity.
D. Use technology to communicate and collaborate with peers, parents, and the larger community in order to nurture student learning.

VI. SOCIAL, ETHICAL, LEGAL, AND HUMAN ISSUES
Teachers understand the social, ethical, legal, and human issues surrounding the use of technology in PreK-12 schools and apply those principles in practice. Teachers:
A. Model and teach legal and ethical practice related to technology use.
B. Apply technology resources to enable and empower learners with diverse backgrounds, characteristics, and abilities.
C. Identify and use technology resources that affirm diversity.
D. Promote safe and healthy use of technology resources.
E. Facilitate equitable access to technology resources for all students.

6.5 - Activities

• Activity One •

Read the "NETS for Teachers" contained in this chapter. Write a one-page, double-spaced reflection addressing how these standards would impact your actions as a teacher. Your reflection should include three sections: Description, Analysis, and Future Impact.

• Activity Two •

Read the "NETS for Students" contained in this chapter. Write a one-page, double-spaced reflection addressing how these standards would impact your students and your expectations of them. Your reflection should include three sections: Description, Analysis, and Future Impact.

• Activity Three •

Examine a copy of the NETS document titled *Profiles for Technology Literate Students*. Write a one page, double-spaced paper that addresses how this document would impact the actions and plans of a school or school district.

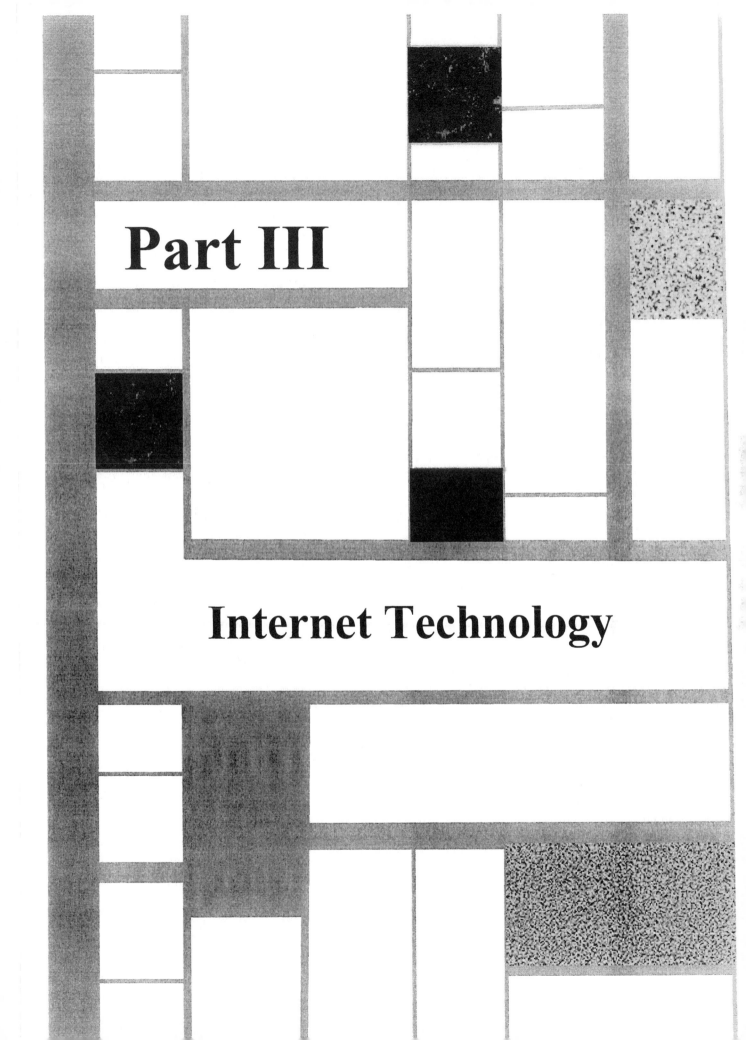

Part III

Internet Technology

CHAPTER **7**

The Internet

7.1 - Introduction

The Internet is a network of computers around the world. It began as an experiment in the late 1960s when the United States Department of Defense, doing military research and needing to access and share information with various units and universities, developed a communication network. In the 1970s, universities and research institutions joined the network, with popularity becoming worldwide during the 1990s. Today, the Internet has permeated every facet of our lives in every corner of the world.

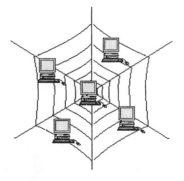

It is often said that the Internet cannot be defined. It is not a place or thing, it is not owned by any person or group, and there is no one in charge. It is a global collection of people and computers linked by cables and telephone lines, all freely exchanging information. This cluster of interconnected networks worldwide gives millions of users access to people, as well as a constantly changing collection of documents, resources, and databases.

The terms Internet and World Wide Web (WWW) are often used interchangeably. They are not the same. The WWW is a part of the Internet, emerging in the early 1990s. E-mail is another component we find in schools and homes today.

7.2 - Connecting to the Internet

Use of the Internet is available to anyone who has a computer with a modem or Ethernet card and connection to the Internet. The higher the GHz speed and RAM (Random Access Memory) of the computer, the better it will function on the Internet.

The speed of accessing the Internet is dependent upon the type of connection one has to the Internet. Dial-up service is available via a computer modem and a connection over a telephone line. This is the slowest connection and ties up the telephone line while using the Internet. If using a modem, be sure the number you call is local and has unlimited minutes. DSL (Digital Subscriber Line) and cable TV deliver the Internet with higher access speeds. A modem is connected to the computer and either the telephone or cable line, resulting in speeds more than ten times faster than a 56K modem. These connections also allow the house phone line to be accessible while the Internet is in use. In addition to speed, another advantage is that the Internet can always be active. You can be connected to the Internet whenever your computer is on.

Any of these connections require a monthly contract with a service provider. Ease of use, speed, accessibility, and the type of services offered vary with providers and connections. Prices for dial-up service are $10 - $20 per month, while higher speed connections could be in the vicinity of $40 - $50 per month. Other considerations are the number of e-mail accounts you receive, space provided for a Web page, customer support, and computer requirements.

Schools are usually connected over networks, allowing them high-speed access to the Internet (using Ethernet cards and often wireless connections).

> ## Free Internet Access for Rowan students— Using a Modem
>
> If you do not want to pay for a service provider, Rowan University offers free dial-up service for students.
>
> - On your computer, click on *Network Connections*.
> - Create a New Connection.
> - Connect to the Internet using a dial-up modem.
> - When asked for an ISP, use *Rowan Dial-Up*.
> - Use one of these two numbers to connect: 856-401-9309 (Blackwood) or 856-863-9016 (Glassboro).
> - Create a connection for *All Users*.
> - Enter your username.
> - It is not recommended that you enable the built-in firewall services—uncheck this box. The other boxes are OK.
> - The final screen tells you if the connection was successful.
> - Add a shortcut to your desktop.

7.3 - Browsing the World Wide Web

Once the computer has a connection to access the Internet, browser software is needed to access and view the Web pages. Most computers come with browser software installed.

The two major browsers are *Netscape Navigator* (a part of *Netscape Communicator*™) and *Microsoft® Internet Explorer*. PCs usually come with *Explorer* installed; however, there is a *Windows* version of *Netscape*. There are also versions of *Netscape* and *Explorer* available for Macintosh (no new versions of *Explorer* will be made for Macintosh). Newer browsers are *Safari*, which comes installed on Apple Macintosh computers, and *FireFox*, available for both *Windows* and *Macintosh OSX*. Software downloads are free from their Web sites. Doing a search for Web browsers will identify many others that are available.

Which should you use? It is a personal choice. They are all similar, and each has advantages and disadvantages. Test them out—Web pages usually appear differently in each browser.

When a browser opens, a Web page appears. At first it is the browser's home page. You can set this to any page you want under *Preferences*. If you always want *Explorer* to open to the Rowan home page, enter http://www.rowan.edu in the *Preferences* of *Explorer*.

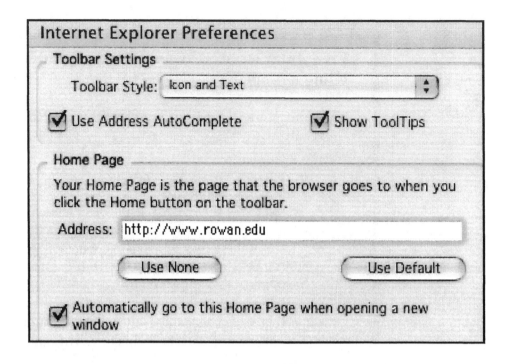

Toolbar Buttons and Menu Items [*Microsoft Internet Explorer*]

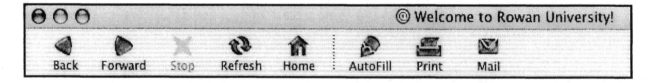

Toolbar Buttons:

Back: Go back one page in the viewed sequence.
Forward: Go forward one page in the viewed sequence.
Stop: Click to stop loading a Web page.
Refresh: Update the page if there have been any changes since last viewed.
Home: Go back to the home page (the first one seen when the browser begins).
      (This page can be set to your choice under *Preferences*.)
AutoFill: Helps to fill out forms.
Print: Print the current Web page selection.
Mail: Opens an e-mail program.

Menu Items:

Window-History: Lists Web sites visited in the last few days/weeks.
Go: Lists sites most recently visited; another way to go back.
Favorites/Bookmarks: A list of favorite sites; bookmarked to return to easily.

Address Bar

Each Web page has a Web address or a URL (Uniform Resource Locator). It must be entered exactly or the Web site will not be found. The majority begin with *http://* (Hypertext Transfer Protocol): a set of rules and procedures that allow Web sites to work. These are the same for all computers and connections. When entering an address, it is not necessary to enter the *http://* in the address; it is understood. The address for Rowan University is www.rowan.edu; the College of Education is www.rowan.edu/colleges/education; the Web address for this book is users.rowan.edu/~levy/tt4t. (Note: not all Web addresses begin with *www*.) The Web address is entered in the Address Bar (also termed the *Location* or the *URL*). Enter the address, then click on *Go* or press the *Enter/Return* key. The site for the address entered should appear in the browser. Some browsers do not require the *www* and *.com* for .com addresses. If the address ends in *.com.* you can just enter the Web name, such as *google*, instead of www.google.com.

> Access hyperlinks used in this book: users.rowan.edu/~levy/tt4t

Bookmarks/Favorites

Any time you locate a site you want to return to at a later time, add a Bookmark (*Netscape*) or Favorite (*Internet Explorer*). It will be stored in a listing in the menu bar for access at a later time. Bookmarks/Favorites can be organized in folders by using *Edit Bookmarks* (*Netscape*) or *Organize Favorites* (*Internet Explorer*).

The *Technology Tools for Teachers* Web site (users.rowan.edu/~levy/tt4t) contains hyperlinks to all sites mentioned in this book. Bookmark this site for easy access.

Saving and Printing Sites

Being connected to the Internet is not the only way to access the information found there. Some alternative ways are:

Downloading Web Pages

To view Web pages at a later time when you are not connected to the Internet, pages can be saved. To save a file, go to *File; Save As: Source (or Text)*. Source saves the entire page as it looks on the Internet; text saves only the text portion.

Sending Files

Some browsers have an option to send pages (look under *File* in the Menu Bar). This allows you to retain the Web address by sending it to an e-mail address. (For example, if you are working at school and find a great site, send it to your home e-mail instead of copying the address.)

Printing

Most pages can be printed with the print command. To determine where the page breaks are, go to *Print Preview*. Some documents allow you to highlight the text, copy it, and paste it into a word processing document. Graphics can also be copied to documents (see Chapter 13: Drawing Tools and Clip Art). If the site is wide (you cannot see all of it without scrolling to the right on the monitor), the entire page will not fit on the paper vertically (two pages will be printed that need to be placed together to read all of the page). When this happens, go to *File; Page Setup*; change the page orientation to print horizontally *(landscape)*.

PDF Documents

Documents on the Internet that are meant to be printed are saved in Portable Document Format (*PDF*). *PDF* formats the text to be printed in a book-like format. Examples include user guides, price lists, articles, and other documents that are meant to be printed for reading off the Internet. To view and print the document, the software *Adobe Acrobat Reader* must be installed on the computer. This can be downloaded for free from the Internet (www.adobe.com). Using *Acrobat Reader*, the document may be saved to the hard drive, desktop, or a disk. The file can then be opened and printed in a readable format.

7.4 - Communicating on the Internet

There is always a need to communicate with other people—colleagues, parents, students, or friends—and exchange information. Frequently, however, problems arise: You do not have time, the other party is not home, now is not a good time to talk, etc. This can be solved by asynchronous communication—sending messages, reading them, and replying to them when the time is available (and you are ready). On the Internet, e-mail, newsgroups, and mailing lists are a few of the tools for asynchronous communication. Other tools, such as chat rooms and instant messaging, are synchronous—messages are sent and received at the same time.

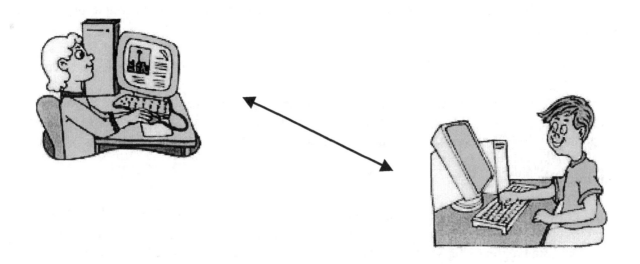

E-Mail (Electronic Mail)

Of the various tools for communication via the Internet, e-mail is the most common for teachers and students. Through e-mail, messages and files are transmitted via a computer network, allowing you to send, receive, and store messages on your computer. E-mail messages not only contain text; graphics, photos, audio, video, computer files, and electronic cards can also be a part of a message. You can compose messages, reply to others, forward messages, store, print, and delete messages.

For anyone with an Internet connection, e-mail is free. You can communicate with friends and colleagues in any state or country. In addition to correspondence with those you know, students can have key pals, while teachers can share ideas and discuss problems with others in their field.

Most browsers, Internet service providers, and portals provide free e-mail accounts. You can have one or multiple accounts. It is a good idea to have different accounts for different purposes: personal, professional, school, etc. An advantage to free accounts from Web portals is that mail can be checked at any time from any computer via the Internet.

E-Mail Address

An e-mail address is needed to receive messages. The mail server for your e-mail places your received messages in a box until you retrieve them. Each address contains specific components so that the mail is sent to the correct mail server.

In the address, each user has a user name (provided with the account) and a domain name (where the mail is sent). The user name and domain name are separated by the @ sign. The domain name ends in a three-letter abbreviation identifying the organization sponsoring the mail server. A few of these abbreviations are: *.edu*=educational, *.gov*=government, *.org*=organization, etc. An example is Lynne Levy at Rowan University, an educational institution: levy@rowan.edu. For addresses outside of the United States, an additional two-letter country abbreviation is added at the end.

K-12 schools with direct mail have their addresses terminating in k12.state.country. A fictitious example of this would be if Lynne Levy taught at Rowan High School in Glassboro, New Jersey. This address might be: levy@rhs.k12.nj.us.

In the Classroom: E-Pals/Key Pals

Schools can set up free, safe e-mail accounts for students. Sites offering these free accounts have filters that block junk mail. Some also block inappropriate language, while others allow teachers to review students' address books. Two examples of these are *Think.com* and *Gaggle.net*.

Using e-mail in the classroom, students can:
- make new friends
- learn about other towns, cities, and countries
- exchange photos
- collaborate on stories and projects
- do research on projects
- communicate with their teachers and their peers

Using e-mail, these exchanges can be with someone in the same town or in another country. Since a keyboard, not a pen, is used, those they communicate with are termed *key pals* or *e-pals* (electronic).

There are a variety of sites on the Internet where the teacher can go to find key pals for students. *Epals.com*® (www.epals.com) is the largest, connecting over 100,000 classrooms and six million students and educators in 191 countries. Students can participate in cross-cultural learning and classroom-to-classroom projects. In addition to e-mail, photographs, and sound and video clips, these sites show the students what life is like in other countries. Another example is *IECC* (www.iecc.org) (Intercultural E-mail Classroom Connections). At this site, teachers link with partners in other cultures and countries for e-mail connections and project exchanges.

Teachers can go to *Teachnet* (www.teachnet.com/t2t) to keep connected with other educators around the world. Those involved exchange ideas pertaining to the K-12 classroom through daily e-mail, a daily e-mail digest, and weekly announcements.

E-Mail Attachments

Attachments are enclosures such as photos or computer files. To send an attachment, click on *Attach* (usually a paperclip) at the top (or side) of the screen; then locate the file on the computer to be attached. Photos must be in the *.jpeg* format.

It is a good idea to send the attachment to yourself first to be sure it works. Computer files must be compatible with the recipient's computer. For example, a file sent that was composed using *Word* can only be opened with *Word* on the receiving computer. Be sure to include the extension, such as *.doc* for this example. Viruses are often sent through attachments on e-mail. Never open an attachment if you do not know the sender of the message.

Address Books

An address book is included with most e-mail programs. This allows you to store frequently used addresses, along with other data about the person. Distribution lists can be created from the addresses to send the same letter to multiple individuals (e.g., a list of all students in your class). By choosing a specific list, the same message would be sent to everyone on the list.

Chatting and Instant Messaging

Chatting and instant messaging take place in real-time when users are online. Chat rooms are virtual areas where people meet and communicate. Areas are topic-specific with two or more people communicating at any one time. On the Internet, real names are not exchanged, and caution must be used to be sure real identities, especially of children, are not revealed. While many chat rooms have poor reputations, others such as *KidsCom*® (www.kidscom.com), are designed for communication among children. Your Rowan professors can set up chat rooms within WebCT for group discussions.

Instant messaging (provided free by *AOL's Instant Messenger*™, *MSN*® *Messenger*, Macintosh's *iChat*®, and others) allows you to write messages back and forth to friends whenever you and the friend are online at the same time. Some also support video and voice conversations. *TaskStream* includes this feature, allowing you to communicate with others while online, asking questions and getting directions.

WebLogs (Blogs)

Blogs are online journals in the form of a Web page. While not a true form of Internet communication, they are Web pages whereby individuals post information. The person maintaining the page is a *blogger*, while the activity of updating the page is called *blogging*. Some types of pages are just for the *blogger* to post information, while others are for discussions. *MyOwnJournal*, *Blogger*™, and *LiveJournal*™ are three examples of free online journals. Blogs encourage students to express themselves, share thoughts and ideas, and write to other students.

7.5 - Internet Terminology

An understanding of the following additional terms will make you more conversant regarding the use of the Internet.

Address: location of a site on the Web.

Domain Name: a unique name assigned to a site, such as *google.com*.

FTP (File Transfer Protocol): a way of transferring electronic files (software, files, pictures, sounds) through the Internet.

Hypertext: a type of document that allows links to other documents.

Hypertext (Hot) Links: words, phrases, or graphics that connect to another page on the Web site or any other site.

HTML (Hypertext Markup Language): the standardized coding language used to create hypertext documents on the WWW.

HTTP (Hypertext Transport Protocol): a communications protocol; used to move WWW documents on the Internet.

Link: an underlined word, phrase, or picture on a Web page; selecting the link takes you to a related page.

Plug-in: software programs, normally downloaded from the Internet, that extend the capabilities of the Web browser. Some come with the browser, others need to be downloaded (free). They usually extend the functionality of the browser for graphics, sound, and multimedia.

Portal: a Web site that offers a variety of services from one location, such as a search engine, news, weather, sports, stocks, maps, e-mail, chat rooms, yellow pages, shopping, and more. Home pages of browsers and search engines are common portals. A portal can be chosen as your home page that comes up each time the browser begins.

URL (Uniform Resource Locator): an Internet address; used to identify locations on the Web.

7.6 - Activities

• Activity One •

Go to Think.com and Gaggle.net. Explore these sites to learn about the features of their free e-mail accounts. Subscribe to each. Compare and contrast their features and ease of use.

• Activity Two •

Go to *Epals.com* (www.epals.com) and *IECC* (www.iecc.org). Explore these sites to learn about connecting your students with students in other countries. What does each site have to offer you for your classroom? How can your students participate in their projects?

• Activity Three •

Go to *Teachnet* (www.teachnet.com/t2t). Subscribe to their daily e-mail digest and weekly announcements. Follow these postings for three weeks. Report your findings.

CHAPTER **8**

Searching the World Wide Web

8.1 - Introduction

Since the World Wide Web consists of several billion Web pages, locating what you want can be a problem. Search engines are software programs that help you find the information you need. Most search engines send *spiders* or *robots* out on the Web to find key words, bringing them back and placing them in a large database of terms. When you enter search terms, the database is searched for your key words. There are thousands of search engines; some are general, and some are for very specific searches. Not all searching can be done from common search engines such as *Google*™. Finding the right search engine for your purpose can be difficult. Once you have located the appropriate search engine, you need a good searching strategy.

8.2 - Types of Search Engines

Regular Search Engines

When users of the World Wide Web talk about using a search engine, they are usually referring to a regular search engine such as *Google*. In recent years, *Google* has become synonymous with searching the Web. One "googles" to find information. In addition to basic searching, *Google* has a number of features on the main tool bar. A few of these are:

- *I'm Feeling Lucky*™: a button on the main search page that automatically takes you to the first Web page returned for your query.
- *Images:* billions of images (photographs, clip art) to search and use (check for permissions).
- *Local:* find maps, businesses, and services in U.S. towns or cities.
- *Language:* get results in different languages.
- *Date:* ask for results in the last three, six, or twelve months.
- *Groups:* discussion groups for online communication.
- *SafeSearch:* filtering to eliminate adult sites from search results.

Alta Vista™ search categories include the *Web, Images, MP3/Audio, Video,* and *News.* You can search worldwide, or just the U.S., and in all languages or English/Spanish. Also included on the home page is *Babel Fish Translation,* where you can translate from/to many languages, whether it is a block of text or an entire Web page.

Directory Search Engines

Directory search engines have the assistance of humans to place Web sites in categories. Rather than searching, they open with a list of categories. Each category has sub-categories. The user works through the categories and eventually is presented with a list of site links.

Arts & Humanities
Photography, History, Literature...

Business & Economy
B2B, Finance, Shopping, Jobs...

Computers & Internet
Software, Web, Blogs, Games...

Education
Colleges, K-12, Distance Learning...

Yahoo® is the most popular and frequently used directory search site on the Web. You can search or browse the directory. A sample of browse categories is shown on the previous page.

Another directory is the *Open Directory Project*. This is the largest human-edited directory on the Web. It was constructed, and is maintained, by a community of volunteers. Anyone can contribute by choosing a topic of interest and contributing their expertise by adding, deleting, and updating links. This directory currently contains over five million sites, 590,000 categories, and 70,000 editors.

About.com is another search engine that utilizes people. Here they serve as *Guides to the Internet*. There are over 500 guides that are experts in their field. They offer information and advice, covering over 57,000 topics.

Metasearch Engines

Metasearch engines search other search engines and report the results. These draw from the top search engines, remove duplicate sites, and compile the results.

Dogpile® and *MetaCrawler*® are two metasearch engines that search other search engines, reporting the results by relevance or by the search engine where the sites were found. Both search *Google, MSN*®*, Yahoo, Ask*®*,* and more.

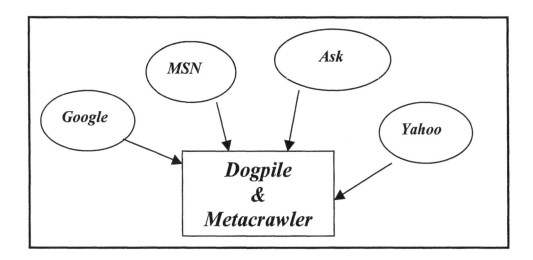

Search Engines for Children

There are specific search engines for children, with searches yielding only *safe* sites. Some of these sites are educational portals, or Web guides, providing much more than a search engine. Often included are sites for specific interests, safe chat rooms, games, activities, sports, news, clubs, and more.

Yahooligans!®, self-named *The Web Guide for Kids*, features a safe search engine for children ages 7-12. Topical areas include *Around the World, Arts & Entertainment, Computers & Games, School Bell, Science & Nature,* and *Sports & Recreation.* Other areas such as news, movies, jokes, games, etc. are also available.

Ask for Kids™ is a search engine where the user asks a question. Sites are identified based on words in the question. The home page includes *Fun & Games, News Resources,* and numerous *Study Tools.*

Two other search engines for children/teens include *KidsClick!*, a directory Web search for kids by librarians, and *Awesome Library for Kids*, a place to search for *School Subjects* or *Fun and More. The Open Directory Project* also has a site for kids and teens.

Search Engine Addresses

About.com	about.com
Alta Vista	www.altavista.com
Ask	www.ask.com
Ask for Kids	www.askforkids.com/
Awesome Library for Kids	www.awesomelibrary.org/student.html
Dogpile	www.dogpile.com
Fast Search	alltheWeb.com
Google	www.google.com
KidsClick	kidsclick.org
Metacrawler	www.metacrawler.com
Open Directory	dmoz.org
Open Directory – for Kids & Teens	dmoz.org/Kids_and_Teens/
Yahoo	www.yahoo.com

Other Search Engines

The search engines listed above are some of the most common examples from the various categories. There are literally thousands of search engines. *Search Engine Watch* is a Web site that provides information on these and many other search engines. Included are ratings, tutorials, daily and monthly newsletters, and links to search engines in various categories. A sampling of these categories are: *News, Shopping, Multimedia, Kids,* and *Specialty.*

NoodleTools.com is a collection of tools that assist with online research. These tools assist in selecting a search engine, along with citing sources in MLA or APA style. *Choose the Best Search for Your Information Need* is a table that provides links to specific search engines. Look up the information you need, and they identify search engines for that need. This need could be anything from *biographical* to *opinions of current issues* or *primary sources* to *radio programs.*

8.3 - The Invisible Web

The search engines previously identified are part of the "visible Web." This is what you see when doing a Web search, or accessing a subject directory. The "Invisible Web" contains information these search engines do not find—they are "invisible" to the searching "spiders." This is not just text, but sounds, images, audio, etc. PDF files are another "find." Spiders are unable to locate these since they are not in HTML format for the Web. There are thousands of specialized databases that cannot be searched by regular search engines. Often, Web pages are generated just for your search; they are not stored anywhere.

An example is searching for books in Rowan's Campbell Library. When you go to the Campbell Library Web site, you can search for all of their books from your computer. At the University of Pennsylvania Web site, you can find *The Online Books Page* (onlinebooks.library.upenn.edu). This leads you to over 25,000 free books on the Web. Other databases are available for magazines (www.magportal.com), music, newspapers, museums, etc. The same concept holds true for reference books. Searching for "dinosaurs" will not take you to Encyclopedia Britannica as part of your search. You must go to the Web site of the reference book and perform a search there.

Databases for academic research can be found at *Infomine* (infomine.ucr.edu), *AcademicInfo* (www.academicinfo.net), and *Librarians Internet Index* (lii.org), to name a few. These all have searchable categories, which also take you to academic sites as well as invisible databases. At these sites, as well as regular search engines, searching for terms and including the word "database" in your search will take you to the thousands of invisible Web databases (i.e., "education database"). *Searchability* (www.searchability.com) provides a list of multi-subject guides (with descriptions) to thousands of search engines covering hundreds of subjects.

When searching for *education database* at *Google*, the first site to appear is ERIC. The introductory text for this site follows:

> *The Education Resources Information Center (ERIC), sponsored by the Institute of Education Sciences (IES) of the U.S. Department of Education, produces the world's premier database of journal and non-journal education literature. The ERIC online system provides the public with a centralized ERIC Web site for searching the ERIC bibliographic database of more than 1.1 million citations going back to 1966. More than 107,000 full-text non-journal documents (issued 1993-2004), previously available through fee-based services only, are now available for free. ERIC is moving forward with its modernization program, and has begun adding materials to the database. [www.eric.ed.gov]*

When using *Advanced Search*, you have the option to choose from publication dates, as well as publication types (shown on the next page).

ERIC Publication Types

Journal Articles	Historical Materials
Book/Product Reviews	Information Analyses
Books	Legal/Legislative/Regulatory Materials
Collected Works - General	Machine-Readable Data Files
Collected Works - Proceedings	Multilingual/Bilingual Materials
Collected Works - Serials	Non-Print Media
Computer Programs	Numerical/Quantitative Data
Creative Works	Opinion Papers
Dissertations/Theses	Reference Materials - Bibliographies
ERIC Digests	Reference Materials - Directories/Catalogs
ERIC Publications	Reference Materials - Vocabularies/Classifications
Guides - Classroom - Learner	Reports - Research
Guides - Classroom - Teacher	Speeches/Meeting Papers
Guides - General	Tests/Questionnaires
Guides - Non-Classroom	Translations

[www.eric.ed.gov/ERICWebPortal/Home.portal?_nfpb=true&_pageLabel=ERIC_Search&Clearme=true]

Another way to access ERIC materials, along with access to *the Gateway to Educational Materials (GEM)* and other sources, is through the *Educator's Reference Desk*[sm] (www.eduref.org).

> *The Educator's Reference Desk builds on over a quarter century of experience providing high-quality resources and services to the education community. From the Information Institute of Syracuse, the people who created AskERIC, the Gateway to Educational Materials, and the Virtual Reference Desk, the Educator's Reference Desk brings you the resources you have come to depend on. 2,000+ lesson plans, 3,000+ links to online education information, and 200+ question archive responses.* [www.eduref.org]

While many search engines cannot locate *Word, Excel, PDF*, and other non-HTML files, *Gigablast* (www.gigablast.com) locates these, along with files regular search engines can find.

> *Founded in 2000, Gigablast was created to index up to 200 Billion pages with the least amount of hardware possible. Gigablast provides large-scale, high-performance, real-time information retrieval technology for partner sites. The company offers a variety of features including topic generation and the ability to index multiple document formats. This search delivery mechanism gives a partner "turn key" search capability and the capacity to instantly offer search at maximum scalability with minimum cost. In addition, the Gigablast Website (www.gigablast.com) provides unique "Gigabits" of information, enabling visitors to easily refine their search based upon related topics from search results. Clients range from NASDAQ 100 listed corporations to boutique companies.* [www.gigablast.com/about.html]

8.4 - Searching at Rowan University

Resources similar to those found on the Invisible Web are in databases and indexes at Campbell Library at Rowan University. Some of these can be located through the Internet from home, while others can only be located when on campus or in the library. This depends on individual licenses. Note the legend in the picture below showing that some are electronic, while others can only be accessed from campus, or at the library. This listing can be found at: www.rowan.edu/open/library/databases/index.htm.

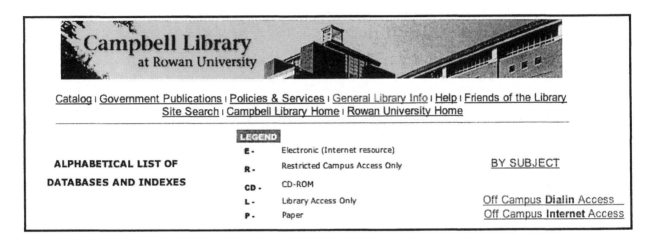

Electronic Resources can be found at:
www.rowan.edu/open/library/databases/historical_abstracts.htm

Electronic Resources

Listed by Subject   Instructions for off-campus access

Listed Alphabetically

A | B | C | D | E | F | G | H | I | J | K | L | M | N | O | P | Q | R | S | T | U | V | W | X | Y | Z

From the library home page (www.rowan.edu/open/library) you can do a search of Rowan's library catalog, or a catalog *Super Search* from *EN[Compass]*.

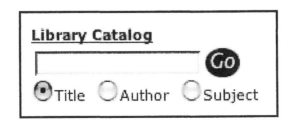

8.5 - Searching Strategies

Basic Search Engine Procedure

Most search engines operate in much the same way. The search engine has a box where the user enters a key word or words for the topic to be searched. When the search is started, the engine searches the resources of the Web to identify those sources that best match the identified search term(s). The result is the identification of the number of matches found based on the keyword and a ranked list of the sites. For each "hit," the following information is usually provided: (1) the name of the document, (2) a brief description of the document, and (3) a direct link to access the document/site. The most difficult part in the search is choosing the terms to search; sometimes this is a "guessing game."

When accessing the results, it is a good idea to look at the first two or three sites listed. If these (or at least the first ten) are not productive then it is doubtful that the others will be of value. If the results are not productive you can either search again using different words, or use the power search/advanced search feature that most search engines have. This, or a search using Boolean operators such as AND or NOT, might produce more accurate results.

Boolean Searches

Most search tools now use Boolean Logic. That means that if two or more words are identified in the search area (e.g., math lesson plans), the tool will search for documents with the words grouped in the identified order (math+lesson+plans). Some search engines, however, still search for each of the words separately, resulting in many hits that are not relevant. To ensure the words are not searched independently, group two or more words together using quotation marks (e.g., "math lesson plans").

By default, *Google* only returns pages that include all of your search terms. The connector "and" is understood. The order the terms are typed is important.

When searching for "math lesson plans" at *Google*, the following number of pages were returned:

- math lesson plans = 5,820,000
- math + lesson + plans = 5,820,000
- "math lesson plans" = 84, 400
- "lesson plans" + math = 3,170,000
- "math lesson plans" + elementary = 84,100
- "elementary math lesson plans" = 642
- "elementary math lesson plans" + grade 3 = 322
- "algebra lesson plans" = 1,150
- "algebra lesson plans" + advanced = 315
- algebra lesson plans advanced = 815, 000

As you can see, "and" is not necessary, but quotation marks keep the phrase together. Using "+" or "-" also helps to narrow the search. Advanced searches, available as an option in most engines, offer the searcher a variety of options, as explained below. However, when using proper Boolean search logic, the same results occur. When quotes are used, the search is the same as that done in an Advanced Search using "with the exact phrase" option.

Google's Advanced Search Tool helps you locate information quickly by selecting various criteria for your search. You can search for pages:

- that contain certain words
- that contain an exact phrase
- that have at least one of the words you list
- that contain some words, but without another (same as minus)
- that are written in a specific language
- that are in a specific file format
- that were updated in a specific time frame
- that have specific terms in various parts of the document
- that are filtered using *SafeSearch*
- from a specific site or domain

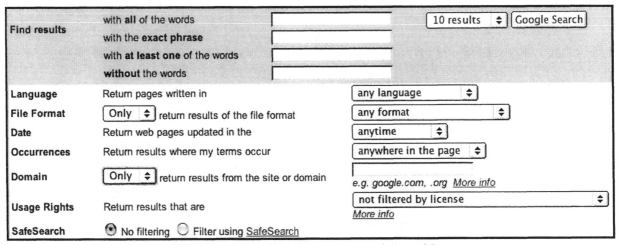

[Screen from *Google's* Advanced Search]

At the bottom of the page, you can also search for the full text of books and search scholarly pages (along with other features).

✓ any format
Adobe Acrobat PDF (.pdf)
Adobe Postscript (.ps)
Microsoft Word (.doc)
Microsoft Excel (.xls)
Microsoft Powerpoint (.ppt)
Rich Text Format (.rtf)

By using the Advanced Search, or adding an extension to any search, you can search for *PDF*, *Word*, *Excel*, *Postscript*, *PowerPoint*, or *Rich Text Format* documents. These will not appear without this extension used in the search.

8.6 - Filtering Web Searches

It is difficult to supervise every student on the Internet while at school. A question for all schools is whether or not to block access to certain Web sites. Parents are concerned that their children might get into sites where they can view inappropriate or dangerous images. Filters are available, most commonly as software programs, to block undesirable key works, phrases, categories, or sites. Most can be customized by the school for age groups, or to block specific words and categories. Most search engines contain filters as an option so sites can be blocked at home or at school. Filters are not foolproof; students often find ways around them. An alternative is to give students specific Web addresses to go to, or to provide them with bookmarks to use in class, rather than allowing them to "surf the Web." Even if a filter is used, students always need supervision when using the Internet. *Google's SafeSearch* screens for adult sites and eliminates them from search results.

8.7 - Activities

• Activity One •

Choose a subject you plan on teaching in the future. (1) Identify a specific topic and grade level. (2) Identify three search terms. (3) Go to three search engines. (4) Perform the same search at each. (5) Reflect on your findings.

• Activity Two •

Choose a research topic you are studying in one of your classes. Using resources from ERIC, search for the topic and report your findings. (1) Identify the topic you searched. (2) What types of results were obtained? (3) Which components of ERIC were searched? (4) Provide a review of the material you found. If one topic yields poor results, use another topic.

• Activity Three •

Search for lesson plans for a specific topic. Think about the best terms to search. Identify the topic and grade level, the search words, and the number of results found. Do this search three times using similar combinations of words, quotation marks, and Boolean searches techniques. Which search provided the best results? Reflect on your findings.

• Activity Four •

Utilize the databases and indexes at Campbell Library at Rowan University to investigate a topic you must research. (1) Identify your topic. (2) Try at least three searches. (3) Reflect on your findings.

The WWW in the Classroom

9.1 - Introduction

Technology tools have always played an important role in the process of education. In recent years, however, the World Wide Web has surfaced as the preeminent resource tool for teachers. With an initial investment of time and effort to surf the Web, teachers can access and infuse a virtually unlimited number and variety of materials into their teaching. Reference material, teaching strategies, lesson plans, virtual field trips, online projects, puzzles, bulletin board ideas, current events, maps, online exhibits, and worksheets are just a sampling of what the teacher can find on the WWW to use in the classroom.

Just as extensive is the wealth of information and resources available for students. They can look up reference material, practice math problems, search encyclopedias, take interactive quizzes, do their homework, and locate primary sources. They may also participate in collaborative projects, virtual field trips, WebQuests, and a myriad of other real time and innovative activities.

The amount of material is so enormous that it would be impossible to discuss all of the possibilities in a single book. This chapter is intended to serve as an introduction to provide guidance for the teacher to begin to explore the multiple resources on the World Wide Web.

9.2 - Educational "Starting Points"

There are a variety of Web sites that are designated as "starting points" for teachers, parents, and students. These often include safe subject resources for students, online projects, curriculum resources for teachers, teaching tips, current events, monthly topics, e-mail, message boards, lesson plans, rubrics, worksheets, and other teacher tools. Some are termed "portals," giving the user a variety of options on the first page. Here, some send teachers, parents, students, or administrators off in different directions to find just what they need. Others are set up as directories of subject resources. Most are totally free, while others have some free resources, as well as those available by subscription. A few sites are by subscription only. A sampling of the most popular (all free resources) are described here.

Kathy Schrock's Guide for Educators (school.discovery.com/schrockguide) is a categorized list of sites useful for enhancing curriculum and professional growth. It is updated often to include the best sites for teaching and learning. This site, now part of *DiscoverySchool.com*, has been the recipient of many awards. Site areas include subject access, search tools, and teacher helpers. The extensive Web links found here are a rich resource and excellent starting point for teachers. Access to the many other sites and tools also available from *Discovery School* is provided at this site. One of the best!

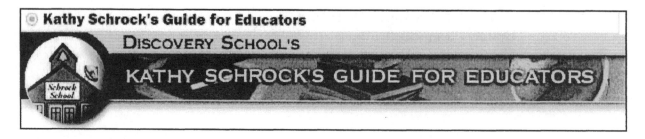

AOL@School® (www.aolatschool.com), available to all, not just AOL subscribers, contains K-12 classroom resources for students, parents, and teachers. Reference materials, tutorials, educational games, and more are available for students. Teachers can find lesson plans, along with classroom resources, tools, and training. For parents, there are resources to assist children with their school work. The home page provides news, monthly features, and learning services. This is an example of a true educational portal.

Education World® (www.educationworld.com) is an excellent site for teachers. Subtitled *The Educator's Best Friend*, this site has six major divisions: *Lesson Planning, Administrator's Desk, School Issues, Professional Development, Technology Integration*, and *Ed. World at Home*. Articles here change often, so check the site daily or weekly. There is a *Joke of the Day, Quote of the Day*, and *Classroom Management Tip of the Day*. Also included are *Article Archives, Subject Resources, Specialties, Reference Center*, and *Featured Programs*. In the *Reference Center* you can subscribe to their newsletters, which will come to you weekly by e-mail. Another weekly feature is *Techtorials*, step-by-step instructions on using some aspect of technology in the regular classroom. These are short, practical, and educationally sound, providing classroom teachers with simple, straightforward tips to use today. An important part of the site contains articles they have published. A search engine takes you to thousands of articles that have been published at *Education World*. Each article also contains links to related sites on the WWW.

Dr. LeBeau's Home Page (www.suelebeau.com) is subtitled "A Resource for Teachers, Students, and Curious Adults." Sue LeBeau, a New Jersey educator, has put together an excellent site for all. Choices on the home page take the user further into additional categories of educational resources for all areas. This site is highly recommended.

Scholastic (www.scholastic.com), known to many for reading resources and books for children, hosts a Web site for Kids, Parents, Teachers, Administrators, and Librarians. *Scholastic News* (for kids) and *BookBeat* are two daily features, along with games, contests, activities, advice, lessons, teacher tools, and more.

Federal Resources for Educational Excellence (FREE) (www.ed.gov/free) provides many free resources for the classroom from the U.S. Government. More than 30 federal agencies put hundreds of federally supported teaching and learning resources together to make them easier to find. An easy-to-follow site map guides in your searching.

Teacher Resources at *MarcoPolo* (www.marcopolo-education.org) provides high quality standards-based resources for teachers and students, including Web resources and interactives.

The sites above are examples of the many resources available for teachers. Additional sites can be found on the *Technology Tools for Teachers* Web site at users.rowan.edu/~levy/tt4t.

9.3 - Lesson Plans

Imagine having a file cabinet containing hundreds of lesson plans. This vision is now a reality. Thousands of teachers have freely shared their lesson plans and teaching ideas by making them available on the Internet as a part of various databases and Web sites. You may not want to use the lesson plan in its entirety; however, online lesson plans can provide ideas, as well as innovative approaches to teaching.

A good starting place is the *Educator's Reference Desk* (www.eduref.org). This combines resources from *AskERIC*, the *Gateway to Educational Materials*, and the *Virtual Reference Desk*. There are over 2,000 lesson plans, 3,000 links to online education information, and 200 question archive responses at this site. Lesson plans can be browsed by subject, or you can search their database by topic and grade level.

Search the Lesson Plan Collection

Describe what you are looking for. <u>Searching Tips.</u>

should contain ▼	the words ▼	all fields ▼

| ☐ Pre-K | ☐ 1st | ☐ 2nd | ☐ 3rd | ☐ 4th | ☐ 5th | ☐ 6th |
| ☐ Kinder. | ☐ 7th | ☐ 8th | ☐ 9th | ☐ 10th | ☐ 11th | ☐ 12th |

There are many other sources of lesson plans on the Web (a few are shown below; see the *Technology Tools for Teachers* Web site for a more complete listing). Other sites can be found through searches. Unfortunately, there is no easy way to search all of the databases and instantly find just what you need. Look through some of the choices and bookmark those that have possibilities for your subject/grade level.

Education World's Lesson Planning Center (www.education-world.com/a_lesson) features new lesson plans (they publish a new lesson plan daily), along with other archives by subject area. Current lessons, lesson plan articles, and lesson planning resources are featured here.

The Lesson Plans Page (www.lessonplanspage.com) houses over 2,500 lesson plans. Choose your subject from the categories: *math, science, music, language arts, computers & Internet, social studies, art, PE & health, other*, and *multi-disciplinary*.

N.Y. Times Teacher Connections (www.nytimes.com/learning/teachers), for grades 6–12, provides daily lesson plans, lesson plan archives, news, puzzles, and more.

PBS Teacher Source (www.pbs.org/teachersource) features over 3,000 lesson plans and activities. A search engine is available, or you can browse by subject.

9.4 - Teacher Utilities

Every teacher can use help in the classroom with daily tasks such as grading; making out tests; and producing rubrics, worksheets, puzzles, certificates, and other handouts. Software can be purchased for these tasks; however, you can find some free utilities on the WWW. As with other sites, some of the utilities are free for teachers, while others have a fee involved. Some companies also offer free trials of their software for the teacher to use, evaluate, and compare the various products. To find those currently available, it is best to do a search, as availability of utilities on the WWW changes frequently.

Puzzles

There are a number of free puzzle-making utilities on the WWW that can be used by both teachers and students.

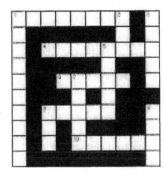

PuzzleMaker is available as a free resource at *Discovery School's* site (www.puzzlemaker.com). Options include *Fallen Phrases, Letter Tiles, Cryptograms, Double Puzzle, Math Square, Number Blocks, Word Search, Criss-Cross Puzzle, Hidden Message,* and *Mazes.*

At *Crossword Puzzle Games* (www.crosswordpuzzlegames.com), you can create your own crosswords, or use theirs.

FunBrain's Word Turtle (www.funbrain.com/detect/) is a seek-and-find word search game. Enter a list of words, and they are hidden in a puzzle. Levels can be selected. Children can play against *FunBrain,* or print the puzzle out on paper.

Other Utilities

Bulletin board ideas are available from *Discovery School, Kathy Schrock's Guide for Educators,* and *Education World,* along with many other sites. Just search for "bulletin board" + the topic you need. *Learning Page* (www.learningpage.com) and *ABC Teach*® (www.abcteach.com) are two excellent sites for worksheets. *RubiStar* (rubistar.4teachers.org/index.php) is a free tool to help teachers create rubrics. They can save and edit them for a year on *RubiStar's* site. *Web Workshop Wizard* (wizard.4teachers.org) is one of several online tools found at *4Teachers.org.* This permits teachers to create worksheets, lessons, and Web pages and post them on the Web.

Sue LeBeau has compiled a long listing (www.suelebeau.com/freetools.htm) of free tools for teachers on her site. These include quiz generators, worksheets, flashcards, games, puzzles, certificates, forms, calendars, templates, and more.

Remember, when you find good utilities, as well as other sites, bookmark them for future use. You might even want to begin a notebook of teaching resources, lesson plans, and ideas you find for classroom use.

9.5 - Sites for New Teachers

As a pre-service teacher and a new teacher, you need basic information about being in a new classroom and being a new teacher. Below are descriptions of some sites to assist you. **Links to these sites are on the *Technology Tools for Teachers* Web site (users.rowan.edu/~levy).** There you will also find a number of articles for new teachers from *Education World*, along with other sites for the new teacher.

Scholastic—Resources for New and Future Teachers: resources and advice for new teachers. At the top of the page are links to the main Scholastic site, along with *Online Activities*, *Lesson Plans*, and *Tools*.

NEA Works 4 Me Tips Library: an archive for *NEA's Weekly Classroom Tips* e-mail. This library contains more than 400 tips offering ideas and solutions that you can use in your classroom.

New Teacher Resources: resources from *TeachersFirst*, a Web resource for K-12 classroom teachers who want useful resources and lesson plans to use with their students.

A New Teacher's Survival Guide: a guidebook; substitutes for a mentor when you need help.

Survival Guide for New Teachers: an online book from the U.S. Department of Education. This is a guide to how new teachers can work effectively with veteran teachers, parents, principals, and teacher educators.

Online Resources for New Teachers: part of a course designed for new teachers at the Oswego City School District, this site can help you by providing you with one-stop shopping for many of the resources that you will find beneficial.

Ideas for New Teachers and Education Students: information ranging from lesson planning and writing behavioral objectives to ideas about classroom management and descriptions of the advantages and disadvantages of different instructional methods. Click on the home page for more categories.

NEA—Helping New Teachers Survive and Thrive: a guide for NEA local affiliates interested in creating new teacher support systems.

The First Days of Middle School: help for new teachers, the first days of school, discipline, and classroom management are the main categories of this site.

Beginning Teachers' Tool Box: while part is an advertisement for a book they publish, the section, *New Teacher's Home Page*, contains good practical tips and resources.

Teacher Resource Center: from the Georgia Department of Education—links to many documents for the first-year teacher.

9.6 - Online Projects

Collaboratively or individually, students can participate in a variety of projects and activities that are posted on the WWW. Collaborative, online projects are one of the most exciting ways to motivate students. Students get involved by posting projects on the Web, e-mailing other students or experts, discussing issues on a threaded discussion, or holding an online chat.

Most collaborative learning projects are placed on the Web at nationally acclaimed sites housing online projects. These projects are for students to collaborate not just with their classmates, but with students around the world. Through these experiences, students learn to use the Web to engage in data exchanges with students from other schools, collaborate on writing projects, and participate in world expeditions and explorations. Most sites and experiences are free; however, some require a registration fee. A few of the most popular are described below.

The *Global Schoolhouse* (www.gsn.org) hosts a variety of collaborative projects each year. The original clearinghouse for collaborative projects, this not-for-profit organization has been linking classrooms around the world since 1984. Free membership provides project-based learning support materials, resources, activities, lessons, and special offers to schools. Over 90,000 educators in over 194 countries now collaborate on projects. Future, current, and archived projects can be accessed on their Web site.

JASON Project (www.jasonproject.org) was founded in 1989. Its mission is to inspire in students a life-long passion for learning in science, math, and technology through hands-on, real-world scientific discovery. It gives educators exciting new ways to teach standards-based mathematics and provides students with hands-on approaches to solving real scientific problems while gaining technology-rich learning experiences.

ThinkQuest (www.thinkquest.org), sponsored by the Oracle Education Foundation, is "all about students thinking and learning together." Working in teams, students compete to create the "best educational Web sites," while they also compete for exciting prizes, including a trip to *ThinkQuest Live*, an educational extravaganza celebrating their achievements. The teams' Web sites are published for the world to see in the *ThinkQuest Library*. This rich online resource contains over 5,500 educational Web sites, created by students for students. You can search the library to find many intriguing sites.

Journey North (www.learner.org/jnorth), from Annenberg Media, engages students in a global study of wildlife migration and seasonal change. K-12 students share their own field observations with classmates across North America. They track the coming of spring through the migration patterns of monarch butterflies, bald eagles, robins, hummingbirds, whooping cranes, and other birds and mammals; the budding of plants; changing sunlight; and other natural events. Standards-based lesson plans, activities, and information help students make local observations and fit them into a global context.

9.7 - Virtual Field Trips

Virtual Field Trips can be taken to places impossible to visit without the Web. Real-life pictures and movies can bring the sites to life. These electronic trips are a way to integrate the Internet into the curriculum by allowing students to "visit" places being studied. Visits can be made to the Smithsonian Institute, the White House, the Louvre in Paris, or the Metropolitan Museum of Art in New York, along with thousands of other places just by entering a Web address.

When having students take virtual field trips, make it clear to them why they are doing this. Give them an assignment or project to do while traveling, such as taking the trip in groups, with resources to locate along the way.

Searching the WWW is one way to locate these trips. Another way is to visit Web sites developed for this purpose.

The *Virtual Tours* site (www.virtualfreesites.com/tours.html) is a good place to start. This is a collection of over 500 tours of the world, museums, exhibits, points of special interest, and the U.S. government. The site's goal is to provide information that will enhance any Internet journey. Included are over 300 museums, exhibits, and points of interest. Many of these offer multimedia guided tours, including text, pictures, sounds, and movies. Cities and countries can also be visited through interactive journeys. Also included here is travel-related information, including traveling tips, world maps, health information, brochures, weather forecasts, restaurant guides, hostels, and more. The government section includes the White House, branches of the U.S. government, House and Senate Web sites, Library of Congress exhibits, historical documents, and much more.

Utah Education Network (www.uen.org/utahlink/tours) also hosts a virtual field trip site. Their field trips are all geared to the classroom and categorized by subjects. Some of these include: *Fine Arts, Foreign Language, Health/PE, Language Arts, Math, Science, Social Studies,* and *Special Ed.* You can visit violin makers, discover artists and their work, take a European vacation, or a journey through the digestive system. Another part of the site provides directions for the teacher to create their own field trip.

Apple Learning Interchange (ali.apple.com/ali_sites/ali/new_events.html) hosts a number of *Digital Learning Events.* They have virtual field trips to dinosaur digs, the Grand Canyon, or a trip through the history of women's baseball. Your students can also tour *Lewis and Clark Then and Now*, featuring Webcasts, videoconferencing, and movie clips from an extensive recreation of their expedition. This site also has content experts to bring to the classroom through Webcasts and video and audio interviews.

Investigate these trips; then read about WebQuests, another form of online projects, in the next chapter. You will see how Internet resources can turn your classroom into an exciting and rewarding learning experience.

9.8 - Student Homework, Reference, and Resource Sites

The WWW is a powerful tool to help with daily homework. It can also assist in locating reference material and resources for projects. Some sites are specifically for reference, while others are divided into subject areas for homework, project resources, and just plain fun.

Homework Helper Sites

B.J. Pinchbeck's Homework Helper (school.discovery.com/homeworkhelp/bjpinchbeck) is a good place to start for homework and reference assistance. Now hosted by *Discovery School*, this site has links for doing homework in any area, along with a *Reference* section featuring over 100 reference books available on the Internet. Homework links include *Art/Music, Computer Science & Internet, English, Foreign Languages, Health & P.E., Math, Science,* and *Social Studies.* Also included are *News, Recess, Reference,* and *Search Engines.* Lots of excellent resource and reference sites can be found here.

Homework Spot™ (www.homeworkspot.com) is a one-site-has-all place to visit. Subject listings are available for elementary, middle, and high school. Also included are menus with links to reference and current events sites. Areas include *Must See Sites, To Do, Field Trips, Exhibits, You Asked for It,* etc. *Must Sees* include B.J. Pinchbeck's (above). Featured encyclopedias are *Britannica.com, Encyclopedia.com,* and *Encarta.com.*

Reference Desk
Almanacs
Ask an Expert
Atlases
Biographies
Calculators
Calendars
Citations
Current Events
Dictionaries
Encyclopedias
Government
Homework Hotlines
Libraries
Lists
Museums
People
Reading Room
Q&A
Quotations
Safe search engines
Statistics
Thesauri
Trivia
Much More...

Subject levels include *Homeroom, Arts & Crafts, Fine Arts, English, Language Art, Foreign Languages, Health/Fitness, Math, Science, Social Studies, Technology,* and more.

MUST-SEE SITES
The Internet Public Library
B.J. Pinchbeck's
Multnomah Homework Center
LibrarySpot.com

Refdesk.com's Homework Helper (www.refdesk.com/homework.html) provides links for grade levels and a *Homework Center* link. This takes the student to Multnomah County Library where they can receive *Live Homework Help* and access a variety of Homework topics. *Refdesk* also provides a listing of Other Homework Links and Tools for Research. Links are available to go to the main *Refdesk* and access *Ask the Experts, Quick Reference/Research,* and *Facts Subject Index.*

Reference Sites

Refdesk (www.refdesk.com), included above as a Homework Helper site, is not just for homework (or kids). It is a comprehensive reference site, with the homework area being only a small part. Some of the site's major areas include *Search Resources, Headlines, Today's Pictures, Daily Diversions, Weather, Breaking News, Potpourri, Reference Resources, Facts Search Desk, Subject Categories,* and *Just for Fun.* A sampling of topics in these areas, helpful to students, appear in the chart below. Their motto says it all: "The single best source for facts on the Net." The best!

Acronyms	Calendars	Grammar/Style	Quotations
Almanacs	Countries	Maps	States
Ask the Experts	Dictionaries	Medical	Thesaurus
Biographies	Encyclopedias	Newspapers	White/Yellow Pages
Calculators	Government	People	Zip/Area Codes

The Internet Public Library (www.ipl.org) contains a variety of subject collections, reference materials, and a Reading Room. Also at the IPL is *KidsSpace @ The Internet Public Library* (www.ipl.org/youth) featuring a reference area, and an area for teachers and parents. *Reference* includes *The World, Computers/Internet, Health & Nutrition, Reading Zone, Math & Science, Art & Music, Sports & Recreation,* and *Fun Stuff.* Each category takes you to topics, each linking to many appropriate Web sites. There is also a link to *TeenSpace,* the *Internet Public Library for Teens.*

Fact Monster™ (www.factmonster.com) from *Information Please*© features an online almanac, dictionary, encyclopedia, and homework help. Areas cover the *World, United States, People, Sports, Science, Math & Money, Word Wise, Arts & Living,* and *Games & Quizzes.* A search engine is also included.

For additional reference work, there are several encyclopedias online. *Encarta*® *Encyclopedia* (encarta.msn.com/artcenter_/browse.html) contains over 4,500 articles, sidebars, literature guides, archives, and homework starters. *Encyclopedia Britannica Online* is also available (www.britannica.com). Searches take you not only to articles in the encyclopedia, but to other references on the WWW. The articles in Britannica include hyperlinks to other articles, photos, and multimedia. Articles are printable and can be e-mailed to others.

Additional dictionaries, almanacs, thesauruses, etc. can be found at *RefDesk, BJ Pinchbeck's Homework Helper,* or through searches.

Primary Sources

Original text, research or writings on a subject, or records of events described or recorded by a participant or witness are considered to be primary sources. These may include letters, manuscripts, diaries, journals, newspapers, speeches, interviews, government documents, recordings, etc. These sources serve as raw material to interpret the past; often combined with other interpretations by historians, they provide resources for historical research. Excellent information on finding primary resources can be found in the history section at the American Library Association (www.lib.washington.edu/subject/History/RUSA).

The *Library of Congress* (www.loc.gov) is the best place to find primary sources. Manuscripts, maps, films, audio recordings, prints, photographs, and music can all be found at this site. With more than ten million primary sources online, there is something for everyone. Teachers can also visit *The Learning Page* for lesson plans and activities using primary sources.

Resource and Fun Sites

Alfy (www.alfy.com), "the Web portal for kids," is geared toward children 3-9 years old. Developed so children this age can safely and easily use the Web, *Alfy* is fun as well as educational. It is stocked with interactive stories, games, crafts, activities, and more. Eight centers entertain and educate children: *Brain Train* (the toddler place), *Music Mania* (play, record, and listen to music), *Storyville* (interactive stories), *Create!* (art studio), *Clubhouse* (communicate with others), *Surprises* (jokes and riddles), *Alfy's Arcade* (game center), and *Alfy's Cool Sites* (gateway to the Internet).

Berit's Best Sites for Children (www.beritsbest.com) provides links to the 1,000 best sites for children. All sites are categorized in topical areas. The home page also includes the 25 best sites chosen by visitors and a search engine for the site.

FunBrain.com™ (www.funbrain.com) is for kids in grades K-8 and teachers. Full of interactive educational resources, quizzes, and games, *FunBrain* is educational as well as fun. *Curriculum Guides* and *Standards Finder* help teachers choose the appropriate games and activities for their students. They can even print out flash cards.

4Kids.org (www.4kids.org) is "your link to the latest tecKNOWLEDGEy on the Web." Here you can find an assortment of safe Web sites, games, and fun for children.

9.9 - Activities

• Activity One •

Identify a unit and grade level you will be teaching. Visit four of the educational "Starting Points" listed to find resources available to teach the unit. At each site locate reference material for the unit and an activity to use in the unit. For each site, provide: (1) an overview of what you found at the site, (2) a description of the specific reference material and activity for your unit, and (3) the Web address for both the reference material and activity.

• Activity Two •

Identify a unit and grade level you will be teaching. Visit four sites with lesson plans, either those identified or others you find through searches. Choose the four best lesson plans you find for your unit. For each, provide: (1) the name of the lesson plan, (2) the site where you found it, (3) the Web address for the lesson plan, and (4) a brief description of the lesson.

• Activity Three •

Identify a unit and grade level you will be teaching. Using vocabulary for that unit, construct a puzzle at one of the identified Web sites. Use a minimum of ten words and definitions in the puzzle. Print out the puzzle and the answers.

• Activity Four •

Identify a unit and grade level you will be teaching. Visit three sites for online projects and/or virtual field trips. Describe three projects (with the Web address) you feel would be useful in your classroom (50 words minimum for each project).

• Activity Five •

Visit the Library of Congress. Go to *Teachers—The Learning Page—Features & Activities*. Choose one activity. Write a reflection (minimum 100 words) about this feature/activity and how it would be an effective teaching resource.

• Activity Six •

Be a kid! Using the Resource and Fun Sites, find two educational games/activities you enjoy. Describe each, including how it could be used in the classroom (minimum 50 words each).

CHAPTER 10

Scavenger Hunts and WebQuests

10.1 - Introduction

Students spend a lot of time on the Internet, with many students using it primarily for e-mail, instant messaging, or games. Teaching students to search properly is one way to assist them in finding what they need for their education; but they must also learn to do something with what they find. Web-based learning activities can help you teach your students to do this. These activities have the potential to enhance learning, while making it exciting to the students. One simple activity is to create scavenger hunts for students.

More sophisticated Web-based learning activities have students do something with what they locate on the Internet. They should be able to determine its meaning, compile and synthesize various sources, and critique the usefulness of the material. Most projects of this type are not just to locate factual information, but also to take it a step further and utilize higher-level thinking skills when synthesizing the information. The most popular form of this type of Web-based learning activity is the WebQuest.

Once these activities have been created, it is helpful to have them published on a Web site for easy student access. *Filamentality.com* is a Web site for teachers to assist in creating WebQuests and other Web-based activities. Teachers can go there to create five different types of activities, which can then be posted for free on *Filamentality's* Web site.

10.2 - Scavenger Hunts

Scavenger hunts, also called treasure hunts, provide students with a fun way to search the Internet, improve reading skills, improve comprehension skills, and practice problem solving. They are easy for the teacher, or even the student, to create. Hunts can be used in any subject area, at any grade level; whereby students learn more about a topic, along with technology at the same time. Individuals, or groups of students, can work on the scavenger hunt. It can be as simple or involved as the teacher wants it to be. While there are different types, all can be developed to be informative and generate knowledge of the subject.

Teachers often find Web pages, with a wealth of educational information on them, useful in a subject they teach. It would be boring for a student to just go and read the material. The teacher can gather a collection of Web pages (specific ones, not the entire site), then pose one or more questions for the student to answer using each Web page. In searching for the specific answer, the student is exposed to photos, videos, and other factual material on the identified page. Questions can get more difficult, having students synthesize what they have learned on other pages. A synthesizing question, needing good comprehension of the subject, can be placed at the end to pull all of their thoughts and research together.

This is one type of scavenger hunt that, along with other types, is illustrated on the following pages.

Sample Scavenger Hunts

The sample scavenger hunts illustrated here use the theme: *History of Rowan University*. Although you are a student at Rowan University, you might not be familiar with some significant events that have happened at this institution in the past.

Each scavenger hunt will utilize the same Web sites and information, but show how you can construct various types of scavenger hunts for your students.

1. **Teaching Searching Skills**
   (disadvantage: students can "roam" the Web without supervision)

   Directions: Search the Web to find facts about Rowan University. Use *Google* to search for answers to the following questions. Provide the answer, along with the site where you found the answer.

Fact to Search	Answer	Web Site Where Found
Two other names for Rowan University before its current name.		
The year the institution was established.		
An event that occurred in 1967 to put the college "in the news."		
The name of the building where this event occurred.		
The year Rowan University got this name. Why did this change take place?		
Who is Robert Hegyes, and how is he affiliated with Rowan?		

2. Searching One Web Site
(advantage: cannot "roam" the Internet; disadvantage: limited information)

Directions: Go to the Web site below; find answers to the questions listed.
http://www.rowan.edu/subpages/about/history/

1._____	What was the mission of the institution when it was established?
2. _____	When was the institution established?
3. _____	How much money was donated by Henry and Betty Rowan?
4. _____	When and how did the institution get worldwide attention?
5. _____	Who is the current president of Rowan University?
6. _____	How long has he been president at Rowan?

3. Search at Specific Web Sites
(advantages: cannot "roam" the Internet; more sites to search and read)

Directions: Use only the sites below to find the relevant information and answers to questions. (Web sites could be hyperlinks on a Web page for easy access. Another way to do this would be to have a specific Web site for each question.)

Rowan University:
www.rowan.edu

Glassboro's History:
www.glassboroonline.com/history_glassboro.html

The History of Rowan University:
www.rowan.edu/subpages/about/history

The Historic Private Gift:
rowanmagazine.com/features/feature5

Wikipedia, the Free Encyclopedia:
en.wikipedia.org/wiki/Rowan_University

1. In the early years, Rowan gained a national reputation in what educational areas?

2. List all of the names the university has had, and in what years the names changed.

3. Identify three areas of interest to you on Rowan University's Web site.

4. Briefly describe the conference held at Hollybush in 1967.

5. Provide the names of three individuals who have been instrumental in the growth of Rowan University.

6. Explain Henry Rowan's background and how/why that is important to the future of Rowan University.

4. Other types of Scavenger Hunts

Another type that could be used, but not applicable for this scavenger hunt topic, would be to make a list of questions, each pertaining to a specific person, place, etc. Provide another list of Web sites for each person or place. The student must read each site to match the answer about the person/place with that person/place. Other examples can include text and photos on a Web site, along with questions and hyperlinks to the sites where additional information can be found; or, placing links in sentences about the topics.

10.3 - WebQuests

WebQuests are inquiry-oriented activities in which students interact with resources on the Internet. They have proven to be a safe and educationally sound way for teachers to take full advantage of the multitude of resources available on the Internet. WebQuests can be short, lasting for only one or two periods, or longer, where the student searches for and analyzes larger bodies of information. WebQuests are often group activities that assign a different role to each member of the group, and are often interdisciplinary, covering several subjects.

Students learn about their WebQuest through an introduction. This explains the project and often provides background information. They are then given a task that is accomplished by searching a set of resources. Most of these are teacher-identified sites found on the Internet (with hyperlinks in the instructions). Other non-Internet references can be provided by the teacher. Students are also provided with instructions and assistance on how to carry out the WebQuest. Fact-finding is not the only activity. As students analyze the variety of teacher-specified resources, they use critical thinking skills to solve the identified problem.

WebQuests were developed by Bernie Dodge at San Diego State University in 1995 as a way for teachers to integrate the power of the Internet with student learning. Tom March later worked with him on the project. They continue to do research in the area and make materials available for teachers. Bernie Dodge hosts *The WebQuest Page* (webquest.sdsu.edu), while *Ozline.com* (www.ozline.com/learning/index.htm) is the home of Tom March's educational initiatives. Both of these should be visited for sample WebQuests, assistance on developing WebQuests, and ideas for classroom implementation. The information in this unit is based on their model.

Learning about WebQuests

Teachers can create their own WebQuests or take advantage of the many WebQuests available on the Internet. Many of these have been developed by students in classes taught by Dodge and March, while others have been developed by teachers who have adopted their model.

One place to learn about WebQuests is to look at the training materials on Dodge's *WebQuest Page* (webquest.sdsu.edu/materials.htm). A good way to begin is to participate in *A WebQuest about WebQuests* for your grade level. Each level provides five WebQuests and has teachers examine each from different points of view:

- the Efficiency Expert (values time in the classroom);
- the Affiliator (the best activities are when students work together);
- the Altitudinist (a proponent of higher level thinking); and
- the Technophile (the WebQuest makes the best use of the technology on the Web).

After completing this WebQuest, investigate other sample WebQuests on the Internet. Dodge's *The WebQuest Page* is a good place to start. Go to webquest.org; on the left of this page click on *Find WebQuests*. There you will find a search engine for various subjects and grades. Tom March's site featuring WebQuests is *Best WebQuests* (www.bestwebquests.com). *Blue Web'n* also has a number of WebQuests (www.bluewebn.com); search for "WebQuests." A few sample topics from these sites are below:

- Poetry Quest
- Weather WebQuest
- Culture Quest
- Smoking Is Cool ... Not!
- Art Exhibit
- The Art of Mathematics
- Staff Development WebQuest
- Should Schools Filter Web Content?
- Animals of the Rainforest
- Trip to Germany
- Museum Mischief
- Math and Stocks
- Women in Science
- Diary of Anne Frank
- The Internet for Teachers
- Ancient Olympic Games

As seen from the titles above, WebQuests can be on any topic, and for any grade level. They could be used to analyze a contemporary problem, or be the basis for role playing a figure in history. Products of WebQuests can be a written or oral report, a multimedia project, a display, artwork, or even a performance. The ideas are endless.

Prior to developing a WebQuest, the teacher should have a clear and detailed answer to the following questions:

- What do I want the students to learn?
- How will the students be motivated to learn?
- What resources are necessary?
- How will I assess students' learning?

Developing a WebQuest

Bernie Dodge has developed six **Building Blocks of a WebQuest**. These should all be included in a WebQuest. Often *Process* and *Resources* are combined, as resources are considered a part of the process.

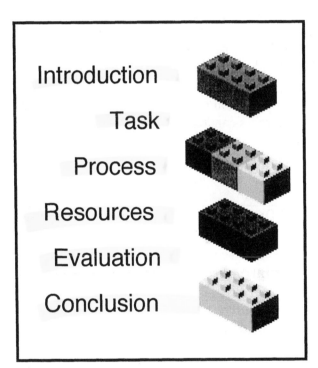

Building Blocks of a WebQuest

Introduction

Task

Process

Resources

Evaluation

Conclusion

In the ***Introduction***, the student is oriented to what will be taking place. It is the time to create interest in the project by emphasizing the relevance and importance of the WebQuest to the student and to making the WebQuest fun and interesting for the student.

The ***Task*** is the most important part of a WebQuest, as it provides goals and focus to the project. What are the students expected to learn? How will they accomplish this? Explain to them what will take place and the sequence of what they will do. What will be the final outcome of the WebQuest?

The ***Process*** includes the steps the students are to follow to accomplish the task. Provide a description of each student's role and their responsibilities in that role. How should they organize the facts they find; what do they do with them? ***Resources*** include hyperlinks to all Web pages the students are to use, along with additional resources they might use. These could include videos, library resources, textbooks, etc. ***Evaluation***, often in the form of a rubric, measures the effectiveness of the WebQuest as a learning activity. The ***Conclusion*** summarizes the experience and reflects upon what was learned.

To understand these Building Blocks better, go to Dodge's Training Materials and go to *Building Blocks for WebQuests* (projects.edtech.sandi.net/staffdev/buildingblocks/p-index.htm). Here each section essential to any WebQuest is described, with examples of WebQuests for each section.

Evaluating WebQuests

Teachers can develop their own evaluation tools to evaluate their own WebQuest. Dodge and March both have rubrics on their sites to help you be sure the WebQuest you create is doing all it should do.

Dodge's can be found at: edWeb.sdsu.edu/Webquest/Webquestrubric.html
March's can be found at: www.ozline.com/Webquests/rubric.html

Below are some of the characteristics of a well-developed WebQuest (in an abbreviated form):

Overall Visual Appeal	Appealing graphic elements are included; differences in fonts, colors.
Effectiveness of Introduction	The Introduction draws the reader into the lesson by relating to learner's interests or setting up a problem; builds on learner's prior knowledge.
Cognitive Level of the Task	Task requires synthesis of many resources, and/or going beyond the data given and making a generalization or product.
Technical Sophistication of the Task	Task requires use of multimedia software, video, conferencing.
Clarity and Richness of Process	Each step is clear; students always know where they are in the project; there are a variety of activities, roles, and perspectives.
Quantity and Quality of Resources	Many resources are provided on the Internet and in the classroom; links make good use of Web resources.
Clarity of Evaluation Criteria	Criteria for gradations of success are stated; often in the form of a rubric for self, peer, or teacher use.

10.4 - Publishing on the WWW

Simple WebQuests, and other Web-based activities, can be created in a *Word* document. Most, however, are developed as Web pages, as seen in examples on the Internet. To do this, you will need Web development software and a location to host your page. *DreamWeaver*® and *Front Page*® are two common Web development packages, but they take a long time to learn and are expensive. You can also use *Netscape* (versions 7.2 or older) that includes *Netscape Composer*, for a free, easy to use Web development program (pp. 106-108). As a Rowan student, you can post your Web page through Rowan (p. 106). Once you have a subscription to *TaskStream*, you can develop a Web page there, which is hosted by *TaskStream* (pp. 110-11)].

Filamentality

Filamentality is an online publishing tool that will let you create online learning activities and post them for free at their site. Originally developed by Tom March in 1996, *Filamentality* now resides on a site that is sponsored by AT & T Education (www.kn.sbc.com/wired/fil/). The name was developed because the site helps the teacher combine the <u>fila</u>ments of the Web with a learner's <u>mentality</u>.

Filamentality helps a teacher create five types of online activity formats:

> *Hotlist:* A list of sites (hyperlinks) for students to access on a Web page. Resources for a unit can be combined and posted for easy access by students. Students can also use this to publish findings of their research.

> *Multimedia Scrapbook:* Sites are organized into categories for easy use; text is incorporated to provide instructions for students or add information about the sites. Students can download items for use in projects, reports, or their own scrapbook.

> *Subject Sampler:* Students are provided with several interesting and interactive Web sites on a particular topic. These sites provide "something for the student to do"; not just read factual information. Students are asked to carry out several of the activities and respond about the activities from a personal perspective.

> *Treasure Hunt:* Similar to scavenger hunts (earlier in this chapter), the teacher finds 10-15 Web sites and constructs a question the students must find on each. It can be used to learn facts, to assist in reading for a purpose, or to review a unit.

> *WebQuest:* A way to put a WebQuest the teacher develops on a free Web page for students to acccess.

Filamentality guides you as you develop a topic, search the Web for resources, and use their fill-in-the-blank tool to make your own online learning activities.

Tom March also developed *Web 'n Flow* ($25 per year). This allows teachers to design Web activities for their students and post them on a Web site. More powerful than *Filamentality*, it includes activity formats and evaluation rubrics. Schools' Web sites can be powered by *Web 'n Flow*, and activities created by the teachers can appear in a matrix on the school Web site. Bernie Dodge has a new online tool: *QuestGarden* ($20 per year). This is also an authoring tool and hosting site for WebQuests. *QuestGarden* helps the teacher set up a WebQuest with the sections discussed earlier in this chapter.

10.5 - Activities

• Activity One •

Design a scavenger hunt as part of a lesson you are developing. Use one of the models in this chapter. Have 15 items in your "hunt." Create a word-processed handout for your students. On a separate sheet of paper, include the answers.

• Activity Two •

Design a WebQuest that will be part of a unit you are developing. Remember, this is not a scavenger hunt where your students just look for facts. This can be developed as a *Word* document or as a Web page in TaskStream. Include a few pieces of clip art, but keep it simple.

- Include the six "Building Blocks" in your project; you may combine Process and Resources.
- Plan to have students work in groups of three or four, with each student having a different "job."
- Include at least six Web links for the students to use.
- When you think you have your WebQuest finished, use Tom March's rubric to see if you have covered all areas.
- It is not necessary to create a rubric for grading your students.

Prior to developing your WebQuest:

- Go to webquest.org; search for similar subjects and grades. Look at three WebQuests for similar topics.
- In Bernie Dodge's Training Materials, look at *Building Blocks for WebQuests*.

• Activity Three •

Use *Filamentality* to create a "Hotlist" for a lesson you are developing. Include it as a resource with your lesson plan.

CHAPTER **11**

Creating Web Pages

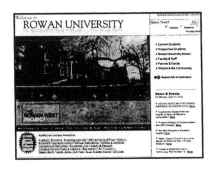

11.1 - Introduction

You (or your students) can design a Web site for your class, your school, your organization, or your family. Having a Web site establishes YOU on the World Wide Web. It is not a difficult task, but in the beginning it can be a bit time consuming. The end result will be worth the effort. Simple, easy-to-follow instructions in this chapter will help you be successful.

Where do you begin?

- There are sites on the Internet that allow teachers and students to create and post classroom Web pages using a template that is provided on their site.
- Simple, free, Web authoring programs, such as *Netscape Composer* (a component of *Netscape Communicator*), are available on the Web to let the user create simple Web pages.
- *TaskStream* allows the user to easily develop a Web page and post it for free on *TaskStream's* Web site.
- Some word processing programs (*Microsoft Word, AppleWorks*®) allow text to be saved as HTML, bypassing the use of a Web authoring program.
- For the advanced user with more complex pages, programs like *Dreamweaver* (Macromedia) and *FrontPage* (Microsoft) are available for purchase (tutorials can be found on the Web for these).

In this chapter, you will learn how to do all of the above, with the exception of the advanced programs. As mentioned above, pages constructed on sites for teachers/students, or with *TaskStream*, are published on these respective sites. For others, you must have a place to publish your Web page. As a student at Rowan, your Web page can be published using your H Drive.

11.2 - Getting Started

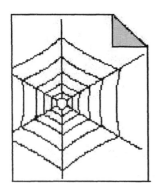

- A Web site is composed of any number of pages; the first page is called the "home page."
- Each page is supported with links to other places on the Internet, images, sounds, or movies.
- It is no longer necessary to be a programmer, or know HTML (Hypertext Markup Language), to construct a Web site.
- The user manipulates the objects, while the program inserts the code as needed.
- Web authoring programs allow the user to place text and graphics on the page, format and reposition the text and graphics, and make links to other sites on the Internet and places within the site being created.

<u>If your students can make Web pages, so can you!</u>

Components of a Web Page

The major components of a Web page are similar in all Web authoring programs:

- Header (similar to the headline in a newspaper)
- Background color, pattern, or texture
- Text: fonts, sizes, and colors
- Images: graphics, photos, sounds, movies
- Links: text or graphics that get the user to another page from the home page, or to other Internet sites
- Tables: easy ways to organize components in rows and columns (divisions do not have to show)
- Horizontal rules: break the page into horizontal divisions

How to Create a Web Site

This section contains generic tips for designing and constructing a Web site. Instructions for authoring programs follow.

Designing a Web Site

1. **Plan and organize**

    Prior to actually creating a Web site on the computer, it is essential to develop an outline, or storyboard, for the project. (Look at other Web pages for ideas.) First, determine the focus of your site. Then plan and sketch out the tentative layout for each page. Don't make the site too complex. Sites can be linear, hierarchical, or in a Webbed design (links going to many locations). Regardless of the format you use, always include links to get back to the home page.

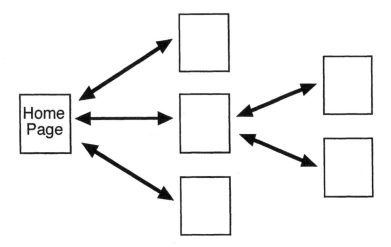

2. **Gather images, links, etc.**

    While in the planning process, find clip art, photos, or other graphics to be used, and determine links to other Web pages that will be needed.

3. **Compose each page**

   Remember this site will be viewed by others; organization and simplicity are of the utmost importance. In addition, each page should be built around a theme or topic, be attractive and easy to navigate, and be linked back to the home page.

4. **Enter and format text**

   Text can be entered directly onto the Web page or pasted from a word processing document (be careful, it might not appear as it did in the original document). Various sizes for headings and text are available. Text styles, colors, and alignments can also be applied.

5. **Add images**

   Images can be digital photos, clip art from CDs, original art, scanned photos, or clip art from the Internet. All must be in *.gif* or *.jpeg* formats. *QuickTime* movies can also be imported into pages. (The larger the images are, the longer it will take the page to load; and the more space it will take to save the page.) Save all components in the same folder as the Web pages.

6. **Add links**

   Links are of two types: those that take the user somewhere else in the Web site and those that link to another Web site on the Internet. When text is linked, the text becomes underlined, indicating a hyperlink (click to go somewhere).

7. **Save the pages as you work**

   From the time each page is created, save often with *.html* or *.htm* as the file extension.

8. **Proof and test the page**

   Check the page with an Internet browser to ensure it looks the way you want it to look when it is published. Try all links to ensure they link properly.

9. **Publish the page**

   Files need to be sent via FTP (File Transfer Protocol) to be stored on the Internet.

10. **Test the page on the Internet**

    Test in several browsers, and on both Mac and PC. Test the links every few months, as Web sites move or expire frequently.

11. **Update pages on a regular basis**

Classroom Tip:
If the design of a Web page is a class project, organize students into groups, each with a specific task. Never undertake a Web design project unless you, the teacher, understand all aspects of the project (even though your students might be better at Web page design than you).

11.3 - Creating Classroom Web Pages

Some educational portals provide templates for constructing school Web pages, which then can be hosted on the portal's site. Even though your school might have its own school site, it might be fun to have one just for your class(es). You can post homework and announcements and keep in touch with parents. Class Web pages can also include rules and policies, news about the school, teacher/staff e-mail addresses, sports information, upcoming events, fun links for students, school calendars, class schedules, cafeteria menus, sites for homework help, student projects, and much more.

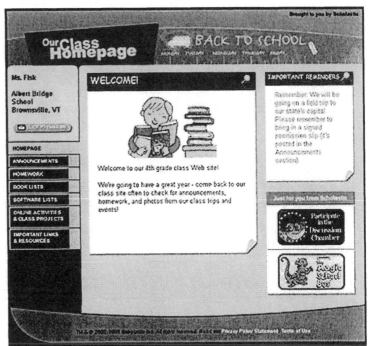

Scholastic's home page, found at teacher.scholastic.com/homepage builder/index.htm includes *Class Homepage Builder*. As illustrated here, this looks like a real Web page with columns and boxes for various types of information. Templates are provided to make your page look like this one. You can even include printable parent forms online.

Another site for teachers is *TeAch-nology.com* (www.teach-nology.com/web_tools/web_site/). This site provides several categories of Web pages. They do have one for free. With this free subscription, they provide 12 MB of Web space and access to their file manager. This does, however, include advertising (which can be removed for a fee) when displayed on the Web. Their other packages, with fees involved, provide additional space, support FTP or *FrontPage* files and offer Webmail accounts and free support. To see if you want to use it in your classroom, try the free version and use their file manager, which means you use their template to create your Web page (the easy way to do it). They also provide links to sites that offer free cursors, backgrounds, clipart, icons, etc.

4Teachers.org (wizard.4teachers.org) has a *Web Worksheet Wizard* that allows the teacher to create a lesson, worksheet, or class page and publish it on the WWW through *4Teachers.org*. For students, they have *Project Poster* (poster.4teachers.org). This free tool allows students to make online school projects and short reports. They can include one image, four links to other Web pages, and a report of up to 3,500 characters. Students can only post a school project; however, they must be registered by their teacher. After being reviewed, the poster is placed on the Web for the public to view.

11.4 - Creating a Web Site with *Netscape Composer*

There are several versions of *Netscape Communicator* available. Any version 7.2 or below includes *Netscape Composer*. This is a free download for both PC and Mac.

At Rowan, you should have a folder in your H Drive titled *public.www*. This is a place to store all of the related files and images that will be on your Web page. Images must be stored separately; they cannot be placed on the page by copy and paste. The first page of your Web site must be saved as *index.html*. By doing this, it is automatically accessed when someone requests it with your Rowan Web address. You are automatically assigned this address, which is *users.rowan.edu/~username* [username = your Rowan username]

1. Open *Netscape* (if you do not have it, it can be downloaded from www.netscape.com).

2. To access *Composer* and create a new page: Go to *File: New: Composer Page*. At the top of the page there is a Composition Toolbar (shown below), along with a Menu Bar. Any time you are editing pages, you must be in *Composer* with this toolbar visible. There is also an Edit Mode Toolbar at the bottom left of the screen.

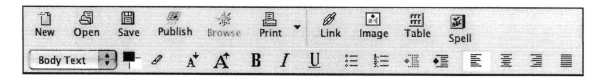

3. To create a new page within *Composer:* Click on *New* in the toolbar.

4. To view your page in a browser to check links: Click on *Browse* in the toolbar.

5. To edit your page: Go to *File: Edit Page* on the menu bar.

6. To add and change text: Sizes and body text styles can be changed in the toolbar. Additional changes can be made under *Format* in the menu bar. Do not use fancy fonts. Times, Arial, Helvetica, and Courier stay the same, while other fonts change on various computers.

7. To save your page: Go to *File: Save*. Enter *index* (Composer will add the *.html*). Save directly to your *public.www* folder. All files names must be lowercase; no spaces.

8. To change text and background colors: Text color can be changed in the Format menu in the menu bar. Background and text colors for the entire page can be changed under *Format: Page Colors and Background*. Specific areas of text can be changed in the toolbar. Go to the icon to the right of body text. The left (black) is for text color.

9. To check spelling: Click on *Spell* in the toolbar.

10. To add a table (tables are used for organizing text and images in rows and columns):
    a. click to place the insertion point where the table will appear
    b. click on *Table* in the toolbar
    c. enter the number of rows and columns needed
    d. enter the width of the table (percentage of window)
    e. click *OK*
    f. add or delete rows and columns under *Table: Insert/Delete*

11. To make changes in a table (first click in table): Go to *Table: Table Properties* in the menu bar (choose *Table* or *Cell*).
    a. in *Table*, change width, alignment, color, border (use 0 pixels for no border)
    b. in *Cells*, change size of cells (use width - % of table to make cells the same width)

12. To add an image: Click on *Image* in the toolbar. (Prior to doing this, you need images in your *public.www* folder. They must have a *.gif* or *.jpeg* (or *.jpg*) extension.) The menu below will appear. Click on *Choose File*; navigate to your *public.www* folder, then open the image. Click on *URL is relative to page location* (if not checked). If you want alternate text to appear if the image does not open, select that option and enter the desired text; if not, click on *Don't use alternate text*.

Image Location:
☐ URL is relative to page location   (Choose File...)
Tooltip: [   ]
◉ Alternate text: [   ]
○ Don't use alternate text

Note:
*   Text cannot be placed directly next to pictures, except at the top, bottom, left, right, and center (see illustration).*
*   To have more flexibility, make a table and put images in the cells.*

text

13. To edit images: Double click on the image. You can then change dimensions and appearance (including text location), or make it a link.

14. To give a name to the page (if your page will be on a Web site, label the page with a descriptive title): Go to *Format: Page Title and Properties*. This will show at the top of the page and as a bookmark.

15. To create links to Web sites: Highlight the text or image to be the link; click the *Link* button in the toolbar; enter the link location. Be sure to begin the address with *http://*. Be sure *URL is relative to page location* is checked.

16. To create links to other pages: Highlight the text or image to be the link; click the *Link* button in the toolbar; choose the appropriate file; click *Open*, then *OK*.

17. To create links (anchors) in the same page (anchors link to text in the same page, usually on a long Web page]:
    a. Click to set the insertion point at the beginning of the line where you want to create the anchor;
    b. Go to *Insert: Named Anchor*;
    c. Enter a name for your anchor; click *OK*; an anchor appears;
    d. Select the text or image to link to the anchor;
    e. Click *Link* in the toolbar; then click on the *name of the anchor*; click *OK*.

18. To enter your e-mail address: *Highlight the text* you want to be the link; click on *Link* in the toolbar; enter: *mailto:youraddress* (enter YOUR e-mail address here).

19. To insert previously saved documents: (There are several ways to do this. You need to try each to see the differences. Since you are working in HTML, text cannot easily be copied in while keeping the original formatting.)
    a. Copy and Paste: Copy your original document; paste into the Web page (this will not be formatted correctly).
    b. Save as a Web page: In *Word*, save the document as a Web page (formatting will be better than copy and paste).
    c. Save as a document: Place your *Word* document in your *public.www* folder. It will not open as a Web page but will be saved as a file on the computer.
    d. Save as a PDF file: In *Word*, go to *Print*, then *Save as PDF*. This will also be saved as a file on the computer.

20. When all is complete, test your site on the Internet, not just through Browse.

Notes:

If you work on your Web site at home and not on your H Drive, you will have to re-link items when you go back to your H Drive (if you want to publish through Rowan).

If you do not want to publish your Web page at Rowan, you can use other free sites such as *Angelfire* or *Geocities*; however, advertisements will appear on these pages.

Web Publishing

After your Web page is created, it needs to be posted on a Web server. This could be on a school's server, a commercial online service, such as *AOL*, or with an ISP (Internet Service Provider). If you are a subscriber to *AOL, Verizon, Comcast,* or similar providers, they normally provide free space for you to post a Web page. Contact them directly for information. If this service is not available, you can purchase space from a service provider. As stated earlier, while you are a student at Rowan, you have free space on the school's server (see p. 106).

Another alternative is to use a free site on the WWW. Sites for teachers were discussed earlier in the chapter. Other sites also offer free space for Web pages. At these locations, Web sites can be created with their tools or uploaded from another Web authoring program (*Netscape, Dreamweaver,* etc), via an FTP program (provided at their site). Unfortunately, these sites include advertisements when the page is seen. Two of these sites are *Geocities* (geocities.yahoo.com) and *Angelfire* (angelfire.lycos.com).

11.5 - Creating a Web Site with *Microsoft Word*

Microsoft Word is not a full-scale Web authoring program, but it has enough options to construct and publish a simple Web page. *Word* has an option to *Save as Web Page*. When doing this, the page is formatted for the Web. However, the document is not the same. Margins change with the width of the Web document, graphics jump, tabs do not exist, fonts change, spaces disappear, symbols change, and so on. Needless to say, the document does not look the same. A document without graphics, formatting, or special features might transfer in a usable format. When working in *Online Layout* (View), the page is seen as it is viewed on the Web. The feature *Web Page Preview* is also available. Try a document and see what happens! This same concept is true when any word processing document is placed on a Web page.

When choosing to prepare a Web document in *Word*, a better choice is to begin the document as a Web page in the *Project Gallery*. When this is done, many of the same concepts explained for *Netscape Composer* are similar for a Web page in *Word*. Some differences follow for a Web page using Word:

1. There is a toolbar customized for the Web. Go to *View: Toolbars: Web* to get this toolbar (see below).

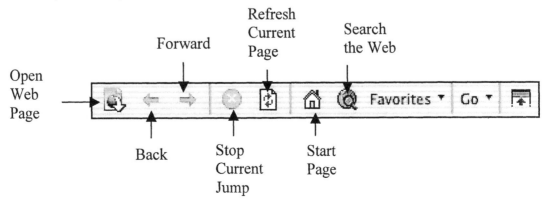

2. When the document is saved, images in the document are converted to *.jpeg, .gif,* or *.png* files, so they are suitable for the Web; all must be kept together in one folder.

3. To insert a hyperlink, enter and highlight the text. Go to *Insert: Hyperlink* in the menu bar. As illustrated below, enter the entire Web address in *Link to:* Other options shown below are to link to another part of the Web page (*Document*) or to link to an E-mail address.

Insert Hyperlink
Link to: http://www.rowan.edu
Display: Rowan University
Web Page	Document	E-mail Address

4. When saving, ensure the file is saved as a Web page with the *.htm* or *.html* extension.

11.6 - Creating a Web Site with *TaskStream*

Refer to Chapter 3 on *TaskStream* for basic instructions on using *TaskStream* and Chapter 4 on creating a Web page with *TaskStream*. Below are additional basic steps for creating a Web page, along with how to include links and receive a Web address for the page you build. The *Web Page Builder* is similar to the *Web Folio Builder*.

1. Choose *Web Page Builder* from the navigation bar.

2. Choose the *Template* and *Style* you want to use.

3. In the *Edit Structure*, add the names of the pages you want. These will appear at the top of your Web site. Each page (category in Edit Structure) is the same as a Web page.

4. Click on the heading in *Web View* to see the different pages.

5. To insert a link to an external Web page (on the Web, not in *TaskStream*), you can do one of two things:
   (a) In the *Edit* mode, click on *Web Links* in the *Content Editor,* then enter the *Name of link* and *Link to outside Web site* (entire Web address).

Web Links

1. Name of link

2. Link to outside website

(b) Within the text, create a hyperlink. Highlight the text to be the hyperlink; choose the link icon in the HTML formatting palette. Enter the URL in box shown below.

Link icon

Hyperlink Properties

To insert a link, you must enter a web address (URL) (e.g. http://www.taskstream.com/)

URL:

6. Complete information for all Web pages. Insert a graphic on each, if desired.

7. *Publish/Share* your Web site; *Publish Options*; then *Publish*. Decide whether or not a password is needed. Clicking on *Publish* at the bottom of the screen sends your request to *TaskStream*. You will receive a Web page address back. It can always be found in *Web Folio Builder* with your Web page.

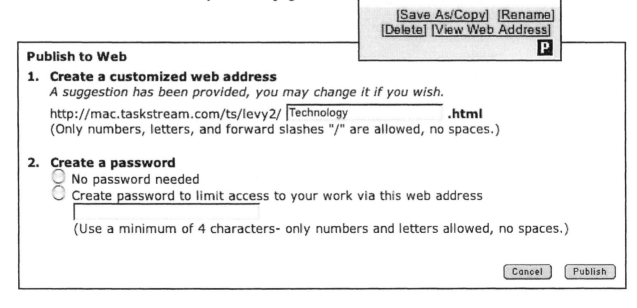

[Save As/Copy] [Rename]
[Delete] [View Web Address]

P

Publish to Web

1. Create a customized web address
A suggestion has been provided, you may change it if you wish.

http://mac.taskstream.com/ts/levy2/ Technology .html
(Only numbers, letters, and forward slashes "/" are allowed, no spaces.)

2. Create a password
○ No password needed
○ Create password to limit access to your work via this web address

(Use a minimum of 4 characters- only numbers and letters allowed, no spaces.)

[Cancel] [Publish]

11.7 - Activities

• Activity One •

Design a Web site for a school. Provide: (1) a home page with basic information and links to other pages; (2) at least six pages that connect from the home page; (3) information for each page and (4) external links for the students. This is not intended to be a real Web site. This is a planning activity. Draw it out as though you intended to use it in the future. Include a drawing of what would be on each page.

• Activity Two •

Go to *Scholastic's Class Homepage Builder*. Design a home page for a classroom where you are doing (or have done) a field experience.

• Activity Three •

Using *Word* or *Netscape*, design and construct a three-page Web site on any topic. Publish it through your H Drive at Rowan.

• Activity Four •

Using *Web Page Builder* in *TaskStream*, construct a Web site with five pages, showcasing some of the work you have done at Rowan.

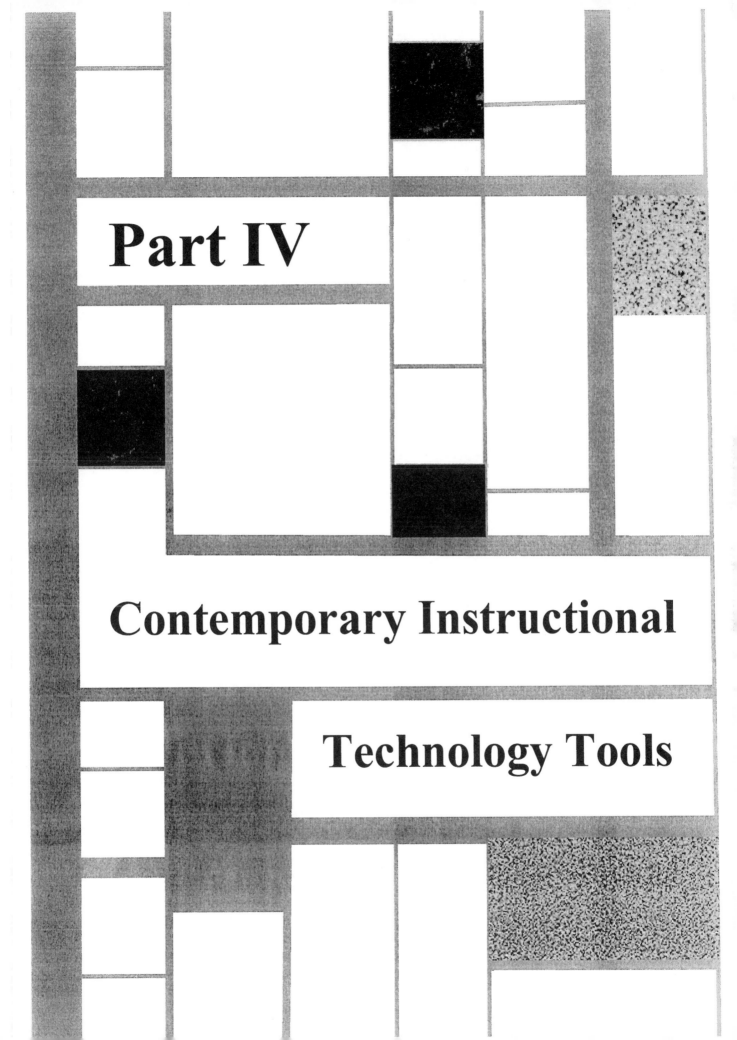

Part IV

Contemporary Instructional

Technology Tools

CHAPTER 12

Productivity Tools: *Word* and *Excel*

12.1 - Introduction

The most common productivity applications are word processing, spreadsheets, and databases. These are commonly found as components of "integrated suites," with all of the components sharing common features, making it possible to move back and forth between the applications. Many also have drawing tools included in all of the components. Some computers come with this software already installed; others can be purchased as add-on packages. The user can write, edit, copy, paste, save files, print, add graphics, convert text to Web pages, and much more.

Word processing is usually the first application introduced in the schools. Using word processing, the students no longer need to write a rough draft, then type their final product; they can begin using a word processor and edit their work in the same place. They receive instant feedback on spelling and grammar and, at the same time, produce a professional-looking document.

Using a word processor makes teacher tasks, from memos and reports to worksheets with graphics and tables, much simpler. Documents can be formatted quickly and easily, editing can be done with a few keystrokes, text can be moved anywhere (even between documents), type sizes/fonts/styles can be quickly changed, and graphics can be added to produce a more visually appealing document.

An electronic spreadsheet is viewed by many as a grid similar to an accounting ledger. Numbers and calculations are stored there, with built-in formulas for calculations. Although it is frequently assumed that the data in a spreadsheet must be numerical, it can be any combination of characters (numbers and/or text). In this context, a spreadsheet can be much more than a calculator to a teacher. It can also house any information normally placed in grids or boxes. In addition to performing numerical operations, most programs also produce charts, showing the numerical data in a graphical format. Line, column, bar, and pie charts are among those that can be made. Formatting capabilities of word processing, such as fonts, text sizes and styles, font colors, graphics, spell check, etc., are also available in spreadsheets.

In the classroom, the most common uses of spreadsheets are for manipulating data in science and math. Charts and graphs can then be produced from this data. Teachers find spreadsheets most useful for calculating student grades, keeping budgets, recording class attendance, and making schedules.

A database is a collection of information, often called an electronic filing cabinet. It is a file where information can be stored, sorted, and retrieved in various ways, then viewed and printed in different formats. Information storage is similar to a telephone book, an address book, or a recipe collection; however, fast retrieval of information can only be done with a computer. Data can also be merged into word processing documents for customized correspondence (mail merge) or used to print out labels.

Schools make use of databases to compile and manipulate student records, while online databases store large amounts of reference material. Students can research information and store it in a database, compile lists of subject material or books, or store results of surveys or experiments. Teachers can use a database to store student information or inventories, mail merge information in letters, or store test questions.

Microsoft Office is the most popular integrated software found in schools and offices today. This software is cross-platform, permitting files created to be used on either a PC or Mac. *AppleWorks* is another integrated program commonly used for the Mac, while *Microsoft Works* has a suite of programs available for the PC.

Microsoft Office includes *Word* for word processing, *Excel* for spreadsheets, *Access* for databases (PC only), *PowerPoint* for presentations, and *Outlook* for e-mail. *Word* and *Excel* for Macintosh are presented in this chapter. Mail merge is a common use for a database. This can also be done with *Word* and will be described in this chapter. Instructions and screen shots in this chapter are for *Microsoft Office for Mac OSX, 2004*, but are similar for other versions.

12.2 - Using *Microsoft Word*

The basics of *Microsoft Word* are not included in this chapter, since they are known by most college students and teachers. Explained here are techniques needed by teachers and students to:
- make columns for a newsletter
- insert and manipulate clip art and other images
- set up a table to present information in "boxes"
- include hyperlinks to link to a Web page
- enter footnotes and endnotes for research papers
- insert headers, footers, and page numbers
- do a mail merge for personalized letters
- save documents in various formats

Basics

Before beginning any document, be sure the toolbars needed for the project are in place. These can be added under *View: Toolbars*. The *Standard Toolbar* includes icons for New Document, Open, Save, Cut, Copy, Paste, Print, Columns, Zoom, and more. This is located at the top of the screen under the *Menu Bar*. Under this is the *Formatting Toolbar* with Fonts, Sizes, Styles, Alignment, Bullets, Text Color, and more. The *Drawing Toolbar* is on the left of the screen to add Text Boxes, Draw Tools, Word Art, and more. Other toolbars are available, often appearing on the screen as needed. The *Formatting Palette* can also be found under *View*. This contains many shortcuts for the items above.

Saving work is of utmost importance. Save at the beginning of a document and every five minutes as you work. If any computer problems, the document is usually retrieved with *Auto Recovery*; but, don't take a chance of losing work. Save OFTEN!

Columns for a Newsletter

The normal layout for a *Word* document is for the text to cover the width of a page, like one wide column. This can be divided into any number of columns by going to *Format: Columns*.

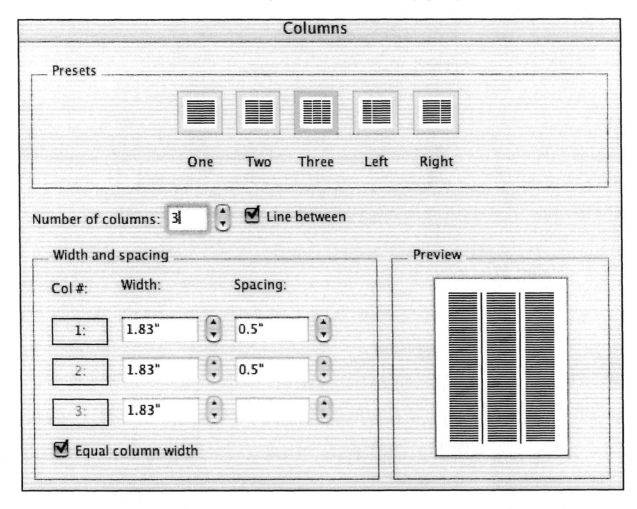

Choices are here for the number of columns (three shown here), the width and spacing, and for a line to appear between columns, if desired. Once this is done, width and spacing can also be changed in the document by dragging the column-related ruler icons that appear. Once the columns are created, use the arrow keys to go back and forth between the columns.

Using the menu above will change the columns for the entire document. If you do not want to do this, when ready to add columns, go to *Insert: Break: Section Break (Continuous)*. Second, choose the number of columns from the *Formatting Toolbar*. This allows you to have text across the full page (the header of the newsletter), then break it into columns when the column break is chosen. If another format is needed later, do the same thing, changing back to one column (or whatever is desired).

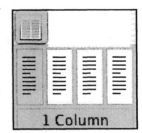

Insert and Manipulate Clip Art and Other Images

Clip art, scanned images, and photos can be added to any document for interest, color, and visual appeal. Images can be inserted from the *Drawing Toolbar* or *Formatting Palette*, or from *Insert:Picture* in the Menu Bar. From each of these, *Clip Art* or *File* can be inserted. In this instance, *Clip Art* is that located within *Word*. *File* is any other object previously saved for insertion. The top graphic here indicates *Clip Art*; the bottom, *Picture* (called *File* in the Menu Bar, *Picture* in the Tools).

When either *Clip Art* or *File* (*Picture)* is inserted, it is inline with the text; the size can be changed, but it cannot be moved or manipulated. It appears where the cursor is when the object is selected. A black line appears around the object. In most cases, this needs to be changed so the object can "float." Floating objects can be moved freely around the page with text wrapping around them.

To set the wrapping style for the object, either double click on the object, or click on the object, then go to *Format: Picture*. Click on *Layout*. The menu below will appear.

Format Picture

Colors and Lines	Size	Layout	Picture	Text Box

Wrapping style

In line with text	Square	Tight	Behind text	In front of text

Horizontal alignment

○ Left　○ Center　○ Right　● Other

Click on any icon except *In line with text* to have the object "float." Normally *Square* is used unless another option is needed. Text will now wrap, as shown with the child here. This clip art could be moved anywhere in the document, with text wrapping around it in various configurations (see Chapter 13: *Drawing Tools and Clip Art* for more details on clip art in a document).

Set up a Table

A variety of tables can be set up in *Word*. These can be used for anything requiring a specified number of rows and columns. For instance, choosing three columns and four rows gives you 12 "boxes" where you can place pictures or any type of information.

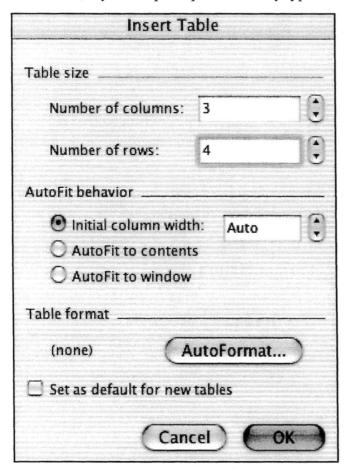

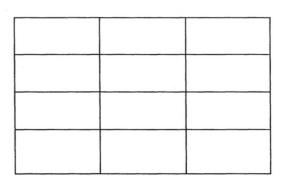

Using the menu under *Table* in the Menu Bar, additional changes can be made: Columns and rows can be added or deleted; cells can be merged or split; text can be sorted alphabetically, numerically, or other; etc. *Table Properties* provides additional choices for formatting. *Auto Format* provides various formats for the table.

Include Hyperlinks to Link to a Web Page

Inserting a hyperlink to link to a Web page is easy in *Word*. This can be done in two ways: (1) When a Web address is inserted in *Word* and the Return key is "hit," the Web address becomes a link; or (2) enter the wording you would like the user (your students) to see. Highlight this, then go to *Insert: Hyperlink*. Enter the Web address. This is better, as the user sees an explanation of the link, not just the address. This address is simple; others could be 50 characters, not telling students what they will find there.

(1) http://www.rowan.edu
(2) Rowan University

Link to:	http://www.rowan.edu
Display:	Rowan University

Enter Footnotes and Endnotes

Footnotes appear at the bottom of each page, while endnotes appear at the end of a chapter or document. Both provide references for text used in the document. Both are entered from *Insert: Footnote*. Choices can then be made for placement and numbering.

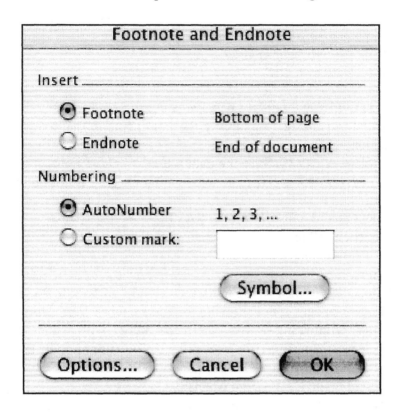

Insert Headers, Footers, and Page Numbers

When added to a document, a header or footer appears on every page of the document. This could be used to insert a page number, chapter name, or title. When Headers and Footers are chosen under *View* in the Menu Bar, the Header/Footer area and AutoText Toolbar (below) appear.

Once a header or footer has been added, page numbers can be a part of this. Choose *Insert: Page Numbers*. Specify the page number and alignment. If "page" is to be part of the numbering, precede the number with "page." Clicking on *Format* (within page numbering menu) will allow you to choose the beginning page number for sections, chapters, etc. Other choices, such as chapter numbers, are also available here.

Mail Merge for Personalized Letters

While mail merge is often a function of a database, it can also be done within *Word*. To create personalized letters, follow the instructions below.

To Set Up the Database:
1. Open a new blank document.
2. In *Tools*, choose *Data Merge Manager*.
   a. Under *Main Document*, click *Create: Form Letters*.
   b. Under *Data Source*, click *Get Data: New Data Source*.
   c. Choose each field you do not need; *Remove Field Name*.
   d. Add other fields as needed by putting the field name in the blank (cannot use spaces or punctuation); *Add.*
   e. When complete, click *OK*; Save the data source.
3. In the *Data Form Dialog Box*, type the information for each field; press the tab key to get to the next field.
4. To get to the next record, click *Add New*. SAVE.
5. When finished, click *OK* to return to the main document.

To Merge into a Letter:
1. A new blank document should be on the screen (if not, go back to 2a, above).
2. If the Data Merge Manager is not showing, in *Tools* choose *Data Merge Manager*.
3. Type your letter, eliminating words where the merge will occur. Where you will be merging data, leave a space and correct punctuation (not enough spaces for the entire word—just one space). SAVE.
4. Go to *Merge Field* in the Data Merge Manager.
5. Where a merge field is needed, drag the name of the field to the proper place in the document. Punctuate as necessary. Do not leave extra spaces. (Pretend the merge field is the text.) SAVE.
6. Click *Preview* in the Data Merge Manager.
7. Click on *ABC*; the first record should appear in your letter. Use the arrows to view the other letters.
8. To Print: click on *Merge*, then the first box—*Merge to Printer*: *Print* (all will print unless you choose *Custom*)

To Make Mailing Labels:
1. Open a blank document; Open *Mail Merge Manager*.
2. Under Main Document, click on *Create: Labels*.
3. Choose the type of printer and label (normal mailing labels are *5160-Avery*).
4. In the Data Merge Manger, *Get Data*—locate data file.
5. Choose *Insert Merge Field*, then construct your label from the choices.
6. *Preview* to see your labels.

For more information, go the HELP: Mail Merge

Save documents in Various Formats

Save

Save As...

Save as Web Page...

Documents are normally saved using the *Save* icon, or *File: Save*. *Save As* saves the document under another name or format, or in another location. Here you could save your file to your H Drive or USB minidrive. Always save in several locations. *Save as Web Page* saves the document in HTML format to use on a Web page.

A document can also be saved as a *PDF* file. To do this, go to *File: Print*. The menu illustrated here will appear. *Save as PDF*.

> **For assistance with any components of Word, go to the HELP menu; enter the topic you are searching for.**

12.3 - Using *Microsoft Excel*

While a spreadsheet has many uses in the classroom for the student, as well as the teacher, the example provided here is for the teacher to use a spreadsheet to calculate grades.

Spreadsheet Basics

- A spreadsheet is composed of a grid of Rows (horizontal: numbers down the side) and Columns (vertical: letters across the top).
- The intersection of the row and column is known as the Cell (column letter and row number ID called the Cell Address).
- The active cell address is displayed in the Cell Indicator Bar.
- The position of the Cell Cursor indicates where data is entered, while the data entered appears in the Entry Bar.
- The Formula Bar is located under the Formatting Toolbar. This is where text, numbers, and formulas are entered and changed. If missing, go to *View: Formula Bar*.
- Cells can contain three types of data: labels (text), values (numbers), and formulas.
- When doing calculations, the user can enter a formula or use a function (a predefined formula within the spreadsheet program that does the calculation required).
- Access to the spreadsheet options is through the Menu Bar at the top of the spreadsheet, the Standard Toolbar, the Formatting Toolbar, or the Formatting Palette.
- When data in one cell changes, calculations for all of the cells dependent on that cell change.

How to Create a Spreadsheet

When a new document for a spreadsheet is opened, cells appear (in opposition to a plain page), as shown (in a modified form) below. This does not look like a traditional format for entering text; however, it is adaptable to both numerical and textual data.

	A	B	C	D	E	F	G	H
1				any				
2		any font		column				
3				width				
4			any row heights	any size font				

A variety of options are available for use in spreadsheet documents. As shown above, columns can be any width, rows any height; fonts can be changed; and text can be any size. Cells can contain any combination of text, numbers, formulas, and functions. Most basic formatting and editing tools such as cut, copy, paste, close, save, print, format, etc. can be used in conjunction with entries in the cells. Graphics can also be added.

Spreadsheet Formulas and Functions

All calculations are done with formulas that begin with the equal sign. Formulas can be entered, or built-in functions in the program (such as SUM or AVERAGE) can be used. In most formulas, cell addresses, rather than numbers, are used. For example, to add the numbers in cells A1 and B1, either of the formulas below could be used. The function AVERAGE could be substituted for SUM to average the numbers. (Upper or lower case letters can be used.)

=A1+B1   or   =SUM(A1,B1)

There are many other built-in functions in *Excel*, as well as in other spreadsheet programs. Consult the program manual or the Help Menu for additional options available to the user.

Create a Spreadsheet to Calculate Grades

The directions that follow explain how a spreadsheet can be used to calculate grades. The basic directions which follow are for *Microsoft Excel: 2004: Mac*. All spreadsheets are similar in design and use.

1. Open *Excel* (or another spreadsheet program); choose the option to create a new spreadsheet (*Excel Workbook*).

2. Enter the information in the chart below in the correct cells. As information is entered, it will appear in the Formula Bar, not the cell. Press the Return key to enter data into the cell and go to the cell below (the Tab key moves the cursor across). To make corrections: click in the cell, make corrections in the Formula Bar.

	A	B	C	D	E	F	G
1	Student Name	Test 1	Test 2	Final Exam	Homework	Average	Weighted
2							
3	Student 1	90	85	60	90		
4	Student 2	88	89	78	80		
5	Student 3	86	90	74	75		
6	Student 4	95	78	90	90		
7							
8	Average						
9	Weights	20	20	25	35		

3. To set the size of the columns for the information to fit, highlight the columns; choose *Format: Column: AutoFit Selection* in the Menu Bar.
4. Save as "Grades"; continue to save every 5 minutes.
5. To average the grades: Click in cell F3 (first calculation for Student 1). Enter the formula: =average(B3:E3). (Average is the function to average all cell addresses housed within the indicated cell range.) Click on the Return key; the average for Student 1 will appear in cell F3.
6. To copy this formula for all other students: Highlight the average in F3; drag to highlight cells for the remaining students: Choose *Edit: Fill: Down* in the Menu Bar.
7. Use a similar formula to get the average for each column in Row 8. To copy across, choose *Edit: Fill: Right*.
8. To give weights to each grade (different percentages instead of all being the same in an average), use the weights identified in the chart for this example. Click in cell G3. Enter the formula: =B3*.2+C3*.2+D3*.25+E3*.35
9. Copy the formula for the other students, as above.

Formatting the Spreadsheet

Once a spreadsheet is set up, it can be formatted in various ways. Fonts, text sizes and styles, and colors can be changed or added as in word processing. Text in the cells can be aligned horizontally, vertically, or with various orientations. Borders and shading can be added to the spreadsheet. Numbers can be formatted with decimals, along with many other formats. These can all be done from the Formatting Palette, which appears with the spreadsheet.

Printing the Spreadsheet

Highlight the cells to be printed; choose the print icon. To change the orientation of the page and print horizontally, go to *File: Page Setup: Landscape Orientation*.

<u>Hint</u>: Once a spreadsheet is set up, formatted, and has formulas added, save it as a template before entering data. Then it can be used many times!

Charts and Graphs

Once a spreadsheet has been developed, charts and graphs can be constructed. You must first decide what data to include in the chart. Rows or columns of data must be next to each other in order to reconfigure the data into a chart. If columns need to be rearranged, highlight the column to be moved, then drag (with the hand tool) to place in a blank area on the right of the spreadsheet; drag other columns as needed.

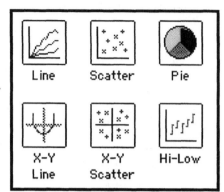

To begin any chart, choose *Insert: Chart* from the Menu Bar. A Chart Wizard appears. Choose the appropriate chart type; click to continue. Other screens in the Wizard will prompt for things such as heading, and X and Y axis. The X axis is at the bottom; the Y axis is on the side.

12.4 - Activities

• Activity One •

Develop a two-page newsletter for a topic you are teaching. Include: (1) Text that is formatted the width of the document; (2) text that is formatted in two or three columns; and (3) a minimum of three photos or pieces of clip art, with at least one exhibiting word wrap.

• Activity Two •

Format a research paper you are working on to include at least three of the following: a page header, a page footer, page numbers, a table.

• Activity Three •

Write a letter to the parents of students in your class. Develop a database in *Word* that includes the parents' name, the home address, the child's name, and two other pieces of information. Merge this into a letter and print it out.

• Activity Four •

Develop a spreadsheet using the sample data for student grades. Calculate the student average and weighted grade, along with the average for each score. Make a column chart showing a comparison of how the students scored in all tests and the homework categories. Make a line chart showing all scores for all students.

Drawing Tools and Clip Art

13.1 - Introduction

All digital images—drawings, photos, graphs—are referred to as *graphics*. Graphics software is used to create, edit, or enhance these images. All assist in adding visual images to your projects. Programs to create images fall into two main categories: paint programs, which are used to create bit-mapped images, and drawing programs, which are used to create object-oriented images.

Paint environments are typically for the artist creating artwork and doing illustrations. They employ computer-based paint brushes, air brushes, pencils, and other tools. Using these paint tools, colors and shapes are "painted" on the computer screen as they would be painted onto a canvas. An eraser is available to remove the artwork. Since some artistic ability, along with specialized software, is required for painting, paint will not be covered here.

Drawing tools are commonly used by teachers and students. They are accessible and easy to use. Drawing environments include object-oriented tools such as lines, rectangles, and circles, along with colors, patterns, and textures. Objects can be drawn on the screen, rearranged, and grouped together.

Drawing and painting programs intended for school and personal use (in opposition to high-ended programs for the artist) are a part of the integrated suites *AppleWorks* and *Microsoft Works*. In these packages, the drawing tools can also be found as components of word processing. The drawing tools illustrated in this unit are components of *Word* and *PowerPoint* in *Microsoft Office* (*Office* does not include painting). Tools in all programs are similar. Once you understand the basics, you can use the tools in any program.

Students can use drawing tools to add interest to writing samples, newsletters, and report covers; draw maps; and develop concept maps, graphs and tables, and organizational charts. Teachers can create classroom plans and seating charts and design bulletin boards, learning centers, flyers, and signs, to mention a few uses.

Clip art includes all ready-made graphics that can be added to documents, signs, flyers, newsletters, cards, Web pages, etc. for interest and creativity. Some clip art is available free of charge, while other clip art is available commercially. Given the large number of choices, it is  often time consuming to locate just the right graphic. Some sources of free clip art are included in this chapter. Teachers and students can make use of clip art to enhance any document, such as newsletters, bulletins, reports, projects, worksheets, instructional handouts, and displays.

Graphic editing software is used to edit and enhance graphic objects. *Photoshop*® is often used for this. An easier version of the program, *Photoshop Elements*, is also available. While these programs are complex and often time-consuming to learn, they are not always necessary. *Word* has a variety of image-editing tools powerful enough for correcting and editing digital photographs, scanned images, and clip art.

13.2 - Using the Drawing Tools

The Drawing Toolbar in *Word* and *PowerPoint* is normally found at the left of the screen. If the toolbar is not visible, go to *View: Toolbars: Drawing* on the Menu Bar.

Drawing Toolbars

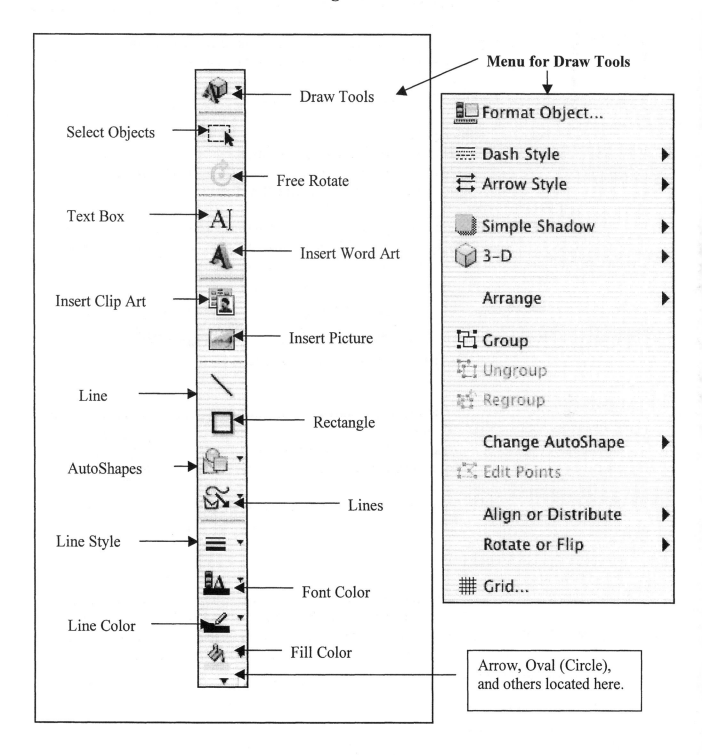

The Drawing Tools

Drawing an Object: Choose the line, rectangle, or oval tool. Place the cursor on the screen where the object is to begin. Holding down the mouse button, drag to form the object; release the mouse button when the size is complete. To draw a straight line, a square, or a circle, hold down the Shift key while dragging. To draw more than one of the same object, double click the tool prior to drawing.

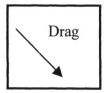

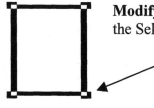

Modifying Objects: To move or change objects once they are drawn, click on the Select Objects Tool (Pointer), then click on the object.

Handles will appear on the object, making it active.

With the object active:
- to resize the object, drag a handle;
- to move the object, click inside (with the hand) and drag;
- to delete the object, use the delete key.

Line Width and Style: Thickness (and styles) of the line (or outline) drawn can be changed with the Line Style Tool. Make the item active; choose the width or style desired. Lines can be changed to multiple lines with the style tool or dashes with the dash tool.

Object and Line Colors: Color palettes, along with fill effects such as gradients, textures, and patterns, are available to fill and color objects and lines.
Fill Color places color (and other fills) inside the object.
Line Color places color or patterns on the line or outline of the object.

Font Colors: Apply colors to highlighted text in word processing or active text in a text box.

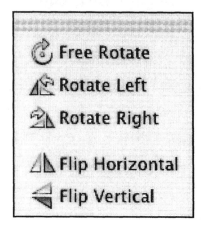

Rotate/Flip: Once clip art, or another graphical object, is inserted, the art can be rotated using the Free Rotate Tool, or rotated/flipped through this menu in the Draw Tools. First select the object, then choose the rotation or flip to be used.

Word Art: Text is formatted in a variety of preset styles to add interest to any document or presentation.

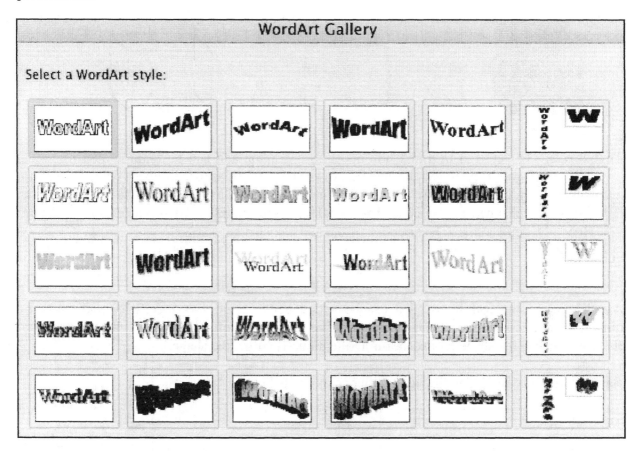

When a style is chosen and text is added, the Word Art is shown, along with the Word Art Toolbar. Colors can be selected, sizing modified, shapes changed and rotated, and more.

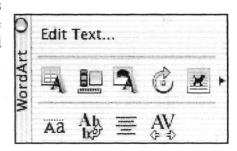

Insert Clip Art and Picture: Images can be inserted from the Drawing Toolbar or Formatting Palette, or from *Insert: Picture* on the Menu Bar. Clip art from *Word* is inserted through *Clip Art,* while clip art files, photos, scanned objects, or any other external objects can be inserted through *Picture* (*Insert: Picture: File* in the Menu Bar). The top graphic here indicates *Clip Art*; the bottom, *Picture*.

Shadows and 3-D: Once an object is drawn, shadows or three-dimensional effects can be added. Select the object; choose the Shadow or 3-D Tool from the Draw Tools.

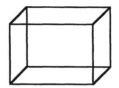

Text Boxes: Text entered in a text box becomes a graphic and can be manipulated like other graphics. It can be moved to various locations or grouped with objects for identification. When the box is active (handles), text can be changed in the same way as when text is highlighted in word processing. The direction of the text can also be changed.

AutoShapes: Graphical shapes that can be added in the same way rectangles and ovals are drawn. In the *AutoShape* menu, there are five categories of shapes (below). Choose the shape to use, then drag the mouse to draw the shape.

Basic Shapes are shown on the right, with one example below.

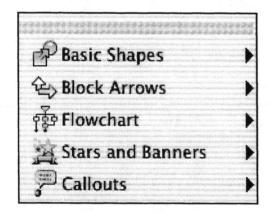
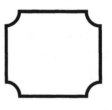
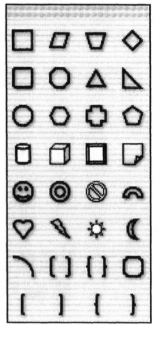

Arrows: With handles on a line or arrow, select *Arrow Style* to make arrows in various styles and directions. The Line Style Tool can be used to change the thickness of the line.

Arranging Objects: Objects appear on the screen in the order they are drawn. To change this order and create various effects, the objects can be arranged. Click on the object; choose *Arrange* in the Draw Tools; move as appropriate.

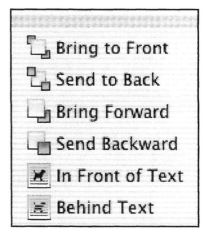

Aligning Objects: To have objects line up on the left or right, the bottom or top, or distribute space between them, use *Align* or *Distribute* in the Draw Tools.

Grouping Objects: When several objects are going to be used together (including text made in a text box), they can be grouped together. When grouped, they all move together for ease of formatting the screen.

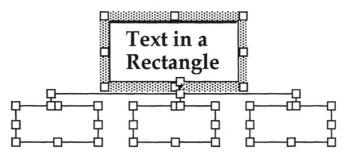

To group objects, click on each object to be included while holding down the Shift key; handles will appear on all objects. An alternative is to drag the Select Object Tool around all objects (like putting a rectangle around all objects). Choose *Group* in the Draw Tools. When grouped, there will be handles around the group, not each object. To take apart, choose *Ungroup* in the Draw Tools.

Design and Draw a Classroom (using tools in any drawing program)

As a part of your education program, an assignment might be to draw and/or design a classroom. This can be done with the drawing tools explained above. Seating charts can also be developed and easily modified. The drawing tools can be used to draw room furniture, doors, windows, and other components. When more than one of an item is needed, copy or duplicate the item rather than trying to replicate it with the drawing tools. For instance: draw a desk; copy and paste it to make more. Make a row of desks; group them; then copy for additional rows.

Make use of textures and fills to indicate specific items. Use the text tool for labeling. A symbol key can be added for easy identification.

Additional icons for furniture, office supplies, computers, etc., can be found on clip art CDs/DVDs or at clip art sites on the Internet.

13.3 - Using Graphics (Clip Art)

 Graphics software (often termed "clip art") includes packaged collections of graphics, usually indexed into libraries by topic. This term originated when art was "clipped" and pasted into documents. Most software (such as *Microsoft Office* and *AppleWorks*) that uses graphics elements contains clip art libraries. In addition to that in the software programs, CDs or DVDs with thousands of images can be purchased. Much more can be located on the Internet. Clip art can be used by the teacher to enhance any document. While there are probably millions of pieces of clip art available, it is often difficult to locate just what you want.

File Formats

Print clip art falls into one of two graphical image categories: bitmapped or vector. Bitmapped images, also known as raster, can only be edited in paint or bitmap editing programs. This limits their resolutions to the size in which they were created. Enlarging the graphic makes it look worse; lines appear jagged. Reducing size does not improve the image; it stays the same. Typical file formats for these are *.bmp* (bitmapped), *.pict* (picture format), and *.tiff* (Tagged Image File). Vector images, also referred to as object-oriented images, are more versatile. These graphics can be edited in draw or object-oriented editing programs. These appear the same at any resolution; their appearance does not change with resizing. Typical file formats for these are *.esp* (encapsulated postscript) and *.pict* (which can also be bitmapped).

Graphics for the Internet are typically *.gif* (Graphics Interchange Format) or *.jpeg* (Joint Photographic Experts Group) formats. Although *.gif* requires less storage space than bitmapped images, it only allows for 256 colors and is used for simple images. Photos on the Web are usually *.jpeg*, which allows for millions of colors.

These file formats will appear after the name of the clip art as an extension. If clip art is not in the correct format for use in a program, it can be translated using a graphic conversion program. Many of these can be found on the Internet as shareware or freeware programs.

Sources of Clip Art

Clip art, available as black and white images, photography, color line art, maps, borders, icons, or cartoons, can be acquired from a variety of sources.

Many application programs, such as *Microsoft Office, AppleWorks, HyperStudio®, The Print Shop®, Kid Pix®*, etc. include their own clip art libraries. To utilize clip art in *Microsoft Office*, go to the Insert Menu; choose *Picture: Clip Art*. A library of clip art will appear. Choose the category of interest. When a piece of clip art is selected, click on it, then choose *Insert*. At this same location, choosing *Online* will take you to Microsoft's online *Clip Art and Media* site, featuring clip art in various categories.

Other clip art can be purchased on CDs/DVDs. When accessing clip art from CDs, DVDs, and other programs, click on the object; *Edit: Copy* (puts the graphic into the memory of the computer); go to the document where you want the clip art: *Edit: Paste*. The clip art is transferred to this document. *Word* also has the option of using *Insert: Picture: From File*. After choosing this, locate the clip art on a CD, in a file, on a disk, etc. Photos and scanned images are also inserted in this way.

There is a multitude of free clip art available on the WWW. There are sites where clip art can be downloaded at no cost, while other sites are by subscription only. Many of the free sites are full of advertisements, making it difficult to locate the clip art. The sites below are for teachers and students, with easy to find and use clip art. Additional links are on the *Technology Tools for Teachers* Web site.

Awesome Clipart for Educators	www.awesomeclipartforeducators.com/
Classroom Clipart	classroomclipart.com/
Discovery School	school.discovery.com/clipart/index.html
Kaboose™	www.kidsdomain.com/clip/
School Clip Art	www.school-clip-art.com/
Teacher Files	www.teacherfiles.com/clip_art.htm

Another source for free clip art is from *Images* files located on Web browsers such as *Google* (www.google.com), *Yahoo* (search.yahoo.com/images), and *AltaVista* (www.altavista.com). The screen for *Google* is below. Click on *Images*; enter the topic to search for; *Search Images*. Limit your topic as much as possible or you could end up with millions of images (a search for "book" found over five million images).

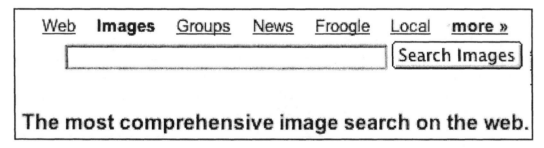

AltaVista Image Search provides even more choices.

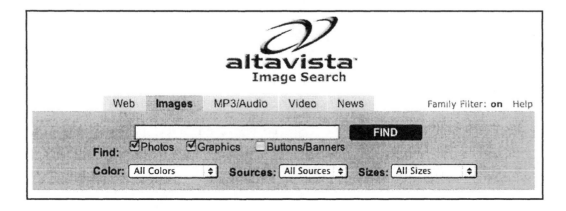

Downloading Web Clip Art

Clip art from the Web can be placed in documents in two ways: (1) inserted directly into the document and (2) saved to disk (or computer), then inserted. When working with a document in *Word*, or other word processors, any of these methods can be used. If inserting to a Web-based document, the image must first be downloaded to a disk (or hard drive), with the file being placed in the same folder as the Web page.

- Locate the clip art on the WWW.
- Hold down the mouse button (PC = right button) for several seconds, or hold down the Control key while clicking on the clip art.
- The menu to the right will appear with options to copy, download, etc.
- If the document where you want to place the clip art is open, choose *Copy Image* on the Web menu, then return to the document where the clip art is to be placed.
- *Edit: Paste* into the document.
- Most programs also support *Drag and Drop,* where you can drag the image to the file where it will be used.
- The clip art can also be saved to the hard drive of the computer or on a disk to use at a later time.

> Open Link in New Window
> Download Link to Disk
> Copy Link to Clipboard
> Add Link to Favorites
>
> Open Image in New Window
> Download Image to Disk
> Copy Image
> Reload Image

Adding Clip Art to a Document

When any type of clip art, photo, or scanned image is placed in a word processing document, it is "inline" with the text. The size can be changed, but it cannot be moved or edited. The graphic must be changed to a "floating" graphic. To do this:

- Double click on the image (or go to *Format: Picture*);
- In the Format Picture menu, click on *Layout;*
- Choose any of the selections except "Inline with text;"
- Click on *OK;*
- Position the graphic within the text (text wrap will also now take place).

Resizing and Moving Images

Once an image is "floating," it has "handles." To resize an object proportionately, drag any corner handle. To resize an object disproportionately, drag any middle handle. Move the object by "grabbing" with the Hand Tool at the edge or center of the object.

13.4 - Editing Images

Using the image editing tools in *Word*, it is possible to edit images (photos, scanned images, and bitmapped pictures images) usually edited in *Photoshop* or other editing programs. Editing tools can be accessed from the Picture Toolbar (*View: Toolbars*), *Edit: Edit Picture*, or the Formatting Palette.

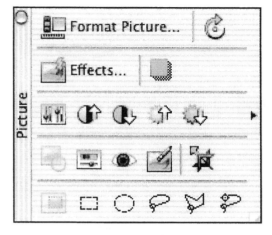

Row 1:
> *Format Picture*: sets image size, text wrap, brightness, contrast, and more.
> *Free Rotate* (also available in the Drawing Toolbar): click on a green handle and rotate in any direction.

Row 2:
> *Effects:* applies a special effects filter to the image (or part of it).
> *Simple Shadow:* adds a shadow behind the image.

Row 3:
> *Image Control:* converts the image to grayscale or black-and-white. *Watermark* dims the picture and places it in the background.
> *Contrast* and *Brightness* icons reduce or intensify contrast or brightness.

Row 4:
> *Set Transparent Color:* makes a specific color transparent.
> *Color Adjustment*: adjusts colors or their saturation.
> *Fix Red Eye:* eliminates red eye in photos.
> *Remove Scratch:* eliminates a scratch in a photo or scan.
> *Crop:* removes unnecessary material from around an object (cannot change size later).

Row 5: Tools to select a portion of an object for editing.
> *Cutout*: cuts out the unused area selected by the tools below.
> *Rectangular* and *Oval Marquee:* select an area to use.
> *Lassos:* select irregular-shaped areas to use.

(see examples on the next page)

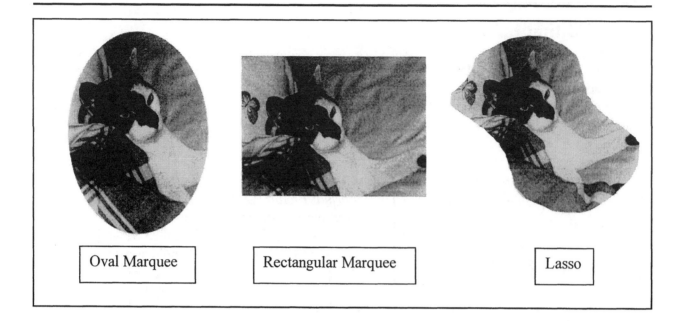

| Oval Marquee | Rectangular Marquee | Lasso |

13.5 - Activities

• Activity One •

Using the drawing tools and clip art, replicate a classroom where you are doing your field experience. Include seating, equipment, computers, windows, doors, teacher area, storage, bookcases, etc. Clip art from the Web can be used for any of the items.

• Activity Two •

Visit five good Web sites for clip art: (1) Review what is available at each site for a teacher to use in the classroom. (2) Copy an image from each into a *Word* document. (3) Using a text box, identify the site where each was found.

• Activity Three •

Produce a worksheet for a lesson you are teaching. Include at least two drawing tools, two pieces of clip art, and two text boxes.

• Activity Four •

Take several photos with a digital camera. Choose the two best photos. For one, use the Crop Tool to crop out the best part of the picture. For the other, crop it using the Oval and Rectangular Marquees and the Lasso, as in the pictures above. Place them on one page and print out.

CHAPTER **14**

Digital Images

14.1 - Introduction

Having a computer in the classroom is only the beginning of what you and your students can do with technology. Digital input and output devices expand the possibilities for using digital images in projects and presentations. Photos can be taken, edited, and printed using a digital camera and peripherals; photos and documents can be scanned for manipulation with the computer; and text can be input without using the keyboard. Any of these images, or anything on the computer, can be sent to a large screen via a video (LCD) projector. These images can be stored on CDs, DVDs, or USB minidrives.

14.2 - Digital Input

Any device that allows the user to enter data, commands, and responses to the computer is termed an input device. Common to every computer is the keyboard and the mouse (laptops, however, have a built-in keyboard and a trackpad in place of a mouse). Other input devices include digital cameras, scanners, electronic whiteboards, touch screens, digital tablets and pens, and more. Once in the computer, the images can be modified with photo editing programs, or in paint or drawing environments. The finished products can be used in various ways.

Digital Cameras

As input devices, digital cameras take pictures that can immediately be saved on a memory card or in the camera. They can be imported into the computer or saved on a disk or a CD for use as a graphic in any application program at a later time, and printed on a home printer or at a processing location for immediate prints. Cameras and/or memory cards can hold hundreds of photos, depending on their size. Photos are less expensive than traditional photos since digital cameras do not require film, thus eliminating processing charges. They are easy to use, even by children. Unwanted photos can be deleted, and photos can be retaken immediately.

When photos are taken, they are usually stored on a memory card within the camera. This card can then be placed in a slot in the computer, or in a card reader that goes into a USB port in the computer, for easy access. Cameras without the memory card are linked to the computer via a USB cable to import the photos into the computer. This method limits the number of photos that can be taken. Using memory cards, the larger the storage capacity of the card, the more photos that can be stored. You can also use several cards before downloading the photos to the computer. Software within the computer transfers the images to the hard drive of the computer, or they can be directly accessed from the memory card.

Most digital cameras store pictures as *jpeg* files, so pictures can easily be sent to friends and family via e-mail, manipulated with editing software, or placed on a Web page. If a digital camera is not available, pictures taken with a 35mm camera can also be processed for use in a computer. When film is processed, photos can be stored on a CD-ROM (PhotoCD) and can be accessed in the same way as those taken with a digital camera.

Camera Features

One of the first things to look for in a camera is the image resolution. Image quality is measured in pixels; in cameras, it is measured in Mega Pixels (MP = million pixels), with the image quality increasing as the number increases. Cameras suitable for classroom and personal use are basic point-and-shoot models, with the MP being under six. Other "high-end varieties" are available for professionals. The point-and-shoot cameras do not have as many features as the more expensive models, but most tend to take quality photos. These cameras are adequate for Web pages and snapshots. A resolution of 640 x 480 pixel images is high enough for pictures used for e-mail and web pages.

Prices are dependent on:

- features included (red eye reduction, auto-focus, flash, self-timer, zoom)
- image resolution
- method of storing photos
- number of images that can be stored (in camera, on card, or on disk)
- type of lenses
- LCD screen for viewing (see large image on screen, as well as in viewfinder)
- capability of storing video clips as well as photos

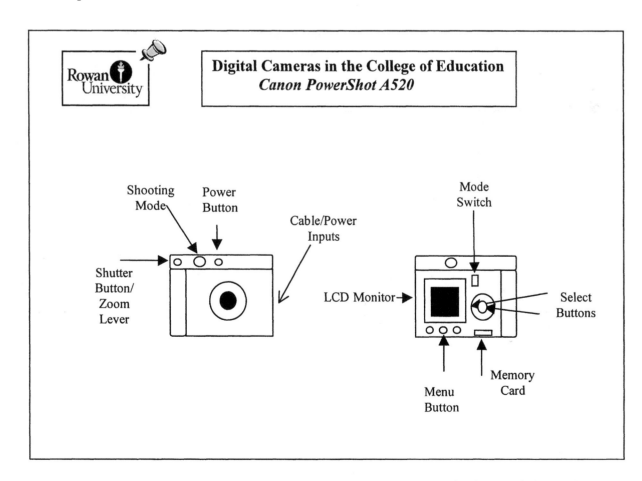

Using a Digital Camera (instructions for the *Canon A520*; similar for other cameras)

1. Insert batteries.
2. Insert the memory card (if applicable).
3. Press the Power Button to turn the camera on.
4. Slide the Mode Switch to the *Camera* icon.
5. Turn the Shooting Mode Dial to AUTO.
6. Aim the camera at the subject.
7. Adjust the Zoom Lever.
8. Press the Shutter Button half way to focus (beeps twice).
9. Press the Shutter Button all the way to shoot the picture.
10. To playback the pictures: Slide the Mode Switch to the *arrow*; use the Select Buttons to display the images.
11. To erase a picture: Press the Function Button (right of the Menu Button); check that *Erase* is selected; press the SET Button (between Select Buttons).
12. Check the instruction book for more detailed instructions.

Downloading Pictures to the Computer

1. Install the software that comes with the camera (Macintosh—photos can be downloaded directly into *iPhoto*®).
2. Connect the camera to the computer using the USB cable that comes with the camera.
3. Slide the Mode Switch to *Playback* (arrow); turn the camera on.
4. The software should recognize the camera and appear (if not, locate the software from the *Start Menu* on a PC, or *Applications* on a Mac).
5. Download the images, following the directions on the menus.

Using a Memory Card

1. Eject the memory card from the camera.
2. Insert it into a slot in the computer, or into a memory card reader that goes into the USB port of the computer.
3. Double click the icon of the drive, or memory card, containing the pictures.
4. Copy the images to a folder for use at a later time.

Image Editing Software

Once a digital picture or image is imported into the computer, it can be edited in various programs. Image editing software can be used, along with easy-to-use drawing and painting programs. New versions of *Microsoft Word* include editing tools (see Chapter 13: Drawing Tools and Clip Art). *Adobe PhotoShop* is the standard for high-end image editing. While this program is quite complex, Adobe's *PhotoShop Elements* is easier for students and teachers to use. These programs provide selection tools, touch-up features, special effects, tools to crop and resize, and ways to brighten or lighten the photo or image. Some programs also provide templates and backgrounds for fun themes and special occasions.

iPhoto for Macintosh OSX

Part of *iLife*® for Macintosh is *iPhoto*. Images can be imported from a digital camera, PhotoCD, or any other source. By plugging a digital camera into a Macintosh with *iPhoto*, photos are automatically loaded into the software. Icons on the Menu Bar below assist in editing, organizing, printing, and sharing photos.

When importing photos, you are given the option to erase the photos after they are imported. However, you should wait to be sure they are successfully downloaded before doing this. They can then be erased from the camera. When importing, a name can be given to the group of photos as they are imported (e.g., Student Portfolios, May 2006). Movie clips can also be imported. Once imported, you can view the photos, delete those you do not want to keep, organize them into folders, or create an instant slide show.

Scanners

Scanners are light-sensing devices, attached to a computer in a USB port, that read documents, photos, and more. Similar in concept to copy machines, they copy a page at a time, producing a graphic image. Images are then sent to the computer and saved in a file format such as *.tiff*, *.jpeg*, *.gif*, or *.pict*, according to their end use. Print images are, therefore, translated to digital images.

Text can also be scanned; however, the end product is still a graphic image. The image can be digitized by OCR (Optical Character Recognition) software for editing in a word processing program. This conversion does not always produce satisfactory results. Accuracy is limited to the fonts used in the original text and the type of document formatting. When the digitized text is opened in a word processor it is often thrown around on the page, and some text is not even recognizable. Higher quality OCR software often produces more accurate results.

Most scanners today are flatbed scanners. There is a glass plate under the lid with a light under it. Light passes under the bed, producing a computer image. Each scanned image is made up of many dots, with resolution measured in dots per inch (DPI). It does not matter if the scanned image is a photograph, magazine, line art, text, or a map; it is made of dots, not lines or letters.

When a scanner is purchased, it comes with software that needs to be installed on the computer. If it is not available, most of it can be downloaded from the manufacturer's site on the Internet.

Images are saved and edited in much the same way as those from digital cameras. Saving as *.tiff* produces a very large document, and is not recommended when disk space is an issue. Anything used for the Internet or e-mail must be saved as *.gif* or *.jpeg*. All photos must be saved as *.jpeg*.

Scanners in the College of Education
HP ScanJet 5590

To use the *HP ScanJet 5590*:

1. Place your image/document to be scanned on the scanner bed and close the lid.
2. Double click on the Macintosh HD icon on your desktop. Open the Applications folder. Find and open the *Hewlett Packard* folder.
3. Click on the *HP Scanjet Pro* icon.
4. When the *HP ScanPro* box appears on the screen, make any necessary adjustments to the scan settings that you wish to change, then click on the "New Scan" button at the bottom right portion of the *ScanPro* box.
5. The preview of your scan will appear. Use the mouse to highlight the portion of the previewed image that you wish to scan. Then click the "Accept" button in the bottom right portion of the Scan Pro box.
6. A "Save" box will appear. Choose the location in which you wish to store your scanned image.
7. Choose the format in which you wish to store your scanned image. *TIFF* is the default. This is a large file; change to another for smaller files.
8. Click *Save*.
9. The scanning process completes and the image is saved to your designated storage location.

Graphics Tablets, Pens, and Touch Screens

A graphics tablet or pad can be attached to the computer. Graphics tablets allow students to create artwork on the tablet, then import the work into the computer. Text can also be recognized by the computer and imported into a word processing document.

Pens, such as those in PDAs, are used to take handwritten notes and place them into a word processor document. The same concept is used in tablet PCs. Although they are a little larger, choices are made and work is done with a stylus.

A touch screen allows the user to input text by touching the screen with a finger or pointer. This is used by the physically impaired or those who cannot use keyboards. Touching icons on a touch-sensitive screen provides input to the computer.

Electronic Whiteboards

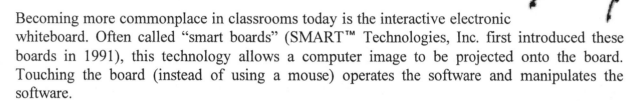

Electronic whiteboards are often found in classrooms. With the standard models, you can digitally capture anything created on the whiteboard. This can then be transferred to the computer and saved or printed. In the classroom, these are often used for discussions and brainstorming sessions, with the products saved and printed for the students.

Becoming more commonplace in classrooms today is the interactive electronic whiteboard. Often called "smart boards" (SMART™ Technologies, Inc. first introduced these boards in 1991), this technology allows a computer image to be projected onto the board. Touching the board (instead of using a mouse) operates the software and manipulates the software.

Using the interactive whiteboard, you can run and display computer programs, surf the Web, and "use" the computer on the whiteboard as you would on the computer itself. Sounds can be heard, and video images can be displayed. Anything on the board can be written over. Software that comes with the boards make it possible to move and manipulate text and objects on the board, save information, and convert handwriting to text. With the built-in scanner, everything on the screen can be digitally captured and sent back to the computer to be saved, printed, etc.

Along with a computer and the whiteboard, a digital projector is also needed for projection. Information from the computer is displayed by the projector onto the touch-sensitive whiteboard instead of the computer monitor.

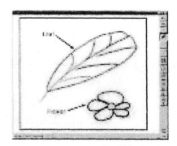

Using an interactive whiteboard, the teacher can be in front of the class (and the board), rather than behind the computer. Students are a big part of the lesson, as they come to the board to enter their own answers and comments. By participating, they feel more a part of their education. They can touch the whiteboard with their finger or a stylus and write notes and comments whenever needed. Since everything on the interactive whiteboard can be saved to the computer and printed, students can pay more attention to what is going on in class and get notes printed out later. Students with special needs are also at an advantage, as they can touch the screen instead of attempting to work with a keyboard. Computer images are also much easier for them to view.

More information can be obtained about SMART Boards at www.smarttech.com. Here you can find out about different types of boards and access educational materials. Their Educator Resources features *Lesson Activities* (hundreds of interactive lesson activities, along with correlated standards), *Software Resources*, *Community* (share with other educators using SMART products), *Professional Development*, and *Online Classroom Resources* (Web sites with free, curriculum-related resources for the classroom).

Hand-held Computing Devices

Personal Digital Assistants (PDAs), Palms, Pocket/Personal PCs, Hand-held Computers, and Hand-held Devices all fall into the category of Hand-held Computing Devices. Small like a cellular phone or pocket gaming device, these are new tools found in today's classrooms. They might contain a personal organizer, a word processor, a digital camera, Internet and e-mail connectivity, and several types of calculators all in one device for the price of a graphing calculator. In addition to these capabilities, free and inexpensive software can be obtained for use in the K-12 classroom. Probes are available for science classes, concept mapping is available for language arts, databases of historical facts can be downloaded for research, and eBooks can be downloaded for reading.

Built-in features include an on-screen keyboard (a larger, external, keyboard can be added), character recognition (data written with a stylus is interpreted and recognized), synchronization (to communicate with a computer), and an infrared port (to transfer programs and data between units). Text is entered using a stylus and a stylized print format called *Graffiti*. Users learn to input stylized letters that can be recognized and transferred to a word processor. Data is synchronized with a computer via a charge/cradle or a USB cable. Output can also be "beamed" to a printer using infrared signals.

Advantages are low cost, size, ease of use, and mobility. Concerns expressed by school administrators include cheating (beam information to others), compatibility, distraction (students do not pay attention to other things), screen size, and security.

Webcams

Mounted on top of the computer, or built-in to newer models of computers, webcams make video chats easy and inexpensive. As illustrated on the right, some cameras sit on top of the computer. Apple's *iSight*® camera, used in the same way, is illustrated below. New Macintosh computers have an *iSight* camera built in above the display. Less than a half inch in diameter, this functions the same as external cameras. With one of these cameras and appropriate software (*iChat*® for Macintosh), you can videoconference with anyone anywhere in the world. Previously used only for communication (no storage), *iSight* conferences can now be recorded as movies and imported into *iMovie*®. In opposition to older technologies, communication can be full screen, with up to four individuals conferencing.

Students can collaborate with students around the world, or the teacher can bring "experts" into the classroom. Students can ask questions, share concerns, or show their work to others without going on a field trip or bringing a speaker into the classroom. Teachers can also use video conferencing to apply for jobs, observe other teachers in their classrooms, or share their teaching practices with pre-service teachers.

14.3 - Digital Output: Video Projectors

After data has been input into the computer, it is processed to become output. This can be seen on a monitor, printed on a printer, or listened to through speakers or headsets. Output to be viewed by a large audience can be transmitted through a video projector and shown on a large screen. These projectors can be mounted in the classroom, or serve as portable units to move from one room to another.

Research has shown that large screen projection is more appealing to students than viewing images on either a monitor or a small screen. The video projector makes large screen projection an option for the teacher. Used in classrooms, lecture halls, and auditoriums, this technology works best in a darkened room, unless the projector has high lumens. In addition to their use with computers, video projectors can be used with VCRs, visual presenters, DVDs, and any other technology that has a video output jack.

Video projectors can be portable or they can be mounted in the classroom. Because of their small size, they can easily be transported within the school or taken out of the school for presentations at other locations. Most video projectors weigh between five to ten pounds; however, newer portable models weigh between three to five pounds. The newest video projectors use Digital Light Processing (DLP), a space-saving alternative.

How to Use Video Projectors

Video projectors are available in many models. The instruction manual for the specific model being used should be consulted for the correct connection/use directions. These directions will usually consist of two series of steps: (1) how and where to connect the various cables and (2) how to focus, use, and control the projection display or image. Generally, the technology being coupled with the projector is hooked directly to the projector with a video cable. Computer users will need a special cable that comes with the projector to convert the computer image to a form the projector can display.

Selection Considerations

Brightness:
The brightness of a video projector is measured in ANSI lumens, with higher lumens being more desirable. Lumens under 1,000 usually require the room's lights being off or dimmed. Projectors with brighter lumens are more expensive but provide brighter projection and eliminate the need to dim the lights.

Image Quality:
The resolution of the projector should be compatible with that of the computer being used. Most of these have XGA resolutions. It is important to check the uniformity of brightness and contrast between black and white.

Size and Weight:
The lighter the projector, the easier it is to carry. Select a projector with a sturdy carrying case. If it will be mounted, the projector size must be compatible with a mounting bracket.

Use with a Laptop

When the projector is connected to a laptop, an occurring problem is getting the computer image on the computer screen and the projection screen simultaneously. Users often have to choose specific keyboard commands to export a signal to the projector. It may mean choosing a Simulscan command or using the function key with another key that represents the monitor. Usually a function key between five and eight is the one needed for simulscan. Consult the user's manual. Because of this problem, it is best to first connect and turn on the projector, then turn on the computer.

14.4 - Digital Storage

Storage devices permit the user to store and access documents and programs. While many of these disk drives are internal, or built-in, external disk drives and other storage devices can be added to the computer system. The hard disk drive is where all programs and data are stored, completely enclosed in the computer itself. Currently sized in terms of gigabytes (GB), the larger the drive, the greater the amount of information that can be stored. To input programs and files, CD drives are the standard internal drive for computers today. Most of these can read and/or write DVDs.

Storage Devices

If you are working between computers, data from the hard drive must be made portable, using one of the following storage devices. The 5.25" floppy disk drive was the original external storage device, followed by 3.5" drives, Zip and Jazz drives, CDs, and DVDs. Newer storage devices are USB (Universal Serial Bus) minidrives, also known as flash drives, keychain drives, jump drives, etc., and memory cards.

Floppy disks, 3.5" in diameter, contain a magnetic media that has read/write capabilities (read from it, or write to it). A high density disk holds 1.44 MB of data, or approximately 720 pages of text.

Zip disks are thicker than floppy disks, holding from 100 MB to 750 MB of data. The 100 MB disk is equivalent to 70 floppy disks.

> **Media Equivalencies**
>
> 3.5" Floppy Disk =
> 720 pages of text =
> 1.4 MB memory
>
> 100 MB Zip Disk =
> 70 Floppy Disks =
> 50,000 pages of text
>
> CD =
> 250,000 pages of text =
> 400 3.5" disks =
> 6-100 MB Zip disks =
> 650 MB memory
>
> DVD =
> 2-8 hours
> high quality video =
> 4.7 GB – 17 GB memory

Compact Disks (CDs) are used in drives that are built-in to most computers. It is necessary to have a CD drive in the computer to install most programs onto the computer. CD-ROM is Read Only Memory; these cannot be written to. CD-R are recordable, and CD-RW are rewritable. The main way to save files as backups or storage (such as photos) is to "burn" a CD. One CD can hold 650 MB of data, or 250,000 pages of text. CD-RW are the most economical to use, as you can reuse them; CD-R can only be written on once.

Digital Versatile Discs (DVDs) are the newest high capacity CD-size discs used for storage of movies, games, audio, and multimedia. DVD drives are becoming common in computers, with the same drive also playing CDs. Similar to CDs, there is also a recordable format available for storage of large amounts of data, such as classroom-produced movies, music, etc. DVD-Video does not lose audio or video quality with extended use, as do VHS tapes. Storage is from 4.7 GB to 17 GB; 2-8 hours of high-quality video.

USB minidrives (Flash Drives, Jump Drives, etc.) and Memory Cards are small, portable storage units. Flash drives are available in 256 MB - 2 GB (and higher) sizes, while memory cards, used primarily to store digital photos, begin at 16 MB. The higher the number of MB, the more photos that can be stored. The resolution of the camera must also be considered. The higher the resolution, the more memory the pictures take up. A camera with a resolution of 3.2, taking high quality photos, produces 1.5 MB files, while a camera with a resolution of 6.3 produces files of over 3 MB. Therefore, a 16 MB card cannot hold many photos.

Using CDs and DVDs

CD and DVD players are easy to use. The disc is placed on a tray in the computer or DVD player with the shiny side down. An icon identifying the CD or DVD appears on (a) the desktop of the computer (Mac), or (b) in "My Computer" on the desktop of a PC. It can then be opened and ejected in the same manner as a disk. When the disc is opened, most will display a menu of choices for the user. Click and go; it's that easy!

14.5 - Activities

• Activity One •

Take a series of digital photos to use when teaching a unit of study. Possible topics could be A Day at the Zoo, Historic Philadelphia, or Trees in New Jersey. Edit and crop the photos to make them more visually appealing. Use them as the basis for a *PowerPoint* presentation.

• Activity Two •

Scan photos or diagrams from books relevant to a unit you are teaching. Use these to construct a bulletin board for your topic.

• Activity Three •

At your field experience site, take a digital photo of each student engaged in an activity. Place each picture on the top half of a sheet of paper. Have the student write about the activity in the space below.

Digital Video

iMovie

15.1 - Introduction

Digital video and audio play an important role in the field of multimedia, as quality video and audio files can be input as files on the computer. Once in the computer, these files can be edited and manipulated to be used in various ways. Titles, music, narration, and transitions can be added. After editing, they can be made into movies.

To use video in the computer, the images must first be captured with a video camera, then digitized to use in the computer. The first technology for this was video sent to the computer from a VCR, or other video device, through a video capture card in the computer. Today, video from a VCR can be digitized for use in the computer. The latest technology is the digital video (DV) camcorder, which eliminates digitizing or the need for a video capture card in the computer. Video from the DV camcorder is sent to the computer via a special cable, known as a FireWire® cable (the computer must have a FireWire port).

Once in the computer, the video is edited using video-editing software. Clips can be arranged in any order; visual effects can be added; and audio in the form of musical soundtracks, voiceovers, or sound effects can be included. Programs such as *iMovie* for Macintosh (free as a part of *iLife* on new Macs) and *Movie Maker* (free as a part of *Windows XP*) for PCs make this a simple process. Edited movies can be stored back on the DV tape; put on a videotape, CD or DVD; shared with friends and relatives via e-mail; used on Web pages; or used as components of presentations. Placing the finished product on a disk for a presentation is not an option. Digital video requires an enormous amount of storage space. A five-minute clip takes over one gigabyte of storage space on the computer.

15.2 - Digital Video Camcorders

Digital video (DV) camcorders are the result of a merger of digital cameras and video cameras. They allow the consumer to make their own movies to use on their computer, put on Web pages to share with others, or merely edit and save for school or family use. DV camcorders also take still images. Video and still images are saved as DV formats, making pictures sharper than those taken with VHS camcorders.

DV camcorders are not totally digital; they store the signal in a digital form, while still recording on videotape. The tape used, the "mini-DV," is the smallest videotape. The camcorder is also smaller than any of the other types, but the quality is higher than other video formats. With more features than analog cameras, they provide better zoom, sound, and more control over color and lighting. Tapes can be copied many times without losing quality; they can also be re-recorded many times. The final product takes up 15-30 GB of hard drive space per hour of tape; however, the editing process could take 100 GB (input, saving, editing, output). Many DV camcorders also take memory cards, where still images are stored.

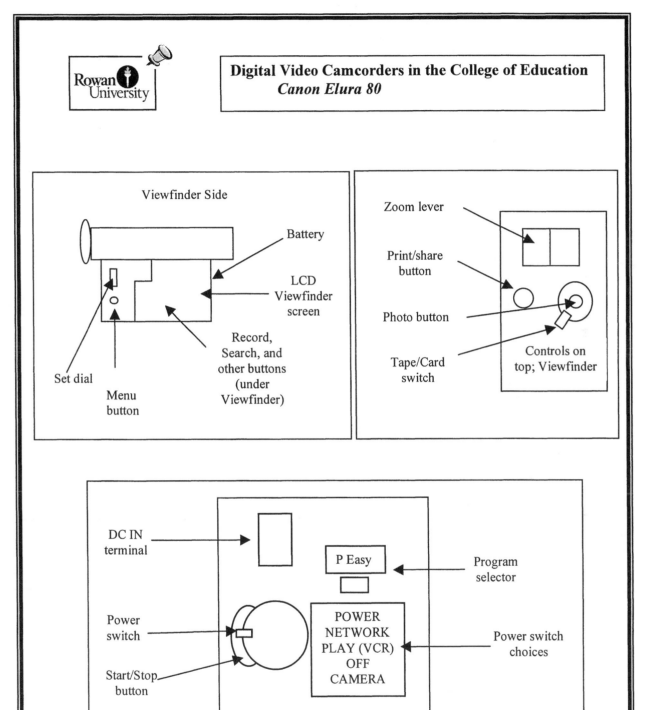

Digital Video Camcorders in the College of Education
Canon Elura 80

Viewfinder Side

Battery

LCD
Viewfinder
screen

Record,
Search, and
other buttons
(under
Viewfinder)

Set dial

Menu
button

Zoom lever

Print/share
button

Photo button

Tape/Card
switch

Controls on
top; Viewfinder

DC IN
terminal

P Easy

Program
selector

Power
switch

POWER
NETWORK
PLAY (VCR)
OFF
CAMERA

Power switch
choices

Start/Stop
button

Controls on handle side

Using a Digital Video Camcorder

(Instructions are for the Canon *Elura 80*; they are similar for other DV camcorders. See the instruction manual with your DV camcorder for more detailed instructions.)

Use tapes labeled *miniDV*.

Attaching and Charging the Battery Pack

1. Raise the front viewfinder. Insert the battery into the camcorder under the front viewfinder (press lightly and slide it in the direction of the arrow until it clicks).
2. Connect the power cord to the adapter; plug the power cord into a power outlet.
3. Connect the power adapter to the camcorder's DC IN terminal (the *Charge Indicator* starts flashing; it glows steadily when charging is complete).
4. When charging is complete, remove the battery by pressing the *Battery Release* button.
5. To save the battery, the camcorder can be used while plugged in.
6. It takes approximately two hours for the battery to charge. This provides approximately one hour of recording time.

To Record and Review a Movie

1. Open the cassette compartment by sliding the *Open/Eject* switch on the top of the camera.
2. Load the cassette with the window facing the handle. (Pull straight out to eject.)
3. Press the *Push* mark unit it clicks and the tape retracts.
4. Turn the camcorder on; remove the lens cap.
5. To begin recording a movie, set the camcorder to the *Camera* mode.
6. Open the LCD Viewfinder screen by pushing the *Open* button.
7. Set the Tape/Card switch to *Tape* (picture of a tape). (*Card* records photos on the memory card; *Tape* records on the DV tape.)
8. Press the *Start/Stop* button to record (and stop recording).
9. When finished, turn the power off. Close the LCD panel, replace the lens cap, and remove the cassette and battery.

To Play Back a Tape

1. Set the camcorder to *Play* (VCR mode). Be sure the *Tape/Card* switch is set to *Tape*.
2. Open the LCD panel.
3. Press and hold the *Record/Search* buttons (top row, left, under the LCD panel). These will rewind (first button) and fast forward (second button) through the tape for viewing.
4. Press the third button to begin playing the tape.
5. Press the fourth button to stop playback.

To Record Still Images (on a Memory Card)

1. Insert the memory card.
2. Set the camcorder to the *Card* mode.
3. Press the *Photo* button halfway. A beep sounds twice indicating focus has occurred.
4. Press the *Photo* button fully.
5. Remove the card and follow instructions in Chapter 14 for working with the images.

15.3 - Digital Video Editing

Digital video editing is the process by which video from a camcorder is taken apart and put back together in another sequence or format. Instead of using all of the video shot, the best parts of it are used and embellished to produce a small movie to be used for a multimedia presentation, shared on the Internet, or saved for other uses.

Video editing software is used to edit the video and audio clips downloaded from a digital camcorder to the computer (or video digitized from a VCR). It can also be used to combine this with still images and music. Footage from a DV camera is transferred to the computer via a FireWire cable. There are expensive video editing programs on the market; however, *iMovie* (Macintosh) and Windows *Movie Maker* (PC) are inexpensive (often free on new computers), easy-to-use consumer software programs that produce quality products.

These programs allow you to:
- transfer video to the computer
- choose the best clips
- arrange clips in any order
- add still images
- add titles and credits
- add screen transitions
- add music and sound effects
- add narration

Finished movies can be used to:
- create a videotape
- make a digital video movie for the Internet or e-mail
- store a movie on a CD or DVD

Once the video camera is connected to the computer with the FireWire cable, the computer recognizes it and loads the software needed. Onscreen controls allow you to view the video and choose the parts to use. As the video is played, it appears in the monitor area of the software. When you see a part you want to use in your "production," it is recorded in the software and stored for later use. Once these video clips are stored, you can begin the editing process. Video clips are further edited and sequenced, with some parts saved and others discarded. Once all the video clips are organized, still images, sounds, music, titles, and effects are added for the final product.

The final movie is saved in a digital video format such as Apple's *QuickTime*®, *Video for Windows*, or *MPEG*. Since digital video takes up so much space (five minutes is approximately one gigabyte), these programs compress the movie to a format that can be used in a multimedia presentation or on the Internet.

The next section provides the basic steps for producing a short movie using *iMovie*.

15.4 - Making a Movie Using *iMovie*

Getting the Video to the Computer

1. Connect the DV camcorder to a computer with a FireWire port, using a FireWire cable.
2. Turn on the camera; set to VCR/VTR/playback mode.
3. Open *iMovie*; *Create a New Project*. Give it a name.
4. The screen should read *Camera Connected* (if not, click *Camera Mode*).

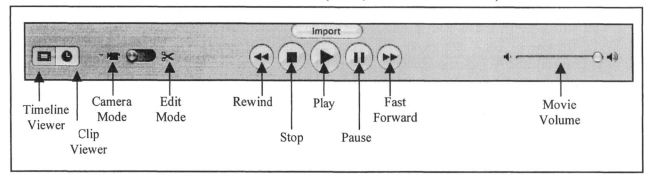

Timeline Viewer · Clip Viewer · Camera Mode · Edit Mode · Rewind · Stop · Play · Pause · Fast Forward · Movie Volume · Import

5. Click on the center arrow—*Play the Camera* (be sure tape is rewound).
6. To import the entire movie, with *iMovie* detecting scene breaks (each time *Record* was pressed when the tape was shot), be sure *Start a new clip at each scene break* is specified in *Preferences: Import*.
7. To enter clips manually, click on *Import*, or press the spacebar to start and end the import of each clip.
8. Each clip is saved to the *Clips Pane*. The icon is a picture of the first scene.   Clips Pane

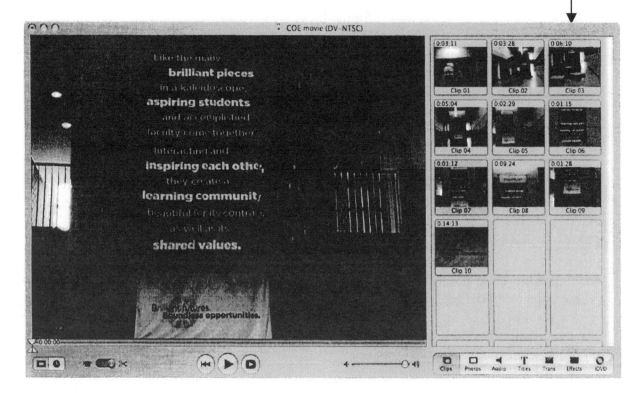

iMovie Work Area

1. Part of the work area is shown on the opposite page.
2. The *Pane Button* area is enlarged below.

3. Video clips are stored in the *Clips Pane* until they are ready to be used. At that time they are placed in the *Clip Viewer* (Movie Track) in the order they are to be seen. Note their length is indicated at the top; the middle one (below) is a still picture.

4. The *Clip Viewer* can be changed to the *Timeline Viewer* by clicking on the clock icon. In the *Timeline Viewer* each clip is represented by a horizontal bar. The length of this bar is proportional to the time the video clip occupies in the movie. (The *Timeline Viewer* adds two audio tracks and controls for other effects.)

5. When you are ready to play and edit a video clip, it is controlled with the buttons below (the *Playhead*):

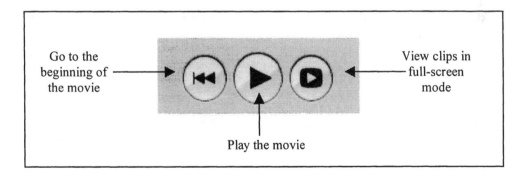

Editing Video Clips

1. Click on a video clip to make it active.
2. Click on *Play* or the spacebar to view the clip.
3. Drag the *Playhead* (arrow under the monitor picture) to view parts of the clip. Using the right and left arrows you can view the clips one frame at a time; holding the shift key jumps ten frames at a time.

4. To crop a clip, drag the crop markers below the *Scrubber Bar* (appears below the monitor area when a video clip is selected) to indicate where the clip should begin and end. Then choose *Edit: Crop* to delete the portions not needed (areas to be cropped will turn yellow). *Edit: Cut (or Clear)* takes away the area between the arrows.
5. To view the entire movie, select *Edit: Select None*. Click on the *Play* button.
6. Select *View clips in full-screen mode* to play on the entire screen.
7. Save the movie and get ready to add titles, transitions, photos, sounds, etc.

Importing Photos

1. When a new *iMovie* is created, *iMovie* creates a folder with the name of the movie. Any other photos, sounds, etc. to be used in the movie must be placed in this folder.
2. In *iPhoto*, choose *File: Export*. Export the photos with *640 by 480* as the image size.
3. Within *iMovie*, choose *File: Import*.
4. Select the photo; *Import*.
5. Each photo is given a length of five seconds. This can be changed in the *Timeline Viewer*.

Adding Titles

1. Click the *Titles* button to display the titles panel.
2. Enter text in the title area at the bottom of the panel.
3. Choose the style of text.
4. Text position and scrolling direction can be selected using the direction arrows.
5. Drag the title name (i.e., *Twirl* in the example) to the Timeline Viewer.
6. To add the title to the middle of the clip, split the clip first.
7. To superimpose the title over the clip, position the title to the left of the clip in the Timeline Viewer.
8. Use the slider to adjust the duration of the title.
9. To have the title on a black background instead of over the clip, click on *Over black*.

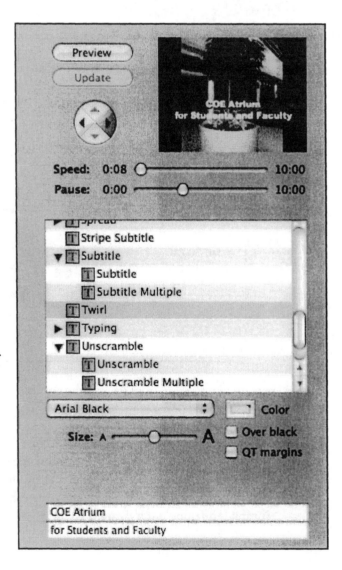

Adding Transitions

1. Click on the button for Transitions (*Tran*) in the Pane button area.
2. The transition is a motion that occurs between clips, in place of going from one clip to another without a break. They can also be put in to imply things like the passage of time, pushing to the left or right, overlapping, etc.
3. Click on the transition; view it in *Preview*.
4. To add the transition, drag it to the Timeline Viewer.
5. Drag the *Speed Slider* to change the duration.
6. To delete, click on the transition in the Timeline Viewer and press *Delete*.

Adding Effects

1. Click on the button for *Effects* in the Pane button area.
2. The effect is added to the video clip itself. Select the clip where the effect is wanted.
3. Choose an effect.
4. View it in *Preview*.
5. Use controls at the bottom of the screen to control each effect.
6. To add the effect, drag it to the Timeline Viewer.
7. Note: These can add strange effects. Use only for a purpose, and do not use too many.

Adding and Editing Sounds

If sound was a part of the video, it will be available in your movie. Sound can also be added from other sources. Using a microphone, narration can be added. To begin recording, click the red button next to the volume meter in the Audio pane. Click the red button again to stop recording. The narration is added to the first sound track.

Importing Music from an Audio CD

1. Insert the CD.
2. *iMovie* will retrieve the disc and track names.
3. Select the track you want and drag it to one of the audio tracks.

Importing Music from *iTunes*

1. Open *iTunes*.
2. Position the Playhead where you want the music to begin playing.
3. Click the *Audio* button.
4. Locate the song you want to import.
5. Click the *Place at Playhead* button.

Highlights From The Phantoi		
Song	Artist	Time
Overture		2:07
Think Of Me		3.09
Angel Of Music		2:20
The Mirror (Angel Of Music)		1:57
The Phantom Of The Opera		4:17
The Music Of The Night		5:12
Prima Donna		3:48
All I Ask Of You		6:39
Entr'acte		2:40
Masquerade		5:27
Wishing You We...ow Here		3:05

Exporting the Movie

1. Go to *File: Share*. You will get the menu on the right.
2. To send the movie back to your digital DVD camera, click on *Videocamera*.
3. Click *Share.* The movie will be sent back to your camera.
4. For the Internet, e-mail, or to save to a CD, it is best to compress the video and save it in a *QuickTime* format.
5. Choose *QuickTime*, then the format desired.
6. Click on *Share*, then save in the desired format.

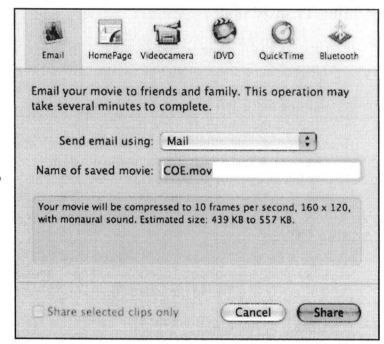

Note: *the instructions above will get you started. There are many other features in iMovie. For advanced work, use the Help menu in iMovie, look for tutorials on the Web, or consult a book on iMovie.*

15.5 - Activities

• Activity One •

Collaborate with your students as they take digital photos of a topic the class is studying (e.g., plants, animals, people, historical spots in the community). Put them together in a movie format that includes titles and transitions.

• Activity Two •

Take digital video of a field trip with your class. This could be a trip to a museum, a trip to the zoo, or just shots of the school. Edit the material following the instructions in this chapter. Display the video during open house.

CHAPTER 16

Presentation Software and *PowerPoint*

16.1 - Introduction

One way to bring variation and interest into the classroom is to use a computer with presentation software to project your lesson. You can demonstrate, illustrate, and clarify information by turning your ideas and lectures into multimedia/hypermedia presentations. Students quickly tire of lecturing when it is used on a full-time basis; they will usually pay more attention, and become more involved, when ideas and concepts are projected onto a large screen. For best results, use a computer connected to a video projector. *Microsoft PowerPoint* is the most common presentation software used today.

16.2 - Presentation Software

Beginning as software to present electronic, non-linear, slide shows, presentation software now has the capability of including elements of multimedia (includes audio/video, photos, graphics, etc.) and hypermedia (non-linear; links to Web sites and other pages within the program).

Presentations can include:

- text
- graphics
- photographs
- drawings
- animations
- charts and tables
- audio
- video
- interactivity
- links to Web pages

Presentation software helps organize and enhance the delivery of content. Basic ideas and content can be turned into vibrant, exciting presentations by adding digital support. If you do not have a video projector in your classroom, most presentations can be converted to color overhead transparencies, printed on handouts, or published on a Web page. When running the presentation from a computer, it can be controlled by the presenter directly from the computer, by using a remote control, or with a timer (used at events such as an open house).

Hypermedia authoring tools began in the late 1980s; early programs were *Linkway*® for PCs and *HyperCard*® for Macs. The next popular program for the classroom was *HyperStudio*, first issued by Roger Wagner and now available from *Knowledge Adventure*. This program, often first used in grades 4 or 5, provides tools for students to work with multimedia/hypermedia elements: cards, buttons, and backgrounds. *Kid Pix Deluxe*, which began as a drawing program for young children, now has slide shows and multimedia included. Today, the most used presentation software is *Microsoft PowerPoint*. There is also a slide show built into *AppleWorks*, and Apple now has another presentation program called *Keynote*™.

Used by teachers and students, most of these programs are similar in that they allow teachers a chance to add creativity and variety to their lessons. Students are given a chance to organize and present their thoughts, ideas, and research in presentations to their class. Presentations can include class notes, flash cards, quizzes, links to Web sites, reviews, and tutorials, to name a few.

16.3 - *Microsoft PowerPoint*

Microsoft PowerPoint, a presentation tool used by professionals in business as well as education, is available for both Macintosh and Windows platforms as a component of *Microsoft Office*. (While instructions are similar for both platforms and all versions, *Microsoft PowerPoint 2004 for Mac* is illustrated in this unit.) Often considered a vehicle to display outlines and notes, there are many other uses in the classroom. As a teacher, you can present tutorials, give quizzes, develop reviews, present games for review and reinforcement, construct flashcards, and much more. Students can produce class presentations on their research, make interactive books, do group projects, or have fun learning to make a presentation showing their drawings and class work.

PowerPoint consists of a series of slides displayed on the screen. The presentation can be self-running or controlled by the speaker. A multimedia lecture or classroom presentation can include text, clip art or digital pictures, video, and sound, along with animation. Slides can be presented in linear, as well as non-linear formats, with the order changed for different presentations as necessary. The screens (referred to as slides) are usually configured for an on-screen or large screen presentation. They can also be printed out to be used as color overhead transparencies or set up to print as presenter's outlines, audience handouts with space for notes, or handouts depicting the screens in various sizes.

A *PowerPoint Viewer* is available to show a presentation without having the program installed. This is a feature whereby the presentation can be saved as a *QuickTime* movie and viewed by anyone having the free *QuickTime* movie player installed. This can be downloaded at the Microsoft Web site. Slide shows in versions after 2000 can be saved as Web pages for viewing by others, or to use as a Web presentation.

A large selection of design templates (backgrounds) is included for presentations, or the user can begin with blank pages for custom page setups. Each template is designed with specific colors and fonts to make creating the presentation easy and visually appealing. Other templates can be found by searching various Web sites.

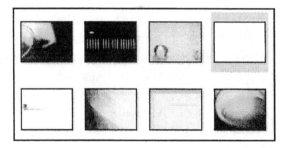

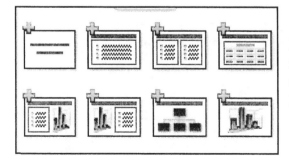

Each template has various slide layouts for inserting clip art, organizational charts, tables, spreadsheet charts and graphs, columns, Web links, photos, *QuickTime* movies, and more.

16.4 - Tips for *PowerPoint* Presentations

- Be sure text is large enough to be seen by your audience.
- Do not put too much text on each slide.
- Have contrast between the text and the background.
- Limit fonts to two per slide.
- Limit the number of fonts in the presentation.
- Restrict the number of items on each slide (text areas, clip art).
- Include only graphics that are part of the content, not just something "pretty."
- Integrate the background with the topic.
- Do not use a complex background with a lot of text or graphics.
- Use the same background throughout, with the exception of solid color slides.
- When using large photographs or charts, use a solid color background so it does not compete with the design template.
- Include only one topic on each slide.
- Keep the same transition throughout.
- Limit sounds to those integral to the presentation.
- Remember, too much of anything distracts (sounds, animations, text, pictures).
- When presenting a lesson using *PowerPoint*, do not read the screens to your audience; use them only as an outline.

Compatibility

PowerPoint is a component of *Microsoft Office*. Since there have been many versions of that over the years, there are an equal number of versions of *PowerPoint*. Although all versions are similar, the newer versions have advanced options and extended capabilities. *PowerPoint* is available for both PCs (Windows operating system) and Macintosh computers. Consequently, while *PowerPoint* is a cross-platform program (files can be used and interchanged on Macintosh and PCs), limitations do exist when moving between computers, or versions of *PowerPoint*. If working between different versions or computers, it is best to make a sample copy and try it on each computer. Animations are the least likely to transfer from one computer to another. Each version also has different backgrounds. This does not matter; once a presentation is started, the background will be saved.

Most screens are similar to those shown on the following pages. Versions prior to *2000* do not show the Outline Pane at the same time the screens are being constructed; however, the outline can always be seen in the *Outline View*. The *Formatting Palette* is available in newer versions for Macintosh, and the *Task Pane* is available in newer versions for PC.

> *Microsoft PowerPoint 2004 for Mac* is illustrated in this unit.

16.5 - Learning to use *PowerPoint*

Most versions of *PowerPoint* begin with a screen similar to the screen below. This shows the workspace and the slide in a Normal view. The top of the screen has the Menu Bar and Toolbars. On the right side (not shown here), Macintosh has a *Formatting Palette*, while PC has a *Task Pane*, which can be moved to various locations on the screen. These contain visual shortcuts to items on the Menu Bar and toolbars.

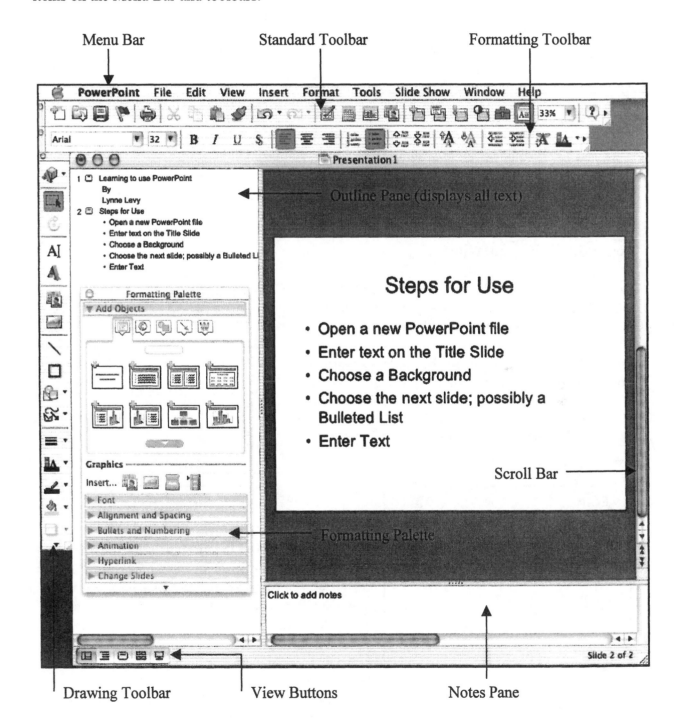

The *Outline Pane* shows text that has been entered. You can also enter and organize text here that will appear on your slides. The *Notes Pane* allows you to type notes about your presentation, or organize items you want to talk about when this slide is shown. Both can be printed out in Outline or Notes views.

At the bottom of the screen are View Buttons, showing the various ways the slides can be seen.

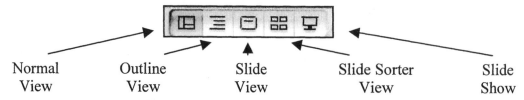

Normal	Outline	Slide	Slide Sorter	Slide
View	View	View	View	Show

Normal View shows the slide, the Outline Pane, and the Notes Pane.
Outline View enlarges the outline area and minimizes the slide.
Slide View shows only the slide.
Slide Sorter View shows all slides in miniature. Slides can be rearranged or deleted here.
Slide Show runs the slide show. Be sure to be on Slide One when choosing this.

Beginning a Presentation

Most new versions of *PowerPoint* open with a blank slide. The first slide to be seen is the Title Slide (right). Click, as instructed, to add text.

Design templates consist of the slide background, along with specific fonts, colors, and layout formats. They can be seen in the Formatting Palette on the Macintosh, the Task Pane on the PC, or accessed from the *Format: Slide Design* menu.

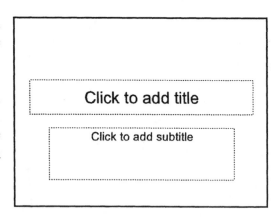

To see a sample of the design, click on the name. When using the Formatting Palette or Task Pane, the design appears on the screen. In earlier versions, a miniature slide appears. The template can be changed at any time; however, some formatting might change, so try to find an appropriate template when you start. Some designs also have several color schemes that can be changed using the menu on the left. Each version of *PowerPoint* has different design templates. Others can be found on the Web.

New slides are accessed from the Menu Bar under *Insert: New Slide*. The layouts for the slide can be changed by choosing *Slide Layout*. A few of the choices for slide layouts appear here. Slides can also be added directly from the Formatting Palette.

The *Chart* options shown on the right exhibit data from an *Excel* worksheet.

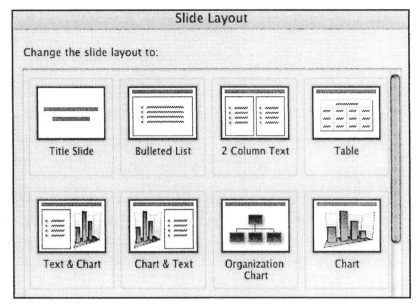

Creating Slides

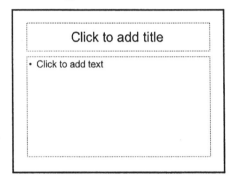

Each slide contains one or more text boxes, indicated by dotted lines. To add text, click inside the text box. Text boxes can be resized by clicking on the box, then using the new cursor and handles. They can be moved by grabbing with the Hand Tool and moving to a new location. Text boxes can be deleted by clicking on the box and hitting the Delete key. The slide shown here is for a Bulleted List. This is also the slide to use when entering text in paragraph form. To do this, remove the bullets by clicking the *Bullets* icon in the Formatting Toolbar.

In the bulleted list, each time the Return key is "hit," another bullet appears. Design templates have varying styles of bullets. These can be changed by going to *Format: Bullets and Numbering* on the Menu Bar, or by accessing the menu from the Formatting Palette. Many different styles of bullets can be created by clicking on

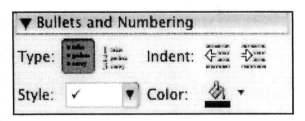

Character in the *Style* menu. Bulleted items can also be indented so they appear in outline form.

Text in any text box can be changed the same as in word processing: highlight the text, then choose a new font, size, color, and/or style.

Graphics can be added to any slide. To add clip art from the Formatting Palette in *PowerPoint*, click on the first icon; to add from a file, click on the second icon. The third is to insert a picture from a camera or scanner, while the fourth is to insert a movie. These can also be inserted from the Menu Bar—*Insert: Picture* (then choose the option).

Organizational charts (*Add Organization Chart Slide*) can be used to illustrate the administrative structure of a school, a family tree, or anything else in a hierarchical structure. This chart can be placed within a presentation or developed as a "stand alone" when a chart is needed.

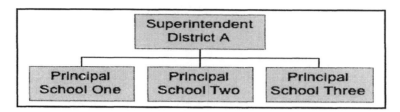

When choosing the Organization Chart slide, you are told to double click—this takes you into the Organization Chart program. When finished, go to *Organization Chart* on the Menu Bar; *Quit Organization Chart*; then *Update*. This places the chart in your presentation. It becomes a graphic with handles so it can be moved on the screen.

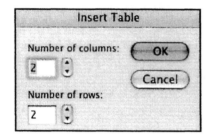

Tables (*Add Table Slide*) organize a slide into boxes or cells. You can make any number of boxes for various uses by choosing the number of columns and rows. A Tables and Borders Toolbar is available to divide or merge cells, add colors and borders, and change the properties of the table.

Adding Slide Transitions

Slide transitions are effects that occur when moving from one slide to another. When choosing *Slide Transition* in the Slide Show menu, the screen to the right appears.

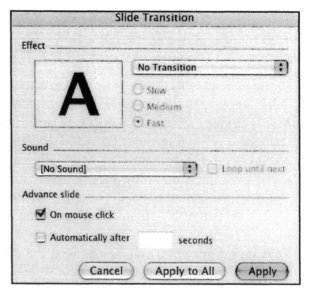

From the *No Transition* pull-down menu, choose a transition to try. The *A* will change to a *B*, displaying the transition. It is best to set the speed on *Slow* and not use too many different transitions in a presentation. To apply the transition to all slides, click on *Apply to All*. To apply to only the slide you are on, choose *Apply*. These can be applied from any slide view. Sounds can also be added here.

Another option from this screen is to have the screens change after a specified number of seconds. This is not recommended when giving an oral presentation, as it is difficult to determine the number of seconds needed (questions might be asked, distractions, etc). This could be used to have a presentation run continuously, such as during a school open house. To set this up, go to: *Slide Show: Set up Show*.

Animation

Text and graphics can be animated in a presentation. Animation options are found under *Slide Show* on the Menu Bar. For example, in a bulleted list, text can enter one line at a time, giving you time to discuss it before going on to the next. On another screen you might combine graphics and text; have a graphic enter, then exit, then one section of text come in followed by another, etc. When animating more than one object on a slide, animate them in the order you want the animations to occur.

Preset animations are quick and easy to do. First click on the text box or graphic you want to animate. Then choose *Preset Animations* from *Slide Show* on the Menu Bar. Choose one of the animations. When you run the slide show, it will appear. Some include sounds, while others do not. *Laser Text* shoots the text in, while *Typewriter* types each letter. Use with caution!

Custom Animation can be used for the same purpose, but there are many more choices. Select what you want to animate, then *Add Effect*.

Movies and Sound

Movies from *QuickTime* files, or music from a file or CD, can be added to your presentation. For either, click on *Insert: Movies and Sound*.

For sound from a CD, have the CD in the computer; click on *Play CD Audio Track*. When the slide show is running, the music will begin when the slide with the music icon appears. Under *Custom Animation*, choose the length: *Effect Options: Media Options: Stop Playing after __ slides*.

Movie from Gallery...
Movie from File...

Sound from Gallery...
Sound from File...
Play CD Audio Track...
Record Sound...

Instead of using a CD, soundtracks can be found on the Web—search for Midi files; *MP3*, *WAV*, etc. can also be used. Copy these files to the same folder as your *PowerPoint* presentation. Go to *Insert: Sound from File*; choose the sound file.

Inserting a Hyperlink (access a Web site by clicking on the link)

Hyperlinks can be inserted to easily access Web sites. To do this, enter the name of the site (use the name, not the address so students can easily understand it). Highlight the site name. Go to the Menu Bar: *Insert: Hyperlink*. Enter the Web address in the *Link to* area, as shown below (copy/paste from the Web page to be sure it is correct).

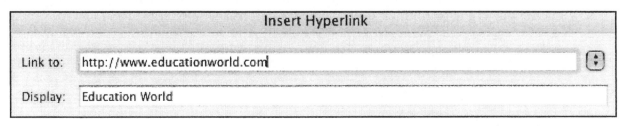

Insert Hyperlink	
Link to:	http://www.educationworld.com
Display:	Education World

Action Buttons (making *PowerPoint* non-linear)

Action buttons allow you to make *PowerPoint* non-linear. For instance, on the first screen, there can be an index. From there, you can go to any page in the presentation or you can make a quiz, going to one screen for the correct answer, another for the incorrect answer.

Custom
Home
Help
Information
Previous Slide
Next Slide
First Slide
Last Slide
Last Slide Viewed
Document
Sound
Movie

• On the slide you want to link from, go to Menu Bar: *Slide Show: Action Buttons;*
• choose where you want to go (next, previous, to another slide, etc.);
• a cross-bar cursor will appear; draw a box on your screen;
• a menu will pop up; choose the slide to link to;
  (if going to a past slide, choose *Previous*; a future slide, choose *Next*; then *Slide* and the slide number);
• save it and try it!

Remember, in many cases you might have to put in two links (as in a quiz—one for the correct answer; another for the incorrect answer).

Saving Your Slide Show

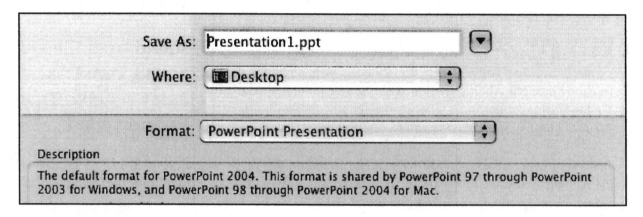

As you progress, every slide should be saved. When saving, the above screen appears. "Presentation 1.ppt" can be replaced by any title, but be sure to keep the *.ppt* extension. Notice that *Mac 2004* is compatible with any versions back to *PowerPoint 97*.

Viewing Your Slide Show

To view your slide show, go to the first slide using the scroll bar. Go to *View: Slide Show*, or use the View Buttons at the bottom left of the screen. Click on the one on the right that looks like a screen and is labeled *Slide Show*. Your first slide will now appear full-screen; use the mouse to navigate through the show. To return to *Normal View* at any time, use the ESC key.

Printing Your Slide Show

If you choose to print, *PowerPoint* will default to print the entire screen. Other options, as shown, can be printed with the correct printer settings. Each printer is different. When selecting the print menu, there will be a choice for printing options. It might indicate "Print What?," have a pull-down menu next to the word "General," or list the *PowerPoint* options. When the correct option is found, this menu will appear.

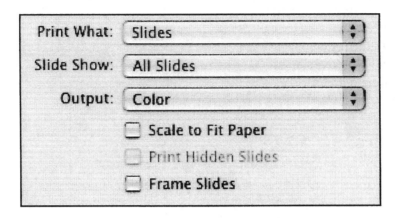

The pull-down menu from *Print What?:* produces the options below.

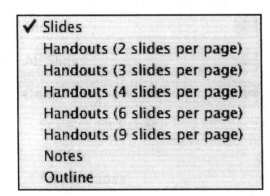

Most of the choices are self-explanatory; *3 slides per page* provides a small space on the right for notes; *Notes* places the slide at the top with a place for notes at the bottom; *Outline* is similar to the Outline Pane, providing your students with the text of your presentation.

The slides in a *PowerPoint* presentation can make excellent overhead transparencies. Transparency film can be purchased for your printer—be sure to purchase the correct type: laser, ink jet, etc. When making a presentation for the overhead, be sure to make light backgrounds so the light shows through and you do not use too much ink.

Save as a Web Page or Movie

Under *File*, you can save your presentation as a Web page or movie. *Save as Web Page* saves it in the HTML format for viewing on a Web page. If you want to save your presentation in a format that can be viewed on computers that do not have Microsoft *PowerPoint* installed, you can save it as a *PowerPoint* movie. A *PowerPoint* movie is a self-running slide show that plays in *QuickTime* Player. It uses the file extension *.mov.*

16.6 – Classroom Applications

- Class notes
- Unit review
- Project reports
- Subject tutorial
- Introduction to the school
- Open house presentations
- Year-in-review
- Personal portfolio
- Sport and club overviews
- Educational games

16.7 – Activities

• Activity One •

Develop a *PowerPoint* presentation in conjunction with a lesson plan or unit plan. (1) Make a title slide. (2) Develop at least six bulleted lists or text areas to present your information. (3) Add clip art that directly relates to the content of the slide.

• Activity Two •

Develop a *PowerPoint* presentation that is a review for a lesson you will teach. (1) Include at least five hyperlinks for information the students can study as a review. (2) As part of your slides, include factual information that is not on the Web sites. (3) Make five sample test questions, with answers provided on another slide.

• Activity Three •

Develop a *PowerPoint* presentation that is an interactive test. (1) Write five questions for your students to answer. (2) For each question, create two action buttons: One will bring the student to a screen that tells them they are correct, the other to a screen that tells them they are wrong and must return to the original question.

CHAPTER 17

Concept Maps
and *Inspiration*

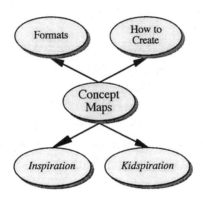

17.1 - Introduction

Concept mapping is a way to give a visual presence to ideas, concepts, facts, etc. Concept maps exist in a variety of types (highly structured to very loosely structured) and are known by a number of different names (idea maps, flowcharts, organizational charts, storyboards, hierarchical diagrams, cognitive maps, star bursts, and webs—to name just a few). They are a planning/organization/presentation tool used in education, as well as in the business community and by government and industry.

Concept mapping is a technique for visualizing the relationships between different concepts. A concept map is a diagram that shows the relationships between the concepts. These concepts, or ideas, are usually connected by arrows and sometimes linking phrases such as "leads to," "results in," "is required by," etc.

Various classroom activities can lead to concept maps.
- While brainstorming, as ideas and concepts are developed, connections can be explored between related ideas and placed in a concept map.
- Flowcharts provide step-by-step actions as a series of events is plotted out, as in a science experiment.
- Storyboards assist in laying out a project before it is created, often on the computer. This could be non-linear slides in a *PowerPoint* presentation, or pages developed for a Web site.

Concept maps can be modified and made especially appealing as a teaching aid for the intended audience if illustrations or photographs are incorporated into the presentation. Illustrations could be cut out of magazines, downloaded and printed from the Web, drawn by students, etc. This approach is often found in learning centers.

A software program that is designed to assist in the creation of cognitive maps is *Inspiration*®, by Inspiration Software. This program combines the planning and the drawing aspects into one process. *Inspiration* is a tool that can be used to develop ideas and organize thinking. It utilizes brainstorming, planning, organizing, outlining, diagramming, concept mapping, and webbing. Another program, *Kidspiration*®, is for grades K-5.

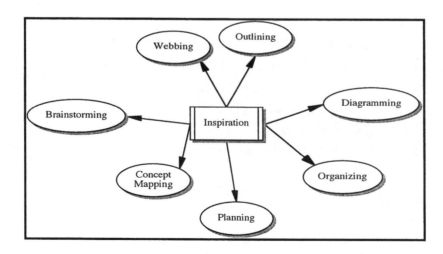

17.2 - Common Concept Map Formats

All concept maps are variations of, and can be grouped under, two basic formats: unstructured maps and structured maps.

Unstructured Concept Maps

Unstructured concept maps begin with a concept, idea, or topic and then branch out into the many related sub-topics or ideas.

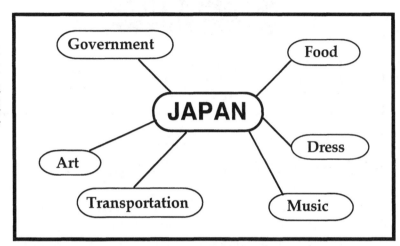

Structured Concept Maps

Structured concept maps also begin with a concept, idea, or topic and then branch out into related sub-topics or ideas. However, there is a discernible structure to the display. It exhibits "levels of consistency." All of the material identified in the map is organized into levels, and each level contains elements of equal weight, meaning, or value. Maps of this type are usually used to present or display information that is already known, or to identify voids in the organization or knowledge structure.

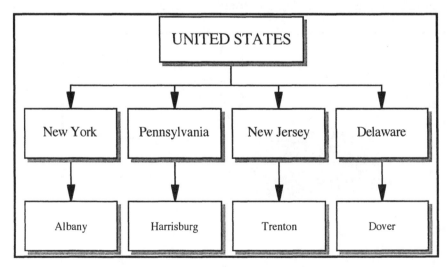

The example here is in a hierarchical structure and begins with the United States as the topic. The next level identifies the names of states. This is followed by the name of the capital of each state. The next level could be the name of the governor. This could be followed by the name of the attorney general, etc.

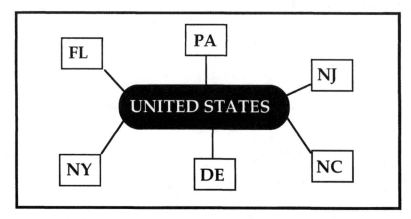

This example could also be displayed as a web or in a sunburst form. However, since it is a structured concept map, the same "levels of consistency" would be evident.

17.3 - How to Create a Concept Map

Concept maps can be created using paper and pen or a pad and a marker. These are the common tools for brainstorming or idea development work. To transform the map for educational/display/presentation purposes, a professional and impressive looking map can be created using the draw tools of any computer program, or a program designed for this purpose. The following steps will facilitate the creation of a concept map:

1. Identify the topic or idea that will be the focal point of the concept map.
2. Select the format for the concept map that best suits the content that will be identified.
3. Using paper and pen, or a pad and marker, develop the map. (Note: It is very acceptable to cross out items at this stage of development. This is not the final product. Neatness does not count at this point.)
4. After all of the desired elements have been identified, redraw a professional looking map using the same tools or using a computer program.

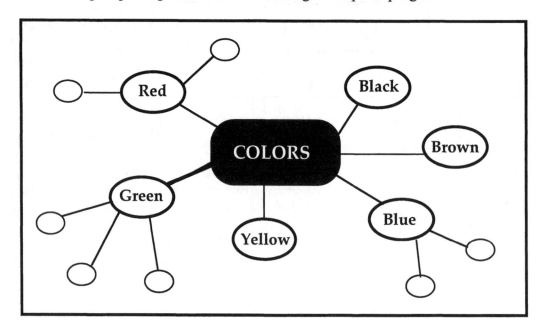

17.4 - *Inspiration*, a "Visual Learning Tool"

Inspiration can help students and teachers develop ideas and organize thinking. As a visual learning tool, it provides graphical ways of working with ideas and presenting information.

Students and teachers can:
- brainstorm
- organize information
- develop an understanding of concepts
- express and share ideas
- plan multimedia presentations (storyboard)

What is created in a diagram can then be converted to an outline. By integrating diagramming and outlining environments, *Inspiration* helps students clarify their thinking, as they better comprehend concepts and information. This also stimulates creative and critical thinking.

Inspiration encourages visual learning through the use of diagrams in the form of webs, idea maps, outlines, concept maps, and storyboards. Through these diagrams, students understand how ideas are connected and how they can be grouped together. The visual diagrams also help in the retention of information.

Webs provide a structure for ideas and show how pieces of information relate to each other. As visual maps, they help students brainstorm and organize information when writing or doing analysis. With a major topic in the center, links are made for supporting information.

Idea maps help to generate ideas and develop thoughts. They help to clarify thinking, as students visually see connections between ideas.

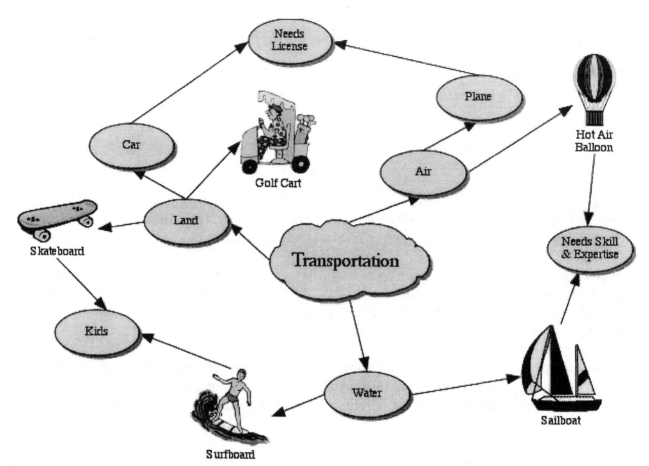

Outlines can help students organize information and present thoughts. Often used for planning a research project, information is gathered then organized in an outline form. The outline can be created and converted to a diagram, or a diagram can be converted to an outline.

Teacher Education Programs

 I. **Foundations of Education**

   A. **Historical Base & Current State of Information**

 II. **Subject Area Pedagogy**

   A. **Content-Specific Teaching Techniques**

 III. **General Pedagogy**

   A. **Generic Teaching Methods**

    1. **Direct Instruction**

 IV. **Subject Area Content**

   A. **Content Structure Information**

Concept maps illustrate ideas and their relationships, beginning with a general concept and working down to specifics. Links with descriptive words on them connect the key concepts.

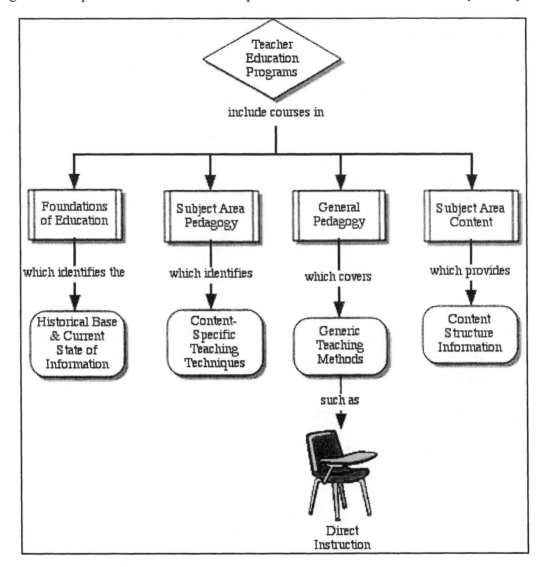

Storyboards help organize projects: what will be done first, next, and so on. Often used in multimedia projects such as a *PowerPoint* presentation, the same concept is used in developing Web pages, or organizing chapters in a book.

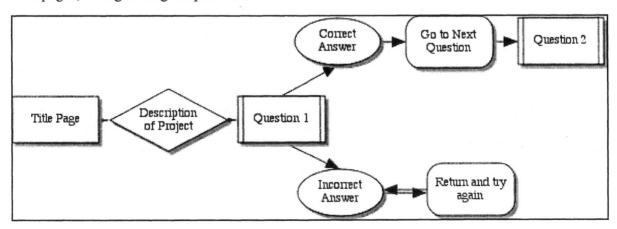

17.5 - Using *Inspiration*

Similar in concept to other drawing programs, *Inspiration* consists of tool bars and symbol palettes where choices are made. In *Inspiration 8*, there are over one million online symbols—illustrations, photos, and animations—that can be used in the diagrams. When the program opens, the *Inspiration Starter Menu* appears. Here you can create a diagram or outline, or open a file, template, training, examples, help, and more. Most users begin with the diagram icon. Beginning in the outline mode allows the user to enter an outline that can then be converted to a diagram.

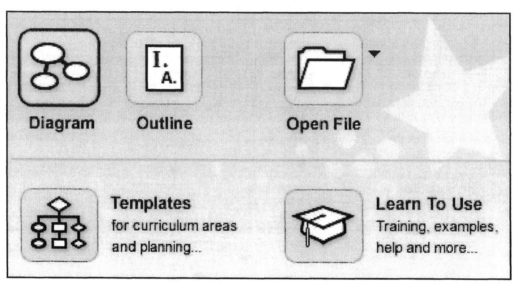

By clicking on *Diagram*, a screen appears with the "Main Idea" symbol in the center, along with several tool and menu bars.

On the top of the screen is the **Diagram Toolbar** (shown below) where symbols and links are found for key tasks. The first, *Outline*, changes from Diagram to Outline View. When in Outline View, *Diagram* will appear, to change back to Diagram View. *Note* attaches a note to a symbol. *Hyperlink* allows text to be converted to a hyperlink to link to a Web page. The *Word Guide* assists in looking up definitions, synonyms, and antonyms and in learning how to pronounce words. *Transfer* allows text in *Inspiration* to be transferred to a word processor. The other Diagram Toolbar icons will be discussed in more detail on the next page.

Adding and Linking Symbols

When the program opens, a "Main Idea" symbol appears. Additonal symbols can be placed on the screen in three ways:
1. Click on the screen and type; this creates an unconnected symbol (no links).
2. Use the *RapidFire* tool in the Diagram Toolbar. Connected or unconnected ideas can be added instantly. Using this mode, you can concentrate on adding ideas, not worrying about where to place them. To use this: click in a symbol (the starting point), position the cursor after the text, choose the RapidFire tool. A red symbol appears. Enter ideas, pressing *Return* or *Enter* after each idea. Symbols appear and can be moved and re-linked later.
3. Click on a symbol (get handles) to make it active; go to the *Create* tool in the Diagram Toolbar. A symbol, with a link, can be added in eight directions.

When any symbol appears, text can be added. This text can be changed using the toolbar at the bottom on the screen. (One click on a symbol gives it "handles to make it active;" two clicks activates the text mode to enter or change text.)

Links (arrows) connect the symbols. If the symbols were not connected when they were placed on the screen, they can be linked with *Link* in the Diagram Toolbar. Click on *Link*, then click from one symbol to the next where links are needed.

Arranging Symbols

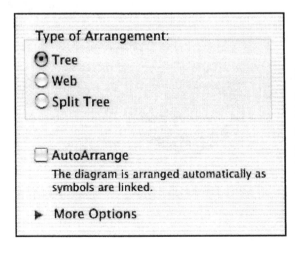

Once symbols appear on the screen, they can be arranged in various ways. *Arrange* in the Diagram Toolbar assists in changing the arrangement. Trees, Webs, and other arrangements can be chosen here.

Formatting Toolbar

Choices in the Formatting Toolbar are available to: change font, size, style of text, and text color. Also available are drawing tools, symbol color changes, and more. The "hand" moves the graphics around on the screen.

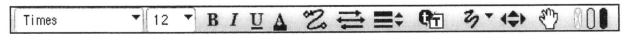

Symbol Palette

On the left of the Diagram View is the Symbol Palette, which contains libraries of symbols for the diagrams. *Inspiration 8* houses over 1,000 symbols in the libraries within *Inspiration* and also has a *Search* to find over one million symbols online.

Clicking on *Basic* provides an index of topics for the libraries. The arrows at the bottom of the screen go through the libraries. One of the libraries is show on the right.

Search searches both the online and built-in libraries.

To change an idea to a symbol, click on the idea to get "handles" (left, below). Choose the symbol desired; the idea will change to the symbol, with the text being positioned below (right, below).

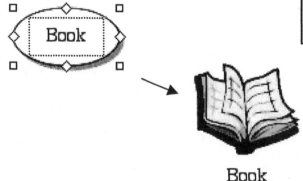

Book

Links

Links can be created with *Link* or *Create* in the Diagram Toolbar. These can be edited by clicking on them (get handles). Go to *Link* in the Menu Bar to: change arrowheads, reverse direction, change angles, make curved links, hide links, and more. Go to *Effect* in the Menu Bar to change thickness, add dashes, add patterns, and change the color. Also, when clicking on the link, a text box appears where text connections can be inserted.

Scan through the Menu Bar for more options, or go to the *Inspiration* Web site (www.inspiraton.com) for more hints.

17.6 - *Kidspiration*

Kidspiration, a companion program for visual learning at an earlier age, is for grades K-5. Younger students can combine pictures, text, and spoken words to represent thoughts and information. Students can categorize and group ideas, express and organize thoughts, and communicate ideas. Use of the program is similar, but with a different graphical appearance (below). The Symbol Palette (left) works the same, with the orange arrow linking to the Symbol Libraries. The icons on the Diagram Toolbar (top) are described below. The Formatting Toolbar is at the bottom. Many icons are the same as those in *Inspiration*.

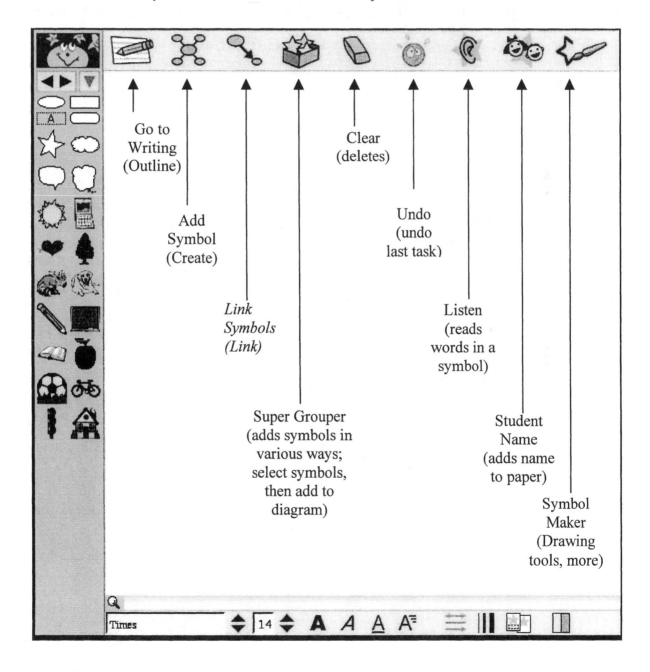

Go to Writing (Outline)

Add Symbol (Create)

Link Symbols (Link)

Super Grouper (adds symbols in various ways; select symbols, then add to diagram)

Clear (deletes)

Undo (undo last task)

Listen (reads words in a symbol)

Student Name (adds name to paper)

Symbol Maker (Drawing tools, more)

17.7 - Other Things to Know

- Files can be exported as *.gif* or *.jpeg* to save the file as a graphic.
- Graphics from the Internet or other programs can be imported.
- Files can be printed; for wide documents, choose *File: Page Setup: Landscape (wide)* format.
- *Inspiration* is also available for handhelds.
- A free 30-day trial for either *Kidspiration* or *Inspiration* is available from *Inspiration's* Web site: www.inspiration.com.
- Templates, Curriculum Packets, Documentation, Examples, and a Training Video are available at the Startup Menu.
- To use text only (no symbol), click on the symbol, then the "a" in the Symbol Palette. The symbol will disappear, leaving only text. Change font size to enlarge for a title on the page.

17.8 - Activities

• Activity One •

Create a web for a book or topic you might teach. Include a main idea, three sub-topics, and three topics under each sub-topic. Include at least three symbols from the library to enhance the diagram.

• Activity Two •

Use *Inspiration* to design a concept map for a lesson you will be teaching. The main idea should be the lesson topic. Include a minimum of 12 symbols and three graphics. Add a title for your diagram and your name (using the text icon ["a"] for both). Arrange the map in a visually appealing manner. Print out the map as a diagram and as an outline.

• Activity Three •

Create an activity requiring your students to use *Kidspiration* or *Inspiration* (depending on grade level). The final product should be an idea map that includes a topic, three sub-topics, six other symbol topics, and four graphics.

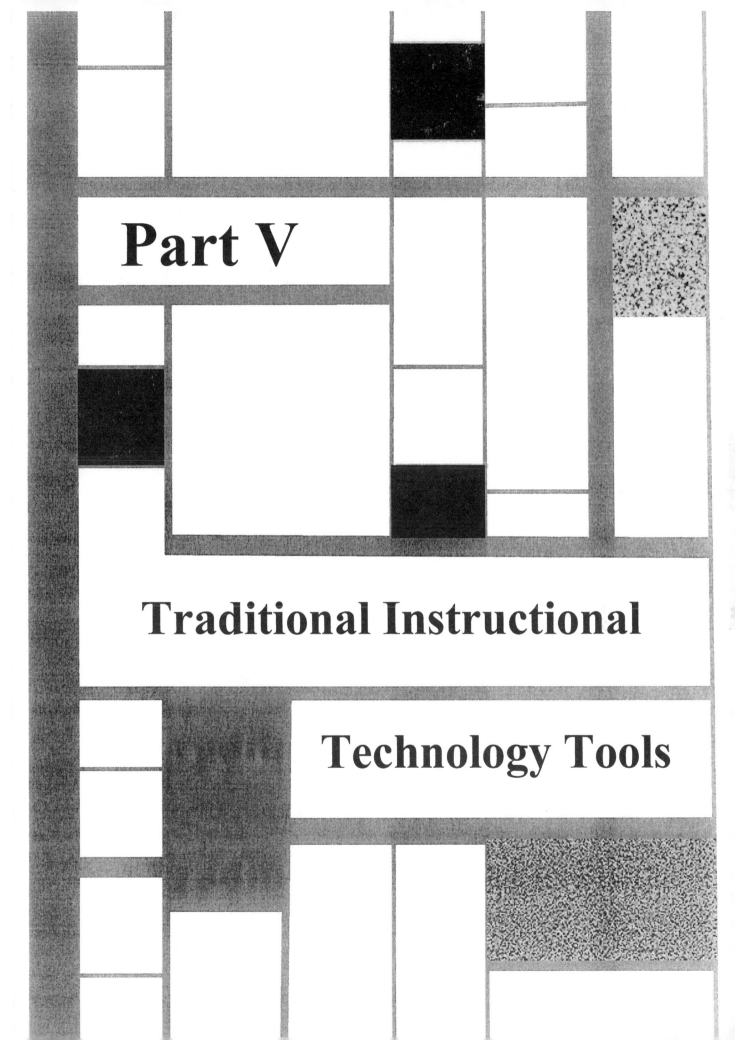

Part V

Traditional Instructional

Technology Tools

Textbooks and Teaching Kits

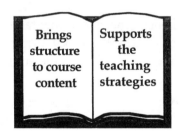

18.1 - Introduction

Textbooks are the most common type of instructional print technology used in the educational process. This is because they:

- can be used at a pace that is determined by the student
- can be consulted repeatedly for content clarification and review purposes
- are organized to bring structure to the content area being addressed
- can be made available to all students at a nominal cost
- are easy to use and do not require support technology in order to be used effectively

The selection of a textbook begins with an examination of the course curriculum. This will identify the course content as well as the instructional strategies for teaching the content. Using this data as the initial criteria, information can be secured from publishers' catalogs regarding appropriate materials.

18.2 - Identifying Textbooks and Teaching Kits

In many cases, textbooks are part of a teaching kit available from the publisher. Whereas the textbook has the student as the audience, the supplemental materials in the teaching kit are resources for the teacher. The content of a teaching kit varies, depending on the subject area, grade level and the publisher. Components, all keyed to the student text, may include:

- copy of the student textbook
- annotated "Teacher's Edition" of the student textbook
- collection of worksheet or activity sheet masters
- transparencies
- quiz and/or test masters
- audio tapes, video tapes, or CDs

Publisher's Catalogs

The first step in identifying textbooks that are appropriate for a course is to identify publishers that produce materials for the subject area or grade level. This can be done by examining materials that are available in the classroom, talking to other teachers, researching materials that are available in a curriculum library, attending professional conferences, etc. Once the names of publishers have been identified, a copy of each publisher's current catalog or a listing of their current materials must be obtained. This can be done in several ways.

All textbook publishers have a catalog that is available free of charge. Print copies of catalogs are often available for examination in the school library/media center or in the school district's curriculum library. Contact information for most publishers, as well as their current catalog, can usually be found online.

A Copy of the Textbook

After the publisher's catalog (and/or other appropriate literature) has been examined, the next step is to secure a copy of the texts being considered and examine them. In most cases a copy of a text can be requested directly from the publisher. In some cases, however, the publisher will provide the name of the regional representative and requests must be placed with that individual. (Note: Materials will only be sent to teachers and will only be mailed to a school address. Texts will not be sent to pre-service teachers.)

When a copy of the requested textbook is sent, it will be identified as being in one of four categories:

- Complimentary copy   - the book is yours to keep, free of charge.
- Examination copy (free)   - the book is yours to keep, free of charge.
- Examination copy (timed) - the book is yours to review for a period of time (usually 30 to 60 days), after which you must either return the book or pay the specified amount.
- Desk copy   - the book is yours to keep, free of charge, providing you order a specified number of books (usually 10 or more) for your class.

At times, the publisher will provide the entire teaching kit to the teacher. This often entails a preliminary face-to-face meeting with the publisher's representative.

18.3 - Preliminary Evaluation of a Textbook

Every textbook evaluation should begin with a "preliminary evaluation." This 20 to 30 minute procedure will allow the teacher to eliminate texts that obviously are not appropriate for the identified situation. Once the preliminary evaluation has taken place, the remaining texts should be examined using a set of detailed evaluation criteria and a related form. Remember, the evaluation procedure can terminate at any point in the process.

How to Do a Preliminary Evaluation of a Textbook

There are nine steps in the preliminary evaluation of a textbook. In many cases you will eliminate between 50 and 70 percent of the texts from consideration after completing this process.

Step 1 - Identify the copyright date for the text

The copyright date for the text is located on the reverse side of the title page. It will appear in one of the following formats:

- © 2005   • Copyright 2005
- © 2001, 2006   • Copyright 2002, 2005

This is the date when the book was registered with the United States Copyright Office. The content of the text was most likely completed during the previous year or earlier. In some areas (health, geography, science, current events, etc.) the currency of the material is critical to the selection of the text. In other areas (classical literature, basic mathematics, etc.) the copyright date is less critical.

Step 2 - Identify the printing number for the volume you are examining

The printing number for a book is also located on the reverse side of the title page. Usually it will appear near the copyright date. The printing number is a good indication of sales for the text. Printing information appears in one of the following formats:

1 2 3 4 5 6 7 8 9	- numbers in ascending order
9 8 7 6 5 4 3 2 1	- numbers in descending order
1 3 5 7 9 8 6 4 2	- numbers in flip-flop order
a b c d e f g h i	- letters in ascending order
i h g f e d c b a	- letters in descending order
a c e g i h f d b	- letters in flip-flop order

When a printing is sold out and more of the same book are printed, the lowest number or letter is removed from the list:

3 4 5 6 7 8 9	- the book is from the third printing
c e g i h f d b	- the book is from the second printing

Step 3 - Read the Preface of the book

If the Preface of the book is done following standard practice, it will identify the author's intentions and purpose when writing the book. It will also provide insight into any unique characteristics that have been incorporated into the presentation and identify the underlying philosophy, school of thought, or model the author used.

Step 4 - Read the Introduction to the book

If the Introduction of the book is done following standard practice, it will provide a brief overview of the content of the text. Major sections should be identified, with key elements for each discussed. A well written Introduction is a book review that is biased in favor of the author. It will stress the high points of the text. (Note: Some books will not include a Preface and an Introduction, but rather will include only one of these two. In many of these cases, the content for both areas has been combined.)

Step 5 - Examine the Table of Contents

Examine the entire Table of Contents. It will quickly provide insight into the organization of the materials and the depth and scope of coverage. The primary concern is whether the scope and depth of coverage in the text aligns with the scope and depth of your course of study.

Step 6 - Visually examine every page of the book

Beginning with the title page and ending with the last page of the index of the book, visually examine every page of the text. Do not skip any pages. This examination can be done as quickly as you can turn the pages. You are not reading, you are imprinting layout design and special features of the book in your mind. You are acquiring a "sense of the text." After completing this process you will have an understanding of the length of the chapters or units and knowledge regarding the use of illustrations, diagrams, and charts; whether key words are in bold type; if concepts are identified throughout the reading; etc.

Step 7 - Read any three to five pages for readability appropriateness

Select any three to five pages of text and read them from the perspective of your students. Your primary concern is whether they will be able to read and comprehend the writing, the presentation, and the organizational style.

Step 8 - Select a topic and read any three to five pages for content

Select a topic from the Table of Contents in which you are well-versed regarding the current state of the research. Select and read any three to five pages from that section of the text. The purpose is to determine the clarity of presentation, currency of content, and accuracy of the material.

Step 9 - Select texts for closer examination

After completing this preliminary evaluation you should be able to eliminate books that clearly do not meet your instructional needs. Use the evaluation criteria in the following section to undertake a more extensive evaluation of the remaining texts.

18.4 - Detailed Evaluation of a Textbook

A number of factors should be considered when doing a detailed evaluation a textbook. Although all of them may not be appropriate in every instance, each will be discussed and each is included in the sample "Textbook Evaluation Form" that appears in this chapter.

How to Critically Evaluate a Textbook

After doing a preliminary evaluation of the various textbooks being considered, use the following evaluation criteria to select texts and support materials that are best suited to your specific teaching situation.

- **Author Qualifications**
  Is the author knowledgeable in the content area? Does the author have practical experience on the level addressed in the textbook?

- **Relevance to Course Curriculum**
  Does the overall content of the textbook correlate with your identified course curriculum?

- **Scope and Depth of Coverage**
  Is the scope and depth consistent with the scope and depth prescribed in your course outline?

- **Objective Presentation of Content**
  Is the content presented in an objective manner and free of bias? Is there a balance of presentation when two opposing points of view are discussed?

- **Currentness of Content**
  Is the material in the textbook current? Do any components "date" the book?

- **Logical Organization**
  Is the textbook organized in a manner that is logical and easy for the students to understand?

- **Clear Writing**
  Is the writing clear and understandable? Is the author's "outline" easily discernible by the reader?

- **Appropriate Reading Level**
  Is the textbook written at a reading level that is appropriate for the class and the students? Is the textbook adaptable for students at differing reading levels?

- **Identified Measurable Objectives**
  Have objectives for each unit or chapter been identified? Are they measurable?

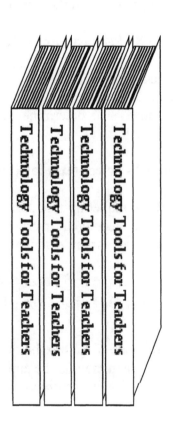

- **Vocabulary Words**
  Are new words and terms highlighted or given special attention in the section where they are introduced? Are the definitions clear and easy to understand?

- **Review Questions**
  Are review questions identified for each unit or chapter of the textbook? Is there a mix of questions that are directly based on the textbook? Are they open-ended?

- **References and Resources**
  Are references for the content of the textbook included? Are additional resources identified for the reader that wishes to investigate the topic more extensively?

- **Illustrations**
  Are illustrations in black-and-white or color? Are they used throughout the text? Are they dated due to clothing, styles, etc.? Do they show individuals similar to the readers of the textbook in terms of age, grade, etc.?

- **Diagrams, Charts, and Drawings**
  Are they in black-and-white or color? Are they used throughout the textbook? Do they clarify the content being discussed? Is there variety in style and use?

- **Overall Layout**
  Is the textbook interesting? Does it draw the reader into its pages? Is there a balance of text, illustrations, charts, diagrams, etc. throughout the textbook?

- **Diversity**
  Does the textbook have a multicultural presentation? Does it include physically and mentally challenged individuals in the discussion of content and the use of examples?

- **Binding**
  Is the type of binding appropriate for the intended use of the textbook? Are various types of bindings available?

- **Cost**
  Is the cost of the textbook in line with other books of a similar type? Is the cost within the budget available?

- **Support Materials**
  Are there support materials such as teacher guides, workbooks, test banks, etc., available?

- **Other Considerations**
  What other factors must be considered due to the uniqueness of your situation?

18.5 - Textbook Evaluation Form

The following example of a textbook evaluation form is based on the content in this chapter. After a preliminary evaluation has been completed, a form such as this will provide a uniform set of criteria for doing a critical evaluation of a textbook. The form would be used to evaluate two or more textbooks and make comparisons that will result in a more valid decision when selecting a textbook.

TEXTBOOK EVALUATION FORM

Part I – Course Information

Course: _____   Grade(s): _____

Brief Description of Course: _____

_____

Part II – Textbook Information

Book One:

Title: _____

Author(s): _____

Publisher: _____

Copyright Date: _____   Edition: _____   No. of Pages: _____

Book Two:

Title: _____

Author(s): _____

Publisher: _____

Copyright Date: _____   Edition: _____   No. of Pages: _____

Part III – Critical Evaluations

Directions: Using the rating system identified below, evaluate each of the selected textbooks. It is important that you are consistent in your interpretation and application of the criteria.

Check the appropriate box for each item:

5 = Excellent   2 = Below Average
4 = Above Average   1 = Poor
3 = Average   0 = Does Not Apply

	Book One						Book Two					
	5	4	3	2	1	0	5	4	3	2	1	0
Author Qualifications												
Relevance to Course Curriculum												
Scope of Coverage												
Depth of Coverage												
Objective Presentation of Content												
Currentness of Content												
Logical Organization												
Clear Writing												
Appropriate Reading Level												
Identified Measurable Objectives												
Identified Vocabulary Terms												
Identified Review Questions												
Identified References/Resources												
Illustrations - Black & White												
Illustrations - Color												
Diagrams, Charts, Drawings - Black & White												
Diagrams, Charts, Drawings - Color												
Overall Layout												
Text/Illustrations - Multicultural												
Text/Illustrations - Disabled Individuals												
Appropriate Binding												
Appropriate Cost												
Support Materials - Teacher's Edition of Text												
Support Materials - Teacher's Guide/Manual												
Support Materials - Workbooks												
Support Materials - Assessment Materials												
Support Materials - Media/Technology												

Total Score Awarded: _____   _____

18.6 - John J. Schaub Instructional Materials Center

To locate teaching kits and other teaching resources visit, the Schaub Instructional Materials Center, located in room 1140, on the first floor of Education Hall. This Center serves the faculty and students of Rowan University's College of Education. The facility houses a wide range of sample teaching materials, teacher's texts and workbooks, teaching kits, print resource materials, professional journals, and instructional audio-visuals.

The specialized collection supports and augments the College of Education's various professional education courses. The Instructional Materials Center offers laminating, binding and copying services, as well as Ellison "lettering machines" and assorted Ellison die cut shapes.

Hours of operation vary due to orientation programs and class sessions. A current two-week schedule is linked to their Website: www.rowan.edu/colleges/education/schaub.

18.7 - Activities

• Activity One •

Identify the names of three educational publishers. Select a grade level (K-12) and a subject area (e.g., math, science, language arts) and go to the Web sites for the three publishers. (Use *Google* to identify the Web address.) Select one textbook from each publisher's online catalog and compare the information provided and the materials available. Based on this information, write a two-page (word processed, double-spaced) report comparing and contrasting the three texts.

• Activity Two •

Go to a curriculum resource center (e.g., John J. Schaub Instructional Materials Center, Education Hall, Room 1140) and select a teaching kit for examination. The kit must include—at a minimum—the student textbook, the teacher's edition of the textbook, and an activity book or workbook. Examine the various items of the kit and write a two-page (word processed, double-spaced) review of the teaching kit. Discuss the advantages and disadvantages of the components.

• Activity Three •

Select two teaching kits that address the same subject and grade level (grades K-12). Make a copy of the "Textbook Evaluation Form" in section 18.5 and do a comparative evaluation of the two student textbooks and their supporting materials.

Instructional Boards

19.1 - Introduction

"Instructional boards" is the name given to the broad array of boards or surfaces that are used to provide information during the process of instruction. The most common types of instructional boards are chalkboards, multipurpose boards (also called whiteboards or marker boards), and bulletin boards. All of these items provide the user with a means of providing information to the class. They also afford the opportunity to easily change the information at any time.

19.2 - Chalkboards

Chalkboards have a long and noble history in the educational tools arena. Traditionally, white chalk was used to write on slate boards called blackboards. Today, chalk and chalkboards are both available in a variety of colors. Despite the fact that this technology has changed little over the years, the chalkboard is still a valuable instructional technology tool for the teacher.

Non-Magnetic Chalkboards

Contemporary, non-magnetic chalkboards consist of a writing surface on a backing of a material that is not magnetic (Masonite, composition board, etc.). These boards are the least costly to purchase.

AaBbCcDdEeFfGgHhIiJjKkLlMmNnOoPpQqRrSsTtUuVvWwXxYyZz

White Chalk is the primary color of chalk used on a black chalkboard.

Yellow chalk is the primary color of chalk used on a green chalkboard.

Magnetic Chalkboards

Many educational settings have chalkboards that are a combination chalk/magnetic board. Unlike the less costly chalkboards, these boards are designed to withstand extensive and long-term use. Since they have a base surface of metal (usually porcelain on steel) they will accept magnetic accessories. This allows the teacher to display posters, charts, maps, student work, etc. on the board without the worry of damaging the writing surface. The materials used in this situation can also be easily and quickly displayed, used, and removed.

19.3 - Multipurpose Boards

Multipurpose boards are also known as "whiteboards" or "marker boards." The name whiteboard is based on the fact that the writing surface is white. The marker board name emerged from the use of dry erase markers as the writing instrument used on the board surface.

The name "multipurpose board" is more accurate because the board can be used for a variety of purposes. It can be written on using dry erase markers (no other type should be used); it can serve as a projection screen for any projection technology (overhead, slide, video, etc.); shapes cut from thin plastic sheets will adhere to the surface if rubbed in place; and those with a steel back can be used as a magnetic display board for posters, student work, etc. Using a split screen approach, any combination of these options is also possible.

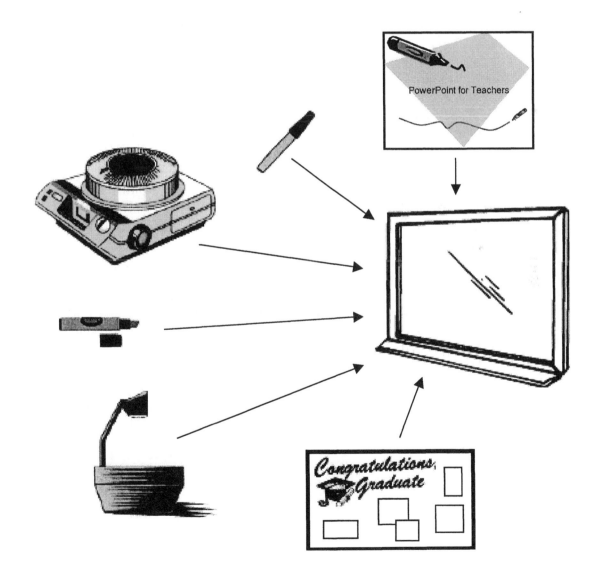

19.4 - Bulletin Boards

Bulletin boards are the most common form of display technology used in the classroom. Although they are intended to provide information or an opportunity for interaction to a large number of students, they can also serve as a link and point of unification for special interest groups.

All bulletin boards can be grouped into one of three categories: decorative, motivational, and instructional.

- **Decorative Bulletin Boards**
  - used to help create a visually stimulating educational environment.

- **Motivational Bulletin Boards**
  - inspire students to reach further in their quest for learning or to take action.

- **Instructional Bulletin Boards**
  - tied to specific curricular objectives and provide instruction.

Motivational bulletin boards and instructional bulletin boards are the two primary categories that all teachers should become proficient in creating and using in their teaching. Bulletin boards in these categories can be either "static" (traditional) or "interactive."

- **Static Bulletin Boards**
  - present information.

- **Interactive Bulletin Boards**
  - require student activity.

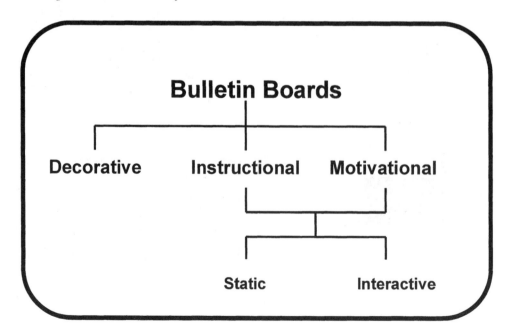

How to Develop a Bulletin Board

Although many books describe the development of bulletin boards, there are six basic steps involved in the process:

1. **Identify the subject and theme**
   Identify this with as much specificity as possible. This will greatly facilitate the remaining steps. Planning at this point will reduce the number of questions that may arise later in the process.

2. **Identify your primary objective(s)**
   What do you want to take place? How? When? Your objective(s) should be clearly stated so that the student has the same understanding of the expectations from the bulletin board as the teacher.

3. **Develop a working layout or plan**
   Brainstorm ideas. Determine if the bulletin board will be static or interactive. Make "thumbnail" sketches of various layouts. Put them aside for a day. Evaluate them again. Needed changes will be more readily evident. Ask another person to look at your plans. Revise. Then, make a detailed plan of your final layout.

4. **Acquire or create the materials needed**
   Gather and/or create the materials necessary for the final layout. Lead time is usually required in order to create an effective bulletin board. The voids that are evident in hastily developed bulletin boards are easy to spot.

5. **Put up the bulletin board**
   When the bulletin board is in place, inform the class regarding its purpose and relationship to the content area under study. Tell the students what is expected of them. Discuss their use of the bulletin board.

6. **Evaluate the success of the bulletin board**
   Evaluate the bulletin board from your perspective as a teacher. Have the students evaluate the success of the bulletin board. (Develop a simple form that asks about content, clarity, interest, etc.)

After the bulletin board has been taken down, save the individual components either for reassembly at another time or for reuse in other bulletin boards. Write down and save your evaluation of the current bulletin board. It will be useful in future planning for other bulletin boards and classes.

Static (Traditional) Bulletin Boards

Static (traditional) bulletin boards present information without requiring the student to directly respond to the information.

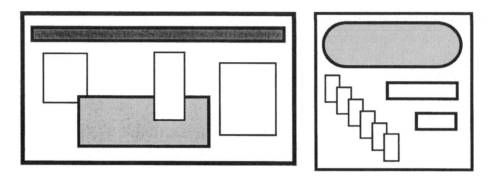

They can be used as an introduction to a topic, a review of the content covered, enrichment regarding a class topic, a means to elicit action from the reader, etc.

Interactive Bulletin Boards

Interactive bulletin boards require the student to engage in some type of activity that is directly tied to the content and materials on the bulletin board. The expected actions are necessary in order to fully benefit from the design of the bulletin board. Like a static bulletin board, the focus could be to introduce or summarize a topic, provide enrichment, etc.

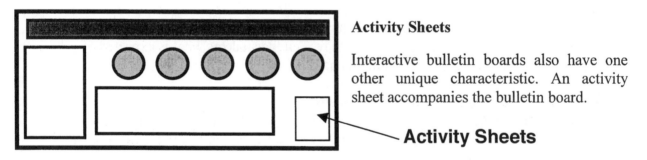

Activity Sheets

Interactive bulletin boards also have one other unique characteristic. An activity sheet accompanies the bulletin board.

Activity sheets identify questions the student must answer and activities that may, or must be, undertaken. Answers to complete some of the activities are found on the bulletin board. Others must be found elsewhere (textbook, almanac, encyclopedia, atlas, internet, etc.).

An activity sheet for an interactive bulletin board on New Jersey might contain the following questions that could be answered using the bulletin board: *What city is the capital of New Jersey? Who is the current governor? Identify two inventors from New Jersey. Name two major companies that are based in New Jersey.* Questions that would require using other sources could be: *Who was the governor of New Jersey in 1950? Identify the bibliographic information for a biography of a New Jersey inventor. Identify a Web site that discusses recreational areas in New Jersey.*

Guidelines for Effective Bulletin Board Design

- ### The "Rule of Thirds"

  Divide your layout area like a tic-tac-toe board. The "rule of thirds" states that the four points of line intersection are good areas to place key elements in your layout.

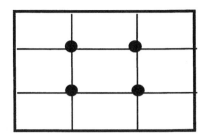

- ### The Reading "Z"

  The reading "Z" principle states that most people read across the top of a page, then diagonally down to the bottom, and finally across the bottom.

- ### The "Upper Third" Rule

  This rule states that the upper third of the layout area is the most powerful place for the title and other key elements.

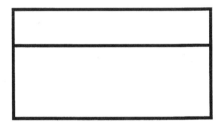

15 Hints for Successful Bulletin Boards

1. **Use one idea or concept for your theme**
    Keep it simple and to the point. When there are many trees in the forest, it's easy to get lost.

2. **Identify one primary objective and stay focused**
    Everything should relate to meeting your identified objective. It is your focal point.

3. **Plan and re-plan on paper, not on the board**
    Identify what you will need to meet your objective and determine how it will be done.

4. **Do not restrict yourself to the materials at hand**
    Find and/or create the needed materials. This should not be a collage of the materials that are available in the classroom.

5. **Follow the rules for lettering and headings**
   Headline lettering should be readable from across the room. The title should draw students near.

6. **Try various layout plans**
   Start with the assumption that you must identify three possible layouts.

7. **Use a layout that is dynamic and visually appealing**
   Take a hint from billboards and ads in popular magazines. Excitement and education do mix.

8. **Make effective use of color**
   Use color to attract attention, show differences, and emphasize content.

9. **Incorporate balance (formal or informal) and unity**
   Use a variety of layout designs in bulletin boards. Examine advertisements for examples.

10. **Capture the viewer's interest and hold it**
    Use the layout, colors, and topic to generate interest. Content should follow through on it.

11. **Identify follow-up or related activities**
    Build on the interest generated by the bulletin board by having required and/or optional activities.

12. **Don't overload the layout or design**
    Too much of any element can be confusing and undermine the layout.

13. **Address issues that are timely and interesting**
    Build on student interests and concerns by addressing them in a bulletin board.

14. **Talk to the class about the bulletin board**
    Teacher/student discussion is essential if you are to get the full value from a bulletin board.

15. **Take the bulletin board down in a timely fashion**
    Once the bulletin board has served its purpose, replace it.

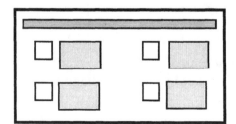 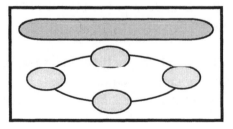

Ideas for Content Area Bulletin Boards

Social Studies	• State History • Current Events	• Map Skills • Government
Language Arts	• Poetry • Famous Writers	• Science Fiction • Types of Writing
Science	• Solar Energy • Electricity	• Plants • Recycling
Math	• Metric System • Geometric Design	• Graphs • Calculators
Health	• Foods • AIDS	• Personal Hygiene • Family Planning
Art	• Art Deco • Famous Painters	• Cartoonists • Art Museums
Music	• Famous Composers • Instruments	• Rap Music • ASCAP
Vocational Education	• Technical Careers • Apprenticeship	• Unions • Tools of the Trade
Physical Education	• Famous Athletes • Evolution of Games	• Rules and Regulations • Baseball
Safety	• OSHA • First Aid	• Rules of the Road • Bicycle Safety

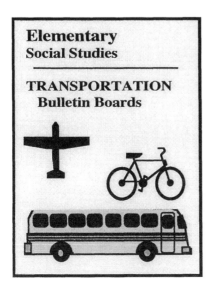

Elementary
Social Studies

TRANSPORTATION
Bulletin Boards

Bulletin Boards
for **Secondary**
Science

Grades
9-12

19.5 - Activities

• Activity One •

Design a static instructional bulletin board that relates to a lesson or unit you will be or could be teaching. Start by creating three preliminary layouts. Select the best idea and develop it on a large piece of paper. Identify the grade level, course, unit topic, lesson topic, and the bulletin board objective(s) on the back of the paper.

• Activity Two •

Design an interactive instructional bulletin board and the related activity sheet. Sketch the layout of the bulletin board, develop an activity sheet that has a minimum of 10 questions, and prepare an answer sheet for the activity sheet questions. Identify the grade level, course, unit topic, lesson topic, and the bulletin board objective(s).

• Activity Three •

Design a motivational bulletin board intended to solicit donations of canned goods for the victims of a natural disaster.

CHAPTER **20**

Learning Centers and Learning Stations

20.1 - Introduction

The constructivist classroom has received considerable attention in recent years. Far removed from the rote memorization approach to learning, constructivism is concerned with students learning "how to learn." Constructivists believe that knowledge acquisition and learning result from hands-on experiences. The student "constructs" an understanding of concepts and a knowledge base as a result of his/her interactions in the real world.

Classrooms that support a constructivist approach to learning are places where individual, collaborative, and competitive activities are commonplace. One of the major questions for constructivists is "How can I provide meaningful educational experiences for a variety of interests, in many areas, on different levels?" The use of learning centers and learning stations is a viable answer to this question.

20.2 - Learning Centers and Learning Stations

One of the first questions asked by anyone researching this topic deals with the use of the phrases "learning center" and "learning station." Is a learning center the same as a learning station? And if not, what is the difference? Articles can be found that will take either side of this issue and defend that stand. The majority of the research does view a learning center as different from a learning station.

Generally, a learning center deals with a broad area of knowledge or study. There can be learning centers dealing with mathematics, science, social studies, art, physical education, music, etc. However, learning centers could also deal with areas such as the state of New Jersey, the Civil War, space exploration, etc.

Learning stations are usually narrow in scope and are frequently found as subdivisions of a learning center. Although learning stations are often smaller than learning centers, that is not always the case. In some instances, a learning station can be as extensive in scope and size as a learning center. As a general rule, the guidelines for a creating a learning center can be directly applied to a learning station.

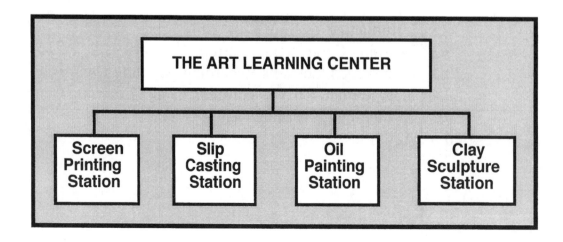

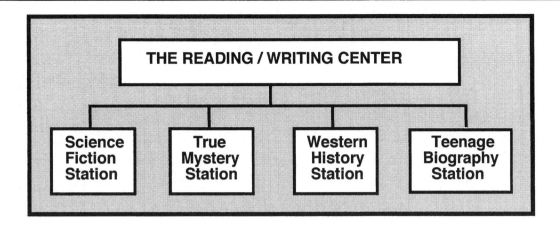

THE READING / WRITING CENTER

| Science Fiction Station | True Mystery Station | Western History Station | Teenage Biography Station |

20.3 - Five Basic Questions Regarding Learning Centers

There are five basic questions that must be answered before the teacher can plan, create, and implement a learning center. (Note: When the phrase "learning center" is used in this chapter it will mean "learning center" or "learning station.")

    1. What is a learning center?
    2. What are the major characteristics of a learning center?
    3. What types of materials are found at a learning center?
    4. What does a learning center look like?
    5. How is the work or progress of the student assessed?

What is a learning center?

A learning center is a self-contained learning environment where one student, or a small group of students, can independently investigate an area of study in order to meet a predetermined objective. The center includes all the materials, supplies, equipment, and directions needed to undertake a series of activities.

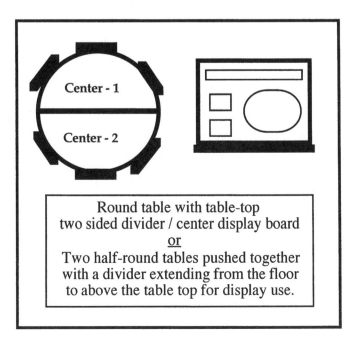

Round table with table-top two sided divider / center display board
or
Two half-round tables pushed together with a divider extending from the floor to above the table top for display use.

A table with file cabinets on either side is ideal for a quiet learning center.

What are the major characteristics of a learning center?

All learning centers have:

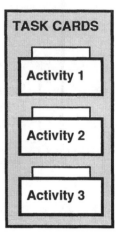

- a clear label or title
- sequenced activities
- optional activities
- all needed supplies
- information resources

- identified objectives
- basic/required activities
- all needed materials
- all needed equipment
- directions for activities

Directions for learning center activities can be presented in a variety of ways: videotapes, audiotapes, instructional notebooks, photograph series, task cards, etc. Task cards can be made using 5" x 8" index cards. They can be laminated and/or held together with a notebook ring.

Learning centers are:

- Structured for individual or small group participation, determined by the teacher.
- Self-instructing—the teacher is not needed for successful center use.
- Self-correcting—he student has immediate feedback regarding success in undertaking or completing an activity.
- Paced by the student—starting and stopping is at the discretion of the student.
- Designed for different purposes—they can introduce, develop, or reinforce a concept; foster enrichment; develop awareness; create interest; etc.

What types of materials are found at a learning center?

Learning centers may include:

- textbooks and resource books
- teaching kits
- a concept map
- manipulatives to undertake the activities
- support materials (paper, scissors, tape, card stock, etc.)
- photographs of other students engaged in the activity
- directions in multiple formats (task cards, a video, etc.)
- technology to instruct (VCR, audio cassette player, videodiscs/player, slide viewer)
- technology to record results (camcorder, camera, tapes)
- computer
- Internet connection
- individual logs or record sheets/folders
- examples of previous student work
- lists of selected Web sites
- lists of resource/reference books in the school library

What does a learning center look like?

The structure, location, and appearance of a learning center is determined on a case-by-case basis. The examples in this chapter are representative of commonly found learning center designs. Tables and desks are the natural starting point for creating a learning center.

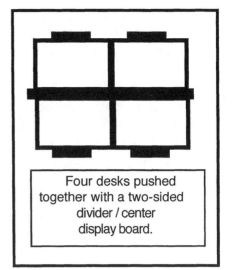

Four desks pushed together with a two-sided divider / center display board.

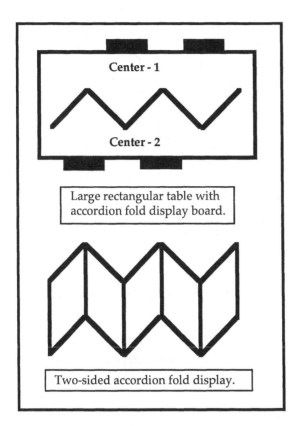

Large rectangular table with accordion fold display board.

Two-sided accordion fold display.

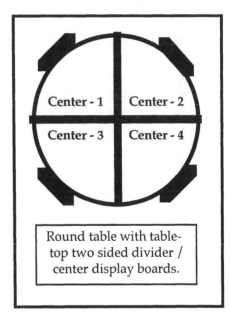

Round table with table-top two sided divider / center display boards.

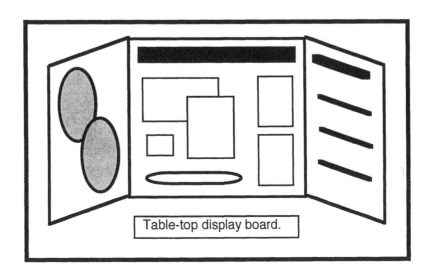

Table-top display board.

How is the work or progress of the student assessed?

Student progress at a learning center is assessed on two fronts: by the student and by the teacher.

Self-assessment by the student should be completed at the end of each and every work period at the center. This can be done in a number of ways. The student could:

- keep a journal of his/her center activity
- record activity in individual logs or folders at the center
- keep an audio record of the activity
- keep a photographic record of results
- maintain a portfolio

Assessment by the teacher is a periodic process. This can be done by:

- reviewing student logs or journals
- listening to audiotape reports
- viewing photographic or video tape records
- meeting with students individually to review progress
- reviewing individual portfolios
- keeping an ongoing photographic record of student activity

20.4 - How to Plan, Create, and Implement a Learning Center

Planning and preparation are the key components to effective lessons. They are also the keys to successfully using learning centers as an educational tool. The following steps are essential to the process:

1. Identify the center area, topic, or concept.
2. Identify the center title.
3. Identify the center objective(s).
4. Identify the basic activity.
5. Identify the optional activities.
6. Determine a physical location.
7. Develop a concept map/web showing the place of the center in the larger area of study.
8. Design the center layout.
9. Design and create a display board.
10. Identify and assemble/create the materials and supplies required to do the basic and optional activities.
11. Gather the equipment/technology required to do the basic and optional activities.
12. Develop an instructional package (task cards, video tapes, activity flow charts, etc.) that will guide the student through the successful completion of the activities.
13. Gather the support resource materials.

14. Develop a system to record individual student activity at the center (log, journal, report folders, etc.).
15. Set up the center to be visually appealing.
16. Do a "dry run" of all the activities using only the directions, materials, supplies, and equipment provided.
17. Revise the directions and add needed materials to assure correct completion of the activities.
18. Develop a plan for infusing the center into the instructional schedule.
19. Introduce the center to the class with a brief presentation.

20.5 - Evaluating a Learning Center

One of the most valuable activities that a teacher can undertake regarding a learning center is to have other teachers and/or users of the center complete an evaluation form. This will not only provide input when restructuring the center the next time it is used; it will provide valuable insight when you undertake the development of additional learning centers, as well. What follows is an example of a learning center evaluation form. Note that the name of the evaluator is not part of the form.

Learning Center Evaluation Form

Center Name_____

Overall Visual Appeal; Setup	5	4	3	2	1
Title and Objective(s)	5	4	3	2	1
Basic Activity; Directions	5	4	3	2	1
Optional Activity; Directions	5	4	3	2	1
Grade Level: Appropriate, Value	5	4	3	2	1
Materials, Supplies, Equipment	5	4	3	2	1
Procedure to Record Progress	5	4	3	2	1

What is the most appealing element of this learning center?

What is the weakest element of this learning center?

What one suggestion would you make that would improve the effectiveness of this learning center?

Additional Comments:

20.6 - Activities

• Activity One •

Identify a broad topic for a learning center and discuss the purpose and objectives the learning center will address. Name and describe three learning stations that could be part of this center. For each of the stations, identify your objectives, the basic activities, and the optional activities.

• Activity Two •

On a large sheet of paper, draw the layout of a learning center for a topic of your choice. On the back of the paper identify the center name, objectives, and grade level. Briefly describe two basic activities and two optional activities for this center. The layout on the front of the paper must reflect the material identified on the back of the paper.

• Activity Three •

Plan and create a learning center for a lesson or unit you will be teaching. Test the center by having two students use the center as intended. Watch the students as they undertake the activities. Make note of any problems that occur during this test phase. Have each student evaluate the center. Redesign the center using your notes and the student evaluations.

Lettering and Die-Cut Letters

21.1 - Introduction

Lettering is an important element in virtually every teacher-made instructional aid used in the classroom. Posters, bulletin boards, handouts, learning centers, and transparencies all rely on lettering to help convey the intended message. If the letters are too small, difficult to read, or amateurish in their presentation, the instructional aid will fail to fulfill its intended purpose.

Lettering techniques can generally be grouped under one of four primary categories: (1) handmade letters, (2) ready-made letters, (3) mechanical letters, and (4) computer-generated letters. Regardless of what technique is used to produce the letters, there are some basic rules that apply to all situations.

In the first part of this chapter we will discuss lettering guidelines that apply to the development of all instructional aids that incorporate the use of lettering. The second part of the chapter will concentrate on die-cut letters, with emphasis on the family of *Ellison*® lettering machines and tools.

21.2 - Lettering Guidelines

Guidelines for effective lettering deal with letter size, letter style, and the spacing between letters and words. Letters must be of a sufficient size and style to allow for easy reading. Each element contributes to an effective and readable product.

Lettering Styles

When selecting a letter style, often called a face or a font, the rule is "simple is better." Sans-serif (without the end stroke) letters and gothic letters are bolder and easier to read than letter styles that have a serif or ornamental style.

This is Century Gothic in 12 point, 14 point, 24 point

This is Chicago in 12 point, 14 point, 24 point

This is Helvetica in 12 point, 14 point, 24 point

This is Librarian in 12 point, 14 point, 24 point

This is New York in 12 point, 14 point, 24 point

This is Marker Felt in 12 point, 14 point, 24 point

This is SignBoard in 12 point, 14 point, 24 point

Additional options include selecting plain, outline, heading, or italic lettering formats.

This is Plain lettering in 14 point

This is Outline lettering in 14 point

This is Heading 1 lettering in 14 point

This is Italic lettering in 14 point

For short titles, use all capital letters. If four or more words are used in the title, it is better to use lowercase letters with capital letters used for the first letter in the primary words.

• AMERICA •

GEORGE WASHINGTON

America: Yesterday, Today, and Tomorrow

When longer headings or entire sentences are a part of the display, serif (with the end stroke) letters should be used. They are more readable when longer text is involved.

The Civil Rights Movement in America: A History

Lettering Techniques

Posters, bulletin boards, displays, and learning stations all depend upon letters to identify their theme and present content to the student. These letters can be produced using a variety of techniques that can be grouped into four categories. The primary methods for each category are discussed here.

Handmade Letters

Handmade letters can be made using a marking instrument (pen, crayon, marker, brush), or they can be cut out of a variety of different materials using scissors.

- **Felt pen lettering** is usually done directly on the surface where the letters will be used. Markers are available in two types: permanent ink and water-based ink. Permanent ink markers are used to either draw the entire letter or draw the outline of a letter. When the outline only is drawn, the letter can be filled in with color using a water-based marker.

- **Cut-out letters** can be made in one of two ways. They can be traced from a template, or the letter can be projected onto the selected material using an overhead projector and traced. The letters are then cut out with scissors.

Ready-Made Letters

Ready-made letters require little or no preparation in order to use them. Examples include precut letters and adhesive-backed letters.

- **Precut letters** are available in a variety of sizes, materials, and styles. They are direct cutouts from a material such as cardboard, paper, felt, plastic, etc. Some have a special backing for mounting (pins, hooks, slots) on a particular type of surface.

- **Adhesive-backed letters** are made from a variety of materials (vinyl, paper, felt). The letters are peeled off of the backing sheet and applied where desired. Although there are many sizes and styles that are easy to use, they are one of the more expensive options for lettering.

Mechanical Letters

There are many mechanical lettering systems in use, but the two that are most frequently used in the preparation of posters, bulletin boards, and learning stations are stencils and die-cut letters.

- **Stencils** are commonly used in the elementary classroom. They are available in many sizes and are usually made of heavy paper, plastic, or metal. The stencil is used to outline the letter on the desired surface. Then the letter is completed with markers, crayons, paint, etc.

- **Die-cut letters** are made using a metal cutter mounted in a wooden holder. These are discussed in the next section of this chapter.

Computer-Generated Letters

All word processing programs will allow the user to generate letters, words, and titles using various type styles (faces or fonts) and in almost any size desired. In addition, software packages that have special features to create banners and posters are available.

21.3 - Die-Cut Letters

Die-cut letters and shapes can be used for signs, bulletin boards, posters, and many other educational projects. They are made using a die that consists of a metal cutter that is mounted in a wooden holder. The material is cut using the die, producing perfect letters, numbers, or shapes every time.

For more than 25 years, the most popular letter and shape die-cutting tools used by educators have been made by *Ellison*. In addition to manufacturing several styles of die-cutting tools, the company has a catalog of nearly 10,000 dies. The content in this section is based on materials produced by *Ellison*.

Dies: Alphabet, Number, and Shape

Dies are available in a variety of sizes. Alphabet and number dies are the starting point for any collection. Shape dies to fit the educational needs of the situation are then chosen to round off the collection.

3" to 8" alphabet and number dies are formatted as "single-up"—one letter is contained on each die.

1-1/4" and 2" alphabet and number dies are formatted with multiple letters and numbers on each die.

Music			
Fall			
Presidents			
Science			
School			

• Examples of Shape Dies •

Materials

The most frequently asked question regarding using die-cutters is: "What materials can I cut using these dies?" The answer is simple. If you can cut the material with a regular pair of scissors, you can cut it with a die-cutter. Examples of materials commonly cut with die-cutters include:

- construction paper
- wall paper
- aluminum foil
- static cling vinyl

- file folders
- shelf paper
- fabric
- card stock

- oak tag
- felt
- poly foam
- greeting cards

How to Make Die-Cut Letters

When cutting out letters or shapes, place the material (paper, card stock, poster board, felt, plastic, wall paper, etc.) under the cutting edge of the die and insert the die and material packet in the hand-powered machine. (Note: The material must be precut to the size of the die, since both the die and the material must be placed in the machine.) When the handle of the machine is lowered, the die cuts the material. When the handle is raised, the die and the die-cut shapes can be removed.

1. Raise the handle all the way up.

2. Place the paper, or other material, against the rubber side of the die.

3. Turn the die over and slide it into the machine, rubber side down.

4. Center the die under the pressure plate of the machine.

5. Bring the handle down to cut through the material.

6. Raise the handle slowly in order to prevent it from springing back and causing injury.

7. Remove the die and the material from the machine.

21.4 - Activities

• Activity One •

Design a bulletin board that incorporates different die-cut letters or shapes. (1) Use large die-cut letters for the title. (2) Use a different style and size letter in the layout of the bulletin board. (3) Incorporate three or more die-cut shapes in the design.

• Activity Two •

Create a poster that uses die-cut letters for the title and incorporates four different die-cut shapes in the layout.

• Activity Three •

Design a display board for a learning center that: (1) Uses die-cut letters for the title. (2) Incorporates three or more shapes in the display board design. (3) Uses the shapes to connect to other materials at the center (e.g., activity book, resource materials, record sheets, etc.).

CHAPTER 22

Overhead Projectors and Transparencies

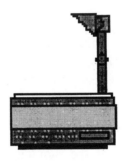

22.1 - Introduction

The overhead projector is not only very easy to use, but it is also the most common type of projection technology available in schools. Unlike other projection technologies that are "dated" and have limited current resources available (16mm films and filmstrips) or are costly (video projectors), overhead projectors are available in many models and at affordable prices.

Overhead transparencies are used with an overhead projector. They are one of the most frequently used and popular instructional tools employed by teachers. In addition to being easy to make and use, overhead transparencies offer a number of other advantages to the teacher. They can be interspersed with other forms of technology, they can be customized and manipulated in a number of ways, and the pace is fully controlled by the teacher.

Visual presenters are also used in the classroom for projection. In addition to projecting overhead transparencies, they can also project books and other paper documents, photographs, 35mm slides, and 3-dimensional objects.

22.2 - Overhead Projectors

The broad appeal of the overhead projector in both the educational community and the business sector is largely tied to its unique advantages as an instruction/presentation tool. Normal classroom lighting can be maintained while using the overhead projector, thus the instructor can have better control of the class.

Moreover, because the projector is placed in the front of the classroom, with projection taking place over the shoulders of the presenter, the instructor is always facing the class. The variety of uses and the control afforded the instructor over the presentation of materials when using the overhead projector is enhanced by its light weight, ease of operation, and reasonable cost.

The basic design consists of a box with a glass platen (called the stage) on the top surface. A powerful lamp is mounted above a reflector on the floor of the box. When the overhead projector is turned on, the light is reflected off the reflector, through a fresnel lens (causing the light to be evenly distributed across the stage), and through the stage. The light continues through the transparency on the stage and the image is transferred to a projection lens and mirror that is mounted above the box. This mechanism turns the image 90 degrees and projects it onto the screen.

The stage area of most overhead projectors is 10" by 10", allowing the user to project images that are this size or smaller. Focus is attained in two ways: (1) moving the overhead projector closer to or further away from the screen and (2) raising or lowering the projection lens using the focus knob.

Using the Overhead Projector

There are many models of overhead projectors available, ranging from the standard tabletop models to the collapsible/portable models. The following procedures apply to most overhead projectors. Prior to using any overhead projector, consult the manufacturer's operator's manual for product-specific directions.

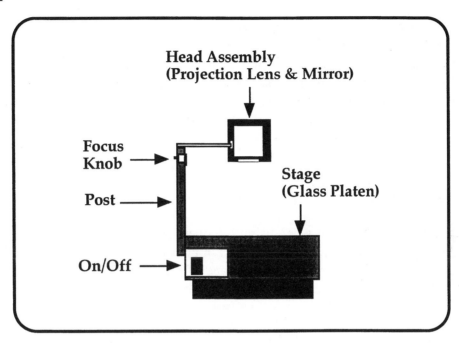

Standard tabletop overhead projectors are generally larger in size than the collapsible/portable models. Although these models do not "fold up," many have a handle to allow for easy transportation from one location to another.

1. Position the projector in front of the screen.
2. Uncoil and plug in the power cord.
3. Turn on the projector.
4. Move the projector and/or tilt the projection lens/mirror so the image space fills the screen without distortion.
5. Place a test transparency on the stage.
6. Focus the image using the focus knob.
7. USE the overhead projector.
8. Turn off the projector.
9. Unplug the power cord and return to storage area.

Collapsible/portable overhead projectors are less cumbersome than the standard tabletop models and are specifically constructed to be portable. To begin using a portable model, the stage door must first be opened. The stage and head assembly are then locked in place. When finished using the projector, the stage cover is opened; the head assembly and post are unlocked and folded in, and the stage cover is closed.

Overhead Projector Lamps

The most common "problem" when using the overhead projector is a burned out lamp (bulb). Most projectors have a spare lamp installed as part of the lamp assembly; others house only a single lamp. If a spare lamp is available, switch to this alternate or second lamp. Procedures vary depending upon the model.

If the lamp is burned out and must be replaced:
1. Unplug the projector.
2. Open the cover or panel to reveal the lamp. (Be sure the lamp is cool.)
3. Release the lamp from the locking device and remove it.
4. Replace the lamp with one having the identical lamp number or one identified as an acceptable substitute.
5. Close the lamp cover or panel.

The Keystone Effect

The most common mistake made when using the overhead projector is not having the projector at a 90 degree angle with the screen. This results in poor projection and a distorted image called the keystone effect or "keystoning." The keystone effect can be corrected by repositioning (1) the overhead projector, (2) the head assembly, or (3) the projection screen.

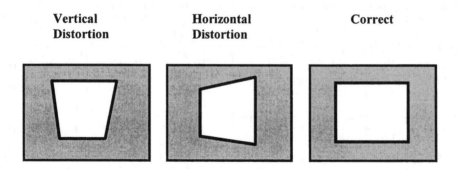

Vertical Distortion   **Horizontal Distortion**   **Correct**

22.3 - Designing Overhead Transparencies

The first step in creating transparencies is designing their layout. The following 12 guidelines will produce transparencies that will be effective technology tools for teachers.

- Use one concept or theme per transparency.
- Use bold or block lettering that is easy to read.
- Use more than one letter size on each transparency.
- Use lines and white space to place emphasis on content.
- Use a horizontal or landscape orientation for frames.
- Use a horizontal lettering layout, not vertical.

- Place drawings off-center, using the "rule of thirds."
- Place headings at the top, either in the center or to the left side.
- Mix formal and informal balance when creating a series.
- Use color to create a mood and/or emphasize a point.
- Create a feeling of unity or oneness in the overall layout.
- Keep text to a minimum.

Materials for Making and Using Transparencies

Types of Transparency Film

There are a variety of transparency films available; each is designed to be compatible with one or more specific transparency production methods. The transparency making equipment may be damaged if an inappropriate film is used when making the transparency. The most common types of transparency film are:

- Write-on transparency film
- Transparency film for plain paper copiers
- Transparency film for laser printers
- Transparency film for ink jet printers
- Film for infrared (thermal) transparency makers

Some transparency films are also available in various "weights." These include standard weight, medium weight, and heavy weight.

Colors of Transparency Film

In addition to the standard clear film, a variety of colored film sheets are available for many of the processes. These are more costly than the traditional clear film formats. Examples include:

- Black image on clear film (traditional film)
- Red, blue, green, yellow, or violet image on clear film
- Yellow image on blue, red, green, or violet background

Transparency Markers

These are special markers that are specifically intended to be used when making overhead transparencies. They are labeled as "transparency markers." Some use water soluble ink and some use permanent ink. Unlike traditional permanent ink markers, transparency markers with permanent ink will allow their color to be projected.

Transparency Framing/Storing Options

Transparency frames can be made of heavy cardboard, thin sheet plastic, or heavy plastic. The cardboard frames are intended to have presentation notes written on the frame. The new "flip-frame" transparency protectors have a sleeve to store the transparency, flip-out borders for notes, and holes for storing in a three-ring notebook. Transparencies can also be protected and stored in regular "plastic sheet protectors."

Formats for Transparency Layout

Various formats can be used when planning the layout of an overhead transparency. The following layout designs represent some of the most common formats for presenting textual (words and/or numbers) material.

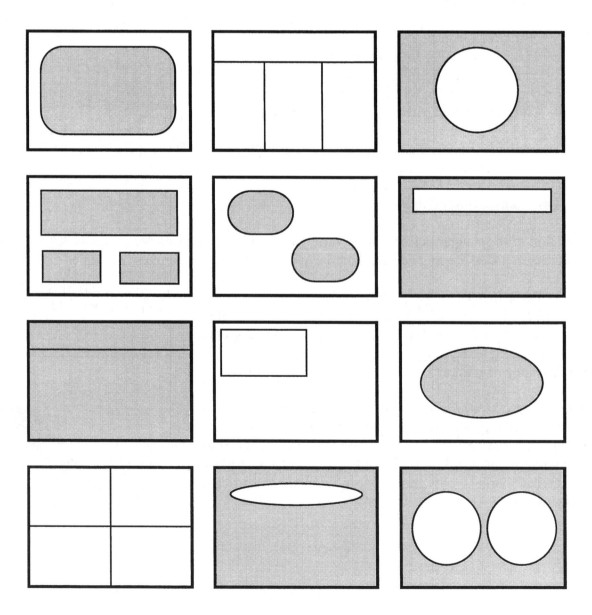

How to Make Overhead Transparencies

There are a number of different ways to make an overhead transparency. Three of the most common methods/categories are: (1) handmade transparencies, (2) transparencies made using a xerographic copying machine, and (3) computer generated and printed transparencies.

Handmade Transparencies

Handmade transparencies can either be done quickly or they can be extremely time consuming; plan first. Plain acetate film should be used for this method. (For an inexpensive alternative, use acetate sheet protectors for three-ring notebooks.)

Handmade lettering and drawings can be made with either permanent ink felt-tip markers or with special transparency markers. Do not use water soluble markers, as they will bead-up. Pointed markers are used for lines, and broad-tip markers can be used to color in small shapes and to do broad-lined lettering. Coloring books, stencils, and magazines are an unlimited tracing library of both letters and objects for those who either are not artistically inclined or want to make the process go quicker.

Xerographic Copying Machine Transparencies

Transparencies made on xerographic copiers are extremely easy to produce. Place the master on the copier just as if you were going to make a paper copy. But instead of feeding paper into the machine, feed the recommended transparency material that is used in these machines. Some manufacturers make material especially for their copiers. However, most copiers will accept film labeled "For plain paper copiers." Check the film box before using any film, as the machine can be damaged if the incorrect film is used. One advantage of making transparencies on larger copiers is their ability to reduce and/or enlarge the copy of the original.

Computer Created/Laser or Ink Jet Printed Transparencies

A transparency master, as well as the actual transparency, can be created using a computer and a printer. The paper printout of a page designed on the computer and printed with a laser printer is the perfect master for making a transparency. However, the process can be shortened by designing the page on the computer screen, placing transparency material into the paper feed tray, and having the printout be on the actual transparency film. This may be done with a laser printer or an ink jet printer. (Only transparency film designated for the particular printer should be used. Incorrect film may damage the printer.)

Technology Tools for Teachers

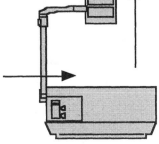

22.4 - Teaching with Transparencies

Overhead transparencies can be formatted to accommodate three different methods of presentation: (1) direct presentation, (2) progressive disclosure, and (3) overlay presentation. The transparency content will determine what format will be used when preparing and using the transparency.

Direct Presentation

Except for the fact that the transparency is either mounted in a transparency frame or placed in a plastic protector sheet, direct presentation is the use of a single transparency in the exact form it was produced. The frame or plastic sheet is used to protect and store the transparency.

Progressive Disclosure

Progressive disclosure is a name that includes many different techniques, all with the same intent: to display or disclose the information on the transparency a portion at a time or progressively. This technique is used when the content is part of a whole, but the teacher wants to disclose the elements as they are explained. To achieve this, sections of the transparency are "masked." This can be simply done by covering all or some of the transparency with a sheet of paper and revealing the content as needed. However, for transparencies that are going to be used on a regular basis and for a more professional presentation, the following approaches can be used:

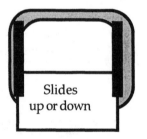

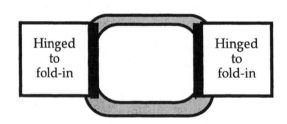

Overlay Presentation

Overlay presentation is used when specific information dealing with a concept is to be presented a portion at a time. Each element is placed on a separate transparency, with the entire set hinged to the lead transparency. The transparencies are then "folded-in" or "overlayed" as they are used. There are two types of overlays: Fixed Sequence Overlays and Random Sequence Overlays.

Fixed Sequence Overlays have two or more transparencies all hinged to the frame and coordinated with the main transparency mounted in the frame. Material is presented in the predetermined sequence of the overlays.

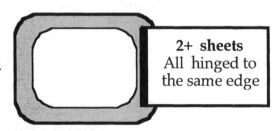

Random Sequence Overlays have two, three, or four transparencies hinged to the frame. Since each transparency overlay is independent of the other, overlays of this type can be used in any combination and sequence the presenter chooses.

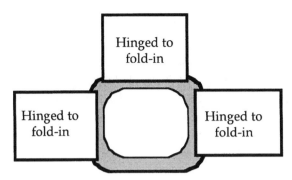

How to Use Transparencies to Resize Art Work

The combination of an overhead transparency and an overhead projector can save the teacher a considerable amount of time when art work is needed for bulletin boards, posters, outlines for wall murals, and other such instances. Existing art work can easily be reduced or enlarged in the following manner:

1. Select the item you want to use (sketch in a newspaper, map in a textbook, picture in a magazine, outline in a workbook, line drawing in a coloring book, etc.).
2. Make a xerographic copy of the artwork. Do not be concerned if there are elements around or with the drawing that you do not want to use. Copy the entire section.
3. Make a transparency from the copy you just made. Again, do not be concerned if items are copied that you do not want.
4. Tape the poster board, paper, or other material you want to have the final art work on, to a wall. If you were creating a wall mural you would use the actual wall as your surface.
5. Place the transparency on an overhead projector and project the image onto the poster board, paper, or wall.
6. Move the overhead projector closer to, or further away from, the paper until the projected image is the size you want. Adjust the focus as you near the desired size.
7. Using a pencil, marker, etc., trace the outline of those parts of the image that you want to use.
8. Complete the line drawing of the art work to meet your needs.

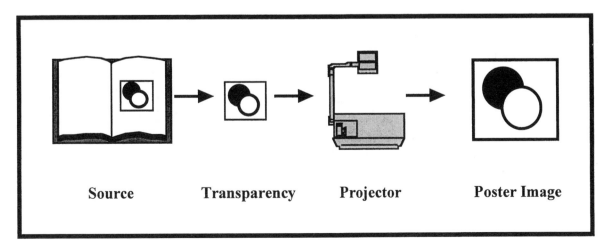

| **Source** | **Transparency** | **Projector** | **Poster Image** |

22.5 - Visual Presenters

Visual presenters are also called document cameras, presentation cameras, and visualizers. They are used in traditional instructional settings as well as in conjunction with video conferencing systems. Their wide appeal is due to the variety of materials that can be shown with this technology. These include all paper documents (books, periodicals, written assignments, newspaper clippings, etc.), transparencies, photographs, 35mm slides, and realia (3-dimensional objects ranging from small tools and coins to plants or a live worm).

A typical visual presenter consists of (1) a stage on which the object is placed, (2) a video camera mounted above the stage, (3) directional lights that illuminate the stage from above, and (4) a light built into the stage that allows it to function as an overhead projector for transparencies and slides.

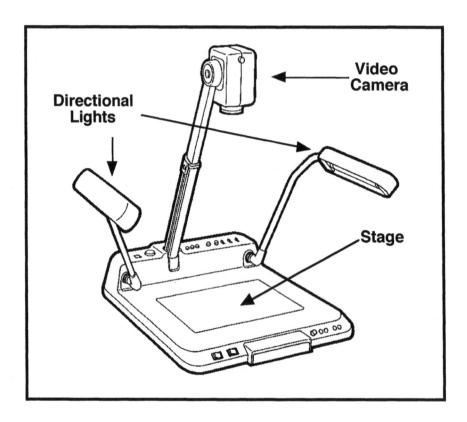

How to Use Visual Presenters

The visual presenter is an input technology and therefore must be coupled with an output technology such as a television monitor or a video projector. Due to the variety of models, the operator's manual for the specific model being used should be consulted. The following are general directions for the two basic uses: presenting opaque materials and presenting transparent materials.

To Present Opaque Materials

Opaque materials are items that light will not project through. This includes books, periodicals, drawings, and all three-dimensional objects such as tools, coins, small plants, insects, etc.

1. Unlock the column arm and set the camera head in position (if required for the model being used).
2. Plug-in the power cord.
3. Connect the visual presenter to the selected output device—TV monitor or video projector. (See the operator's manual.)
4. Turn on the output device.
5. Turn on the visual presenter.
6. Turn on the "directional lights."
7. Place the object to be presented on the "stage."
8. Adjust the "focus" and "zoom" to achieve the optimum image.
9. USE the visual presenter to present opaque objects.
10. Reverse the steps for "shut-down."

To Present Transparent Materials

The most common type of transparent materials are overhead transparencies. These can be either commercial or teacher-made.

1. Unlock the column arm and set the camera head in position (if required for the model being used).
2. Plug-in the power cord.
3. Connect the visual presenter to the selected output device—TV monitor or video projector. (See the operator's manual for the model being used.)
4. Turn on the output device.
5. Turn on the visual presenter.
6. Turn on the "stage light."
7. Place the object to be presented on the "stage."
8. Adjust the "focus" and "zoom" to achieve the optimum image.
9. USE the visual presenter to present opaque objects.
10. Reverse the steps for "shut-down."

Compact and Portable Visual Presenters

The standard visual presenter discussed above is the model most frequently used in schools. It can be a permanent attachment to an instructional counter or desk, or it can have a handle to allow it to be moved from one location to another. In recent years, a number of compact and portable models have become available. These are generally less costly and allow for easy movement from one location to another.

22.6 - Activities

• Activity One •

Design two transparencies for a lesson you will teach. Use a different process to make each of the transparencies. Compare the advantages and disadvantages of each process.

• Activity Two •

Design a transparency that uses progressive disclosure or overlay presentation as the method of presentation. Use the transparency to make a brief presentation to the class.

• Activity Three •

Using the procedure in "How to Use Transparencies to Resize Art Work," select an image from a textbook or a periodical and transfer that image to a poster that is approximately 16" x 24" in size.

Appendix

A-1: Using a Macintosh with OSX Operating System

Turning On the Computer

The power button is located in various places. Some models and laptops have a round button on the top right of the keyboard. Other models have a button on the front of the tower, or in front of the monitor (which turns on the entire system). iMacs (all-in-one units) have a button on the left or right of the base, or on the back left of the monitor.

Turning Off the Computer

The most common way to shut down the computer is to select *Apple: Shut Down* from the Menu Bar. Pushing the power button will also produce a screen with *Shut Down* as an option.

To Force Quit an Application

If an application freezes, hold down the Apple, Option, and ESC keys at the same time. A menu will appear to choose an application to quit.

To Reboot the Computer

If the computer should freeze, it can be restarted by pressing the power button until the computer turns off.

Operating System

The operating system determines how the computer works. Depending on the age of the Macintosh, the system varies. At this writing, there are several versions of OSX, with older models running OS9.

The Desktop

After the computer starts up, the **Desktop** is the entire area you see. The **Desktop** is the working area. The **Menu Bar** at the top contains pull-down menus housing various computer commands. The **Apple Menu** to its left houses important commands like *Shut Down, Empty Trash, Sleep,* etc. On the right of the Menu Bar are **Menulets** showing the date, time, sound, etc. The icon on the right of the Desktop represents the **Hard Drive** (labeled Macintosh HD) that stores all applications, system software, and utilities. Double click each icon to get to what is stored there. At the bottom, left, or right (movable) is a **Dock** that provides access to any applications the user wants to access quickly, along with the **Trash Can** to get rid of documents or programs no longer needed. To empty the trash and permanently remove the items, go to the *Apple Menu: Empty Trash.*

Windows

Rectangular viewing areas on the desktop are called windows. Each time a program is started, or a component accessed, it appears in a window. Each window has a title bar with the program or component name, along with three control boxes on the left. The **Close** button (red) removes the window from the desktop; the **Zoom** button (green) changes the size of the window; the **Collapse** button hides the window, sending it to the Dock, for access at another time.

The window is moved by positioning the mouse over the title bar of the window and dragging the mouse (with the button down) to move the window to a new position. Scroll bars are available to move through the page. Dragging the *Resize Box* (bottom right) allows you to change the size or shape of the window.

Online Help

The Macintosh operating system, along with most programs, has online help (accessed from the Menu Bar). This is an online manual covering how to use the operating system or application program. Most have a table of contents, an index, and a search option.

Installing Software

Some computers are purchased with software installed, while others have none. At some point, you will need to add new software, usually from a CD-ROM. Most programs have an Install Program, a one-time procedure. Insert the CD-ROM. Click the Install icon; follow on-screen instructions. Programs are removed by dragging the program icon to the trash can.

Opening/Closing Applications

Applications, or programs, help you to perform a task, such as writing a letter on a word processor, or doing a calculation on a spreadsheet. Once the program is installed, it can be accessed by double clicking the program icon in the hard drive (this icon can also be placed in the *Dock*; the program is then accessed there). To end the program, choose *"Program name:" Quit* from the Menu Bar.

CD/DVD

Some models have a CD/DVD tray. To access this, click on the key at the top right of the keyboard for the tray to eject. Use the same key to eject the CD/DVD. Others have a slot for the CD/DVD. Place the CD/DVD in the slot and it will be pulled into the computer. Eject by dragging the icon of the CD/DVD to the trash.

Saving Files

Files can be saved to the hard drive, a USB minidrive, a disk, or other media. Go to the File menu; select *Save*, then choose the disk or folder where the file is to be saved. It is important to have the folder where the file is to be saved shown at the top of the screen.

Ejecting Disks/Drives

All disks and USB minidrives must be "put away" by dragging the icon to the trash can.

Opening Files

Double click on the file you want to open. An alternative is to first open the application, then go to *File: Open*. Locate the file to be opened; click *Open*.

Printing a File

Choose the file to print (or have the file active in the application). Under File in the menu bar, choose *Print*. Modifications can be made to print more than one copy, or to print specific pages.

A-2: Using a PC with Windows XP Operating System

Turning On the Computer

The power button is located in various places. On a tower computer, the button is often at the top near the CD-ROM; most laptops have a small button on the top or side. Monitors also have a switch that must be turned on.

Turning Off the Computer

Never turn the computer off with the power switch. It is necessary for the computer to go through a shut down process. Using Windows, choose the *Shut Down* command from the Windows *Start* menu at the bottom left of the screen.

To Reboot the Computer

If the computer should freeze, it can be restarted by pressing the CTRL, ALT, and Delete keys at the same time.

Operating System

The operating system determines how the computer works. At this writing, most PC computers use Windows XP.

The Desktop

After the computer starts up, the "Desktop" is the screen you see. It then becomes the background for all work done on the computer. Various icons appear on the screen (those that appear depend on how your computer is configured). These icons allow you to use various parts of the PC environment. They represent programs, documents, printers, etc.

My Documents

A place to store all documents created in application programs.

Recycle Bin

As a part of the Windows desktop, the recycle bin is a holding area for files and/or programs deleted from the hard drive. To empty, choose *File: Empty Recycle Bin.*

Start Button

Quick access to all programs, applications, find file, etc.

Taskbar

Buttons at the bottom of the screen to easily access windows open on the screen; switch back and forth between programs.

My Computer

Gives access to all drives, printers, scanners, and other hardware available.

Control Panel

Assists in various tasks, such as add/remove programs, set the date and time, change display options, find files, add new hardware, view accessibility options, view fonts, change sounds, and much more.

Windows

Rectangular viewing areas on the desktop are called windows (different than the operating system). Each time a program is started, or a component accessed, it appears in a window. Each window has a title bar with the program or component name, along with three control buttons. **Minimize** and **Maximize** change the size of the window; **Close** removes the window from the desktop. The window is moved by positioning the mouse over the title bar of the window and dragging the mouse (with the button down) to move the window to a new position. Scroll bars allow you to go up and down, or right and left, in the window.

Online Help

The Windows operating system, along with most programs, has online help. This is an online manual covering how to use the operating system or application program. From the Start menu, choose "Help and Support."

Installing Software

Most programs have a Setup Program, a one-time procedure. Insert the CD-ROM. From the Start menu, go to *Settings: Control Panel*; choose *Add/Remove Programs*. Click the *Install* icon; choose the program to install; follow on-screen instructions. Programs can also be removed at this menu.

Opening/Closing Applications

Applications, or programs, help you to perform a task, such as writing a letter on a word processor, or doing a calculation on a spreadsheet. Once the program is installed, it can be accessed by choosing *Programs* from the Windows *Start* menu. To end the program, choose *File: Exit*.

CD/DVD

Most models have a CD/DVD tray. To access this, push the button next to the opening.

Saving Files

Files can be saved to the hard drive (C drive), a floppy disk (A drive), or other media such as USB minidrives (E drive, or other). Go to the File menu; select *Save*, then choose the disk or folder where the file is to be saved. The *Save As* command allows you to keep the original, and also save the file under a different name.

Ejecting Disks/Drives

To remove a disk, close the disk with the *Close* button; press the eject button next to the disk drive. To remove a USB minidrive or CD/DVD, go to the taskbar. Right-click on the "Safely Remove Hardware" icon. Select the device to remove, then click *Stop*.

Opening Files

Double click on the file you want to open. An alternative is to first open the application, then go to *File: Open*. Locate the file to be opened.

Printing a File

Select the file to print (or have the file active in the application). Go to *File: Print*.

A-3: *TaskStream* Summary

To Create a Lesson Plan
1. Choose *Lesson Builder* from the Navigation Bar.
2. Give a title; then choose a Format (e.g., *Rowan University Lesson Plan*).
3. Follow instructions (see p. 22-24).

To Create a Unit Plan
1. Choose *Unit Builder* from the Navigation Bar.
2. Enter the basic information; add lesson plans under *Learning Activities* (see p. 26).

To Create a Rubric
1. Choose *Rubric Wizard* from the Navigation Bar; follow instructions (see p. 25).
2. Attach to your Lesson Plan under *Student Assessment* (Rubrics tab).

To Add a Lesson Plan, Unit Plan, or Rubric to a Folio
1. Choose *Edit*; then *Attachments*.
2. You want to attach "My TaskStream Work" (choose a category).

To Create a Folio/Portfolio
1. Choose the category for your specific purpose.
2. Name the folio; *Create It*; choose the type of portfolio to create.
3. Next Step; Choose a Style; Next Step.
4. Add, Delete, or Rename headings in the Edit Structure.
5. Click on *Edit* to enter your information (see p. 28-31 for additional information).

To Access a Folio or DRF created by your Professor
1. Follow the steps above (To Create a Folio/Portfolio).
2. Modify #2 by choosing the name of the folio created by your professor (instead of type).
3. Note: You will not see the folio until you provide a name.

To Add Text to a Folio
1. Choose the Topic; Click on *Edit*.
2. Add text under the *Introductory Text* or *Main Text* areas (it will go in the same place).

To Add an Attachment to a Folio (from *Word, PowerPoint*, etc.)
1. Click on *Edit*; then choose *Attachments*.
2. *Browse* (this takes you to files on your computer, USB minidrive, etc.).
3. Choose the file you want; *Add File*.
4. This remains in "My Previously Uploaded Files."

To Add Hyperlinks in a Folio
1. Click on *Edit*; then choose *Web Links*.
2. Enter the name of the site; enter the entire web address under "Link to outside Web site."
3. Alternate: Place the name of the site in the text; choose the *Link* icon (see p. 110-111).

To Add an Image to a Folio (*.gif* or *.jpg*)

1. Save the image on your computer, USB drive, etc. It must be a *.gif* or *.jpeg* (*.jpg*) format.
2. Click on *Edit*; then choose *Image*.
3. Click on *Browse*; upload as above for an Attachment.
4. Stock images from *TaskStream* can also be used from the Image area.

To Send your Folio to Your Professor

1. At the top of Folio Builder, click on *Publish/Share*.
2. Choose *Request Feedback/Share with Reviewer*.
3. Choose *Entire Folio* (unless given other instructions).
4. Choose your professor; *Share with Reviewer*.

To Get Feedback from Your Professor

1. Choose *My Programs* from the Navigation Bar; click *My Work*.
2. A "New" icon will appear next to items with comments to read.
3. Click on the title of your folio to read the comments.

To Submit a DRF to Your Professor

1. At the top of the folio, choose *Evaluation*.
2. Click on *Submit*. This will lock your work; you can no longer make changes until it is returned.

To Get Evaluation on Your DRF from Your Professor

1. Go into *Web Folio Builder*; find the DRF that is being evaluated.
2. Click on *Evaluation* to get your assessment results.

To Create a Web Page

1. Choose *Web Page Builder* from the Navigation Bar; choose a template and style.
2. Add Web page names in the Edit Structure.
3. Add information as needed (see p. 34-35 and p. 110-111 for assistance).

To Get a Web Page Address

1. Click on *Publish/Share* at the top of the page; choose *Publish Options*, then *Publish*.
2. Provide a password, if desired.
3. Click on *Publish* at the bottom of the page.
4. *TaskStream* will send back a Web address confirmation.

To Convert a Folio to a Web Page

1. At the top of Folio Builder, click on *Publish/Share*.
2. Follow the steps above (To Get a Web Page Address).

To Place your Web Address in a Folio

1. Choose the appropriate topic; *Edit*.
2. Choose *Web Link*; insert your Web address here (copy and paste from Web Folio Builder).

Index

• A •

• B •

• C •

• D •

• U-V •

• W •

• X-Y-Z •